D1715061

THE UNCOMPLETED PAST

THE UNCOMPLETED PAST
Postwar German Novels
and the Third Reich

Judith Ryan

WAYNE STATE UNIVERSITY PRESS
DETROIT 1983

Copyright © 1983 by Wayne State University Press,
Detroit, Michigan 48202. All rights are reserved.
No part of this book may be reproduced without formal permission.

Library of Congress Cataloging in Publication Data
Ryan, Judith, 1943-
    The uncompleted past.

    Includes index.
    1. German fiction—20th century—History and criticism.
2. National socialism in literature.   I. Title.
PT772.R9   1983   833'.914'09358   83-6744
ISBN 0-8143-1728-6

Recipient of the Second Basilius Award in Germanics

CONTENTS

ACKNOWLEDGMENTS

This book began as an attempt to resolve some puzzles that appeared with persistent regularity in my courses on postwar German literature. At first, I planned to write separate articles on a number of individual novels, but gradually it became clear that the articles revolved around a single problem and thus required a common methodology. This was not easy to develop since it demanded a more radical linkage between theme and form than most critics in this area are accustomed to make. Without the help of my friends and colleagues, the process would have been more prolonged and the product more imperfect. I am particularly indebted to Reinhold Grimm, who read the entire manuscript with an unfailingly critical eye and whose suggestions have added to the scope and precision of the book. Extremely valuable was the critical debate with my colleague Hans Rudolf Vaget, who, by taking issue with me on a number of points, helped me to sharpen my argument and consolidate my case. Of those who encouraged me during the writing of this book, I would also like to thank Gertraud Gutzmann, whose conversations on literature and methodology were always a useful sounding board. The manuscript was read in one version or another by Ehrhard Bahr, Willy Schumann, and Egon Schwarz, and individual chapters were read by William Crossgrove, Klemens von Klemperer, Albert Schmitt, and Jane Wiebel; their corrections, criticism, and most particularly their encouragement were very important to me. The Wayne State University Press helped in a crucial way to clarify the focus of the book and pull it into its final shape. Those notorious last stages in the preparation of this book, when everything seems to be done but isn't, were made much easier in practical ways by substantial help with the index from my son, Antony Ryan, and by the loan of a large work surface from Catherine and Peter Bloom; in less tangible ways they were aided by the unflagging cheerfulness of Lawrence Joseph and the unquestioning faith of my parents and children in the value of the project.

In making these acknowledgments, I should not like to forget my students, past and present, whose willingness to wrestle with these difficult novels and to help in the working out of my ideas has inevitably left its mark on this book. It is for them, and for others like them, that the book has been written.

Two sections of the book have already appeared in print in a slightly different form: the chapter on *Cat and Mouse* in *Germanic Review* 52 (1977) and a shortened version of the chapter on *The German Lesson* in *Expressionism Reconsidered,* ed. Gertrud B. Pickar and Karl E. Webb (Munich: Wilhelm Fink Verlag, 1979). I am grateful for permission to reprint this material here. The poetry of Günter Grass is quoted by courtesy of Hermann Luchterhand Verlag; the poetry of Dylan Thomas is quoted by permission of New Directions Publishing Corporation and J. M. Dent & Sons Ltd.

NOTE ON TRANSLATIONS

For the convenience of readers who are not fluent in German, quotations from the major works under discussion are from English translations whenever possible; however, in instances where the published translations do not reproduce nuances necessary for interpretation, I have provided my own. Certain works referred to briefly in Chapters One and Ten have not appeared in English: in such cases, their titles are given in a literal English rendering for easy identification with the German originals. A translation of Alfred Andersch's *Sansibar*, entitled *A Flight to Afar*, is no longer in print and could not be consulted: I have retained Andersch's more suggestive version. To avoid confusion, I have used the translators' title, *A Model Childhood*, for Christa Wolf's *Kindheitsmuster*, even though I regard this title as inadequate and misleading. Since the chronology of the novels' appearance in German is central to the argument, dates given in the text are those of their first appearance, not the publication dates of the translations.

INTRODUCTION
In Search of Heracles

In his vast novel, *The Aesthetics of Resistance* (1975–81), Peter Weiss describes a group of young working-class resistance fighters contemplating the frieze of the Pergamene Altar, with its massive depiction of the ancient struggle between the gods and the giants. As they explore the sculpture in all its various aspects, the boys make a telling discovery:

> Heracles was missing, the only mortal, as legend had it, to join forces with the gods in the battle against the giants; and we searched among the stony bodies and the remains of limbs for the son of Zeus and Alcmene, the mortal helper who would end the age of oppression by his brave and persistent efforts. But we could only find a sign with his name on it and the paw of a lion skin he had worn as a cloak. Apart from this there was nothing else to indicate where he had stood between the four-horse carriage of Hera and the athletic body of Zeus, and Coppi said it was an omen that it was Heracles, the one most like us, who was missing and that we now had to make our own image of this proponent of action.[1]

Later, the boys come to recognize the somewhat equivocal nature of this mythic figure, but they never give up their search for the missing hero, who becomes a symbolic reminder of their own hopes for the resistance.[2]

In many ways this scene could serve as an emblem of the German novel in its reflection on nazism. Remembering the past means at the same time reconstructing the past—searching for missing pieces, filling in gaps, re-creating lost images. From the outset the German novel has aimed for more than simply a straightforward depiction of life under Hitler. In its attempt to complete the picture it has attacked a whole range of problems that assumed forms peculiar to the unique situation of postwar Germany: the inadequacy of memory, the limitations of subjective perception, the lack of appropriate literary models, the discrepancy between what had actually happened and what one might have wished to have happened. If at first the tendency was to view the historical development culminating in nazism as an inevitable process (Thomas Mann's *Doctor Faustus* presents a sophisticated modification of this view), a shift in emphasis soon became evident, and German writers, especially Günter Grass and his successors, began to grapple in both a thematic and a formal sense with the problem of the "missing Heracles." The reckoning with the past now involved not so much accepting the actualities of history as probing its problematic aspects, its unrealized possibilities. Thus began the search for Heracles, the mortal who had dared to take on battle with the giants; by presenting, if not his image, then the gap in the historical frieze where he might have stood, perhaps literature could bring about a readjustment of attitudes towards the past.

In concentrating on this search for Heracles, I hope to shift the focus of discussion about literature and nazism away from theories of the genesis of nazism and problems of giving expression to evil. Both of these have been dealt with adequately elsewhere.[3] My main concern here is the question of individual responsibility, in particular the specific contribution of literary works to our understanding of it.

The difficulties faced by writers who wished to deal with individual responsibility were considerable. Retrospection revealed that notions of free will and choice had been imperfectly developed and expressed during the Nazi period, yet it would not do to write as if these concepts, however viable theoretically, would always be doomed in practice. A new problem thus arose for a familiar genre, the historical novel. It would be necessary for writers to do more than reproduce the fatalist views of nazism that had begun to emerge. Instead, they would need to develop a new kind of historical novel able to provide a corrective to these views. Yet the movement of postwar German writing towards this conception of its own function was not a simple one. To begin with, a model was lacking for the simultaneous reproduction and critique of accepted ways of seeing. How could writers be true to the actual course of history while at the same time indicating paths that might have been taken and that could provide some kind of guidance for the future?

The German novel went through several stages in its reflection on the ethical problems raised by the reckoning with nazism. Lacking a clear focus on the complex issue of determinism versus freedom, the earliest attempts to present nazism in literature tended to rely on theories of mass guilt, giving short shrift to closer scrutiny of the individual under nazism. Notions of a devil-possessed Germany or of a people overcome by an evil and inevitable fate predominated, and these gave rise to a series of novels essentially mythic or archetypal in form. Only gradually did a more critical approach emerge. As the focus shifted to the individual's attempt to maintain personal integrity in the face of mass allegiance to nazism, the reconstruction of the past began to take on a different character. Novelists no longer sought to locate the atrocities of the Third Reich within the framework of a vast, predetermined design, but rather to provide a new view of history as it had actually been. Some of the subtlest versions of this critique and corrective take a form not unlike Weiss' description of the Pergamene frieze, with its missing image of Heracles left to be filled in by the viewer's imagination. These novels present, not the positive counter-image of a successful resister, but the tantalizingly blank spot where he might have stood. And in forcing us to form our own image of this proponent of action they create a new kind of reader-oriented rethinking of the Nazi period.

Of course this development did not occur in a vacuum. It naturally followed the intellectual, social, and political course of postwar Germany, reflecting, but also instigating, new ways of understanding the past. The earliest novels and stories about nazism were hampered by a kind of pervasive numbness characteristic of immediate postwar Germany that made differentiated reflection on the past extremely difficult. Objective information on the Nazi period was only slowly forthcoming, and the idea of a totally passive citizenry trampled underfoot by the inevitable march of history was a widespread and tenacious misconception. Until the more precise results of historical research began to filter through into public opinion, German literature was shaped by, and itself actively nourished, this perception of the past. In so doing, it was able to attend to the psychological problems of involvement, guilt, and atonement, but ethical and political considerations remained relatively clouded.

The fifties and sixties present a different situation. Now the economic recovery of the Federal Republic and the consolidation of the Democratic Republic created a feeling of having at last escaped from the shadow of the past. But this was only the surface appearance. Anyone who read the West German press in these years cannot fail to have been struck by two conflicting attitudes: the aggressive confidence of a rebuilt society and its misgivings about the actual depth of this ideological change. Questions about the past affiliations of those still in political office were merely one manifestation of this anxiety about a possible political continuity; its other face was a complacent, politically apathetic generation, the observation of which prompted writers in the Federal Republic to respond with a renewed interest in reconstructing the past. Now, as writers became more painfully aware of the missing Heracles, a number of incipient, halfhearted, or ambivalent resistance figures began to crop up in texts whose main focus was the nazified bourgeoisie. The complex nature of individual responsibility began to be explored, at first tentatively, then more insistently. A new question was raised: what might have happened if people had acted differently? Exploring questions like this is a task especially suited to literature. The hypotheses which thus emerged prompted new ways of thinking about nazism by bringing to light the unexploited potential of the masses and showing the double optics of the real and the ideal.

In the German Democratic Republic, this phase took on a different shape, presenting the past in a more controlled way from a perspective that assumed greater congruence between the ideal and the real. The focus was on the Communist resistance to Hitler and the supposed continuity between that movement and the present East German state. This predominantly positive vision glossed over the actual experience of most GDR citizens, but the discrepancy was not allowed to become truly disturbing.

As the seventies approached, both German states became less absorbed with the past. Contemporary social and political problems became increasingly pressing, and when the Nazi past was invoked, it was primarily to provide a kind of contrastive model for reflections on issues of current relevance. In the Federal Republic, torn by student rebellion and an increase in terrorism, the debate on individual responsibility was taken up again in an entirely new context, but it was not as if the issues were now substantially rethought. The assumption was, rather, that one could fall back on conclusions already drawn from the past. In the face of this situation renewed scrutiny of these conclusions in terms of their ability to illumine our thinking about basic ethical questions, to help us in our search for the missing Heracles, is clearly opportune.

Before examining the works themselves, some thought must be given to the function of literature as a reflector of history. It should be established from the start that the actualities of history are, in a sense, peripheral to a study of this kind. More significant is the transmutation of history into opinion and ideology. We are faced, in effect, with a double displacement: first, of historical events into specific perceptions of history; second, of these perceptions into literary form. This second displacement, the complex mutual interaction of perception and fiction, is the subject of this book. We shall be exploring, through the lens of literature, the changing understanding of the Nazi period and the changing answers to the question whether individual action was at all possible and how. What I shall try to show in each case is the peculiar contribution that fictional modes of expression have to make to the rethinking of this issue.

This will require much closer analysis of texts than a more thematic orientation would have done. Hence, the burden of the argument is borne by separate studies of a number of central novels representing various approaches to these more general questions. Supporting these analyses, as a kind of framework, are an introductory critique of certain trends in the early postwar period and some concluding reflections on the problems of realism. While some chapters refer to a comparatively wide range of material, the aim of the book is not to provide a literary survey. It should be read as a set of essays on selected works

and special aspects of a particular problem, presupposing the more
general knowledge of cultural and literary developments that can
readily be obtained from other sources.[4]

In studying the complex mechanisms by which these novels undertake their reckoning with the past, one must bear in mind that the
significance of literature, its prime contribution to an attempt to understand our present and our past, lies in something quite different from
direct representation. Where historiography tries to minimize the subjective element implied by written perspective, canceling it out as
much as possible by its own self-criticism, literature points up the
subjective nature of our view of reality by deliberately clothing it in a
fictional guise. What retrospective novels reveal are thus not the facts
of a particular historical period, but specific views of it. Taking into
account the workings of perspective is an important task allocated to
the reader. Furthermore, the aesthetic form—by nature some kind of
attempt at unity—that novels bestow upon views of the past inevitably
bears a discrepant relation to what we understand as reality. The distortions thus generated are themselves revealing: the discrepancy between the presumed unity of our perception, highlighted by literary
form, and the otherwise inaccessible reality of which it is an imperfect
mirror enables us, as readers and critics, to gain some insight into the
problematic nature of current attitudes about this historical period.[5]

Aesthetic modes, in other words, are not merely a formal issue.
Instead, they provide both the vehicle for accepted views and the
mechanics by which their limitations can be recognized. In looking at
literary forms, we come straight to the heart of our concern, asking not
what aspects of history are reproduced in this literature, but *how* history is viewed by the authors and their audience. Whether these views
mirror contemporary attitudes or diverge from them in turn determines
the narrative techniques selected, and this brings about yet another
diffraction of the material. Further, the reader's reception stands in
more or less direct proportion to the writer's attempt either to meet
established expectations or to provoke the development of new ones.
A study of themes alone cannot possibly do justice to these complex
displacements which literature undertakes.

This is especially true of the literary rethinking of the Nazi past, and
one of the crucial issues is the way it has been understood. It will be
my thesis that certain of these works have been misread, not only by
the general public but by many critics as well. I will argue, for example, that the protagonist of Günter Grass' *Cat and Mouse*, usually
seen as an unwilling dupe of nazism, is in reality a covert, if ultimately
unsuccessful, resister, and that two characters in Siegfried Lenz' *The
German Lesson* who are commonly taken to be opponents of nazism
are in fact more questionable than they at first appear. This type of

interpretation depends upon recognizing the mechanisms by which a literary work performs its critique of perception. The prevalent misreadings of these novels are symptomatic of the extent to which this complex interrelationship between literature and history has been ignored. They indicate, in addition, a certain reluctance in postwar Germany to move beyond accepted views of the Nazi past and come to terms with some of the ethical issues it raises. To recognize the enormity of the Third Reich and to deplore its atrocities is only the first step in what should become a more complex reflection on one's own role in history. Only by a reading that specifically takes into account the nature of literary, as opposed to historical, presentation can the consciousness-building potential of these important texts be released.

On the issue of literary form, critics concerned with the postwar period have generally taken one of two tacks: one extreme holds that the events to be described were so cataclysmic that they can only be expressed indirectly, by transference onto a metaphoric plane; the other calls for a return to realism, for the abandonment of modernist literary techniques which are believed to obscure the presentation of history as history.

Lawrence Langer's book *The Holocaust and the Literary Imagination* is characteristic of the first view, in which the *univers concentrationnaire* can only be rendered through the more bearable mode of metaphor.[6] A continuation of what Langer regards as the Kafkaesque vision, a transference into surrealism, resolves the contradiction between the experience of concentration camp life and the need to express it in some kind of aesthetic form. Such a conclusion is most appropriate for survivor literature or other attempts to depict the experience of persecution and internment. Allegorical representations of concentration camp life or of the flight from Hitler's Germany are of inestimable value for those who underwent those experiences, and they help outsiders see those experiences from within. But this is different from attempting to address an audience that also includes those who participated in the Third Reich, on whatever level of passivity. These readers, as well as many born too late to experience the Third Reich themselves, must see not only that nazism was unspeakable, but also that something might have been done to stop it. Most of the works Langer treats are written from the perspective of the victims, but when he does examine texts from postwar Germany he tends to single out works that also use allegorical or metaphorical modes. Hermann Kasack's *The City Beyond the River* or Ilse Aichinger's *The Greater Hope* are examples of this type. The one work that does not fall into this category is Heinrich Böll's *Billiards at Half-Past Nine*, but this Langer views (erroneously) as a piece of absurdist literature. By giving primacy to Böll's portrayal of the capitulation of three generations instead of to the problem of articulating their wartime experiences, he fails to recognize the book's call for critical engagement. Langer's aesthetics work well in connection with literature about the concentration camps; their limitations become evident when he deals with works that focus on the problem of individual responsibility.

Hamida Bosmajian's *Metaphors of Evil: Contemporary German Literature and the Shadow of Nazism* takes Langer's argument a stage further and makes of it a vehicle better suited to analysis of the German reflection on nazism. Again the emphasis is placed on the aesthetic transformation of experiences that seem to defy expression. In Bosmajian's view, the "metaphors of evil" simultaneously lay bare the horrors of nazism and form a psychological defense against memories that threaten to become overwhelming. In devoting her section on the novel to Günter Grass, Siegfried Lenz, and Uwe Johnson, she also introduces an aspect of aesthetic displacement not treated by Langer: the pervasive ironic mode through which the metaphors are filtered. She understands that the narrators in Grass and Lenz are unreliable, but she sees them as all too effective deceivers, whose account of the past is itself a defense mechanism. Even in ironic guise, the metaphors of evil continue to function as screens obscuring the full reality. "The ironist as trickster is finally as self-deceptive as those whom he wishes to expose."[7] The fault of this argument lies in its identifying the ironic author too closely with his trickster-narrator, thus underestimating the novels' dialectical potential. That casual readers have been duped into seeing only the surface of the screen does not mean that one cannot uncover the hidden image behind it. My readings of the novels attempt to do just this: to reveal the narrative irony, not as a psychological blocking device, but as a deliberate instrument for critique.

Another approach to the reflection on nazism calls for a more straightforward narrative technique that would portray the historical realities of the Third Reich more directly. Critics who take this position—Frank Trommler is one of its most articulate spokesmen— believe that the use of metaphorical analogues obscures the reconstruction of the German past by eliminating the kind of detailed presentation upon which an accurate analysis must be based.[8] From a similar standpoint, other scholars have criticized the use of non-traditional or modernist techniques, which they believe conflict with the reader's need for an accurate picture of historical events.[9] This is an important issue, but, as I hope to show, modernist techniques properly understood need not necessarily preclude a faithful and detailed rendition of the Nazi period. Several postwar novelists have found ingenious solutions to this problem.

From these various critical responses, a line of development begins to emerge. The earliest reaction, most memorably expressed in Theodor W. Adorno's claim that to write poetry after Auschwitz would be barbaric, was the belief that the Nazi crimes were so monstrous they could not be expressed in human language.[10] An awed and horrified silence was felt to be the only possible response. But out of this numbness grew the realization that the horrors of nazism should not be forgotten. One consequence is the recognition, typified by Langer, that transposing the terrible memories into nightmarish images could be a psychologically valid way of articulating them. At the opposite pole is the demand, voiced by Trommler and others, for a new realism that would do justice to the specific historical events and their social and political causes. Beyond these two views, Bosmajian represents a second stage in the argument, since she takes into account the psychological function of ironic displacements, as opposed to surrealist images. But her critique of irony disregards its positive possibilities. In looking again at the various responses to nazism, I hope to take the argument yet a stage further. What concerns me is not just the expressive function of literature, but its influence upon the reader. If keeping alive the memory of Auschwitz is to make any sense, it will surely be as a reminder of the problematic nature of human culpability. What responsibility do we bear as individuals and how much freedom do we have to exercise it? My judgments, which essentially invert those of Langer and Bosmajian, are born of the hope that the course of history is something not entirely out of our own hands.

With this in mind, I have chosen novels for the way in which they deal with the individual's role in history, the way in which they handle such matters as "inner emigration," incipient protest, resistance, and political passivity. All of them employ some kind of innovative literary technique and thus raise questions about the adequacy of traditional ways of representing the past. They form a coherent, if not in every case conscious, chain of action and interaction in the continuing search for Heracles. All of them have fulfilled, to a greater or lesser extent, an activating function. In each case, they have answered questions, filled in blank spots, and expanded upon implications of their predecessors. A paradigmatic example of this type of response-pattern is the interaction between Thomas Mann's *Doctor Faustus* and its successor, Günter Grass' *The Tin Drum,* which takes up, as it were, what Grass regards as the weak points in Mann's argumentation and, by establishing a different context, gives a different answer to the same problems. Although the series does not always move forward mechanically in the order of my treatment, each of the novels harks back to its predecessors and undertakes at least a partial shift in perspective. Each novel's response to its forerunner both indicates contemporary reception and points the way for further reflection. Structural and generic changes in these novels are part of a continuing experiment to find the most appropriate form for their dual-level purpose. Changes in novel form must thus be seen as a response to changes in conceptualized thought: if history is seen as determined by fate or necessity, by recurrent cycles or archetypal configurations, this will be reflected in essentially self-contained literary structures; if, on the other hand, history is seen as subject to change, as a process that can be influenced by individuals or groups, we are most likely to have dialectical forms which mirror this view. So we shall be taking up such questions as whether traditional narrative modes have proved adequate to the task of articulating recent German history; why the historical novel has not been successfully revived for this purpose; and whether more avant-garde forms are appropriate vehicles for dealing with the ethical issues involved. How successfully have German writers emancipated themselves from narrative forms that constrict their perception of history? What techniques have been found to mediate more effectively between past and present problems and direct us beyond them?

A continuing refinement of narrative strategies has been part and parcel of the writers' thematic concerns, their search for Heracles. It is not accidental that *Doctor Faustus* or *Cat and Mouse* have narrators whose own lives are rather questionable. Desperately anxious to find some kind of heroic model in the lives of their friends Adrian Leverkühn and Joachim Mahlke, the two narrators attempt a reworking of the past by means of biography. But, as they write, they begin to discover that Leverkühn and Mahlke are neither transparent nor unequivocal: the real model (if it exists) lies at some remove, just beyond the grasp of narration, a blank spot that can only be suggested, never explicitly filled in. In the entire series of novels, figures who at first appear to be models for imitation turn out to be more shifting, more complex, and less relevant to actual situations than they at first appeared. Whether the exemplars are fully fleshed out, as in the case of the painter Nansen in Siegfried Lenz' *The German Lesson,* or more slightly and suggestively sketched, as are the schoolteachers in Christa Wolf's *A Model Childhood* or the Huckleberry Finn ideal in Alfred Andersch's *Zanzibar,* they are in any event found to be imperfect or non-transferable. And even when the search for heroes leads beyond the bounds of socially accepted norms, as in Johannes Bobrowski's outsider Levin or Heinrich Böll's madwoman Johanna, the models turn out to be poignantly insufficient. The chain of novels is a record of the frustrations and disappointments that marked the postwar search for heroes from the outset. The problem was not where to find appropriate models, but where to locate the meaningful blanks. It was how to make readers aware of the missing figure, how to help them find the place where it might have stood and begin to construct the image that had never quite been realized.

In the face of this problem, with its complex intertwining of formal and thematic concerns, the postwar period in Germany is perhaps best seen as a transitional one. The most interesting writers on the Nazi past are those who experienced this transition in its most acute form. Anyone who spent childhood or adolescence under nazism and saw it through the perspective of school and youth groups, anyone whose original frame of reference was determined by the ideology of the Third Reich, was bound to undergo a profound shock as the transition took place. These are the writers who were forced to alter most drastically the views they had acquired during their formative years. The multilayered nature of their novels reflects this transitional view while simultaneously incorporating a critique of it. These novels, which have come to form the unspoken canon of literature on the Nazi past, reveal most clearly the changing consciousness. The fact that almost all have been best-sellers of sorts indicates that they can be read to a large extent as an expression of contemporary views on the Nazi period; yet, at the same time, their attempt to encompass this phase of history in progressive forms is calculated to provoke rethinking of commonly accepted assumptions. These novels are not just more complex; they are more significant than other German novels on the same theme, for they most tellingly lay bare the problematic nature of postwar Germany's incompletely resolved ideological transition. Such novels point forward, even when they seem to be simply looking backward. And, in a wider context, they also provide a model for literature whose aim is to initiate and develop responses to other political changes that dramatically call a people's self-understanding into question.

CHAPTER ONE

PATTERN AND PARADIGM
History as Design

West German Patterns

In the years immediately following the war, there was much talk, at least in the Federal Republic, of the need to come to terms with the recent past. Once the mental framework of the Nazis was officially gone, a total reorientation of thought became necessary. A particularly difficult problem was the concept of collective guilt; resistance to the Nazis was seen as something that had been virtually impossible. Postwar literature in its early phase was most often a transmutation of historical experience into mythic or metaphorical terms. There were, of course, other attempts to deal with the past in a more direct fashion—Carl Zuckmayer's play *The Devil's General* (1946) comes immediately to mind, but even here, despite the predominant realism, there is an undercurrent of myth in the discreet Satanization implied by the title. Mythic perceptions of the past prevailed by and large, forming a foil against which later treatments, especially the major novels of the sixties, can best be understood.

A complicating factor in the development of postwar German literature was the "zero hour," the sensation that writers were beginning again from a *tabula rasa*.[1] Since Nazi literary traditions had been broken off, while at the same time there was little access to the works of German exiles (due to the strict controls imposed by the Allies), writers felt they were working virtually without precedent, writing almost in a vacuum. Although the notion of the zero hour was overstated, it is certain that these writers were at a loss for appropriate literary models and grasped eagerly at whatever modern literature began to filter into Germany.[2] Some older traditions were still alive, and one of these, the lyric tradition of Rainer Maria Rilke, was already being transmitted by the poets of the "inner emigration" (inward distancing from Nazi ideology). These poets, whose strengths lay largely in the field of a very internalized sort of nature poetry, were among the first to be heard.

The themes and motifs to which they turned after the war remained basically similar to those they had used during their withdrawal—what other reserves did they have to draw upon? But, in the interim, their imagery had undergone a change in meaning and function. Those who wrote lyric poetry in defiance of the political catastrophe around them, sometimes even in concentration camps, could well call upon nature as a force of wholeness and healing, and by positing an identity between the poet and nature, they could find a consistency between outer and inner world which was lacking in their relationship to society and the political regime.[3] And Christian concepts, frequently transposed into nature mysticism, had in themselves the quality of resistance. But when this same use of imagery was continued in the postwar period— Ivan Goll's poetry anthology *De Profundis* (1946) and Walter Höllerer's anthology *Transit* (1956) contain representative samples of such verse—it was more a withdrawal from responsibility than an expression of opposition. One may well ask, therefore, why the reading public did not immediately see it as a suspect form. Partly, it gained legitimacy because it continued the underground traditions whose meaning it now, in fact, sucked dry; it could also be seen as one aspect of the general trend of reviving literary traditions with greater moral integrity than those of the Third Reich; in addition it introduced an element that now seemed lacking, that of myth. The myth sought was no longer the vast and primeval structure of the Germanic past upon which the Third Reich had drawn, nor was it the philosophically demanding superstructure of works like Rilke's *Duino Elegies* (1922). But the nature myth had its own special relevance, for what could be more consoling to this unsettled time than a poetic universe in which individual and nature merged and became one?

Yet a return to nature mythology had inherent within it the tendency to smother, "like a rampant vine," everything within its reach.[4] In the end, both the poet and his imagery were reduced to empty posturing. Wilhelm Lehmann, one of the first poets to gain prominence after the war, epitomizes this trend as he grapples vainly to combine into an evocative, if not logically consistent, network ancient mythology, medieval legend, and a welter of botanical names whose very sound suggests the primeval deities of garden and woodland. In this type of mythological system, both the poet and external reality seem to evaporate before the onslaught of poetic images. It is no accident that when poets such as Paul Celan, Johannes Bobrowski, and Nelly Sachs addressed themselves to the question of the holocaust, weaving into their poetry memories of their experiences in the Third Reich, they were not primarily perceived as political poets. The beauty of their language and imagery lulls the mind away from more than a generalized reflection on the horrors recalled in their verses, and the problems presented, whether embedded in private mythology, in traditional legends, or in mystical thought, are seen as in some way universal, as merely a more terrible repetition of something that has occurred throughout the ages. All three use the elegiac mode, thus raising a serious difficulty, since elegy implies an underlying order that can be re-created in literature. In Nelly Sachs' poetry, suffering is merely a rung on a Jacob's ladder to ultimate transfiguration; Celan's negative godhead is the unknown addressee of the poem, which he sees as a kind of message in a bottle; and if the ancient deities have disappeared from Bobrowski's homeland, their traces still remain, in landscape as well as in memory, to provide the sense of wholeness which serves as a foil to man's sorrow.[5]

In this sense, then, the poetry of the postwar era remained for some time indebted to the concepts of inner emigration. The nature references and the obscure myths and legends that had formed a kind of coded language in opposition poetry had simply been transformed into self-supporting systems of metaphor and myth devoid of genuine political content. How could this have come about? A large part of the explanation lies in a perception of Hitler that was not in any way unique to the German people. Rather than viewing nazism as a social and political evil with a specific historical genesis, they preferred to regard it as a reincarnation of evil itself. But seeing it in this way meant mythologizing history, in effect equating Hitler with the devil. Furthermore, it transposed the individual's struggle against nazism onto another plane, giving it an added dimension of hopelessness: how could mere political action be expected to be effective against the eternal forces of evil? Only gradually, in retrospect, was it seen that this was to a large extent the inverse of the Nazis' own mythology. But by the time other types of political protest poetry were revived in the late sixties and early seventies, the need for reviewing the Nazi past was no longer so pressing.

It may be objected that poetry, even political poetry, is not an adequate vehicle for an evaluation of the historical position in which the Germans found themselves. But it soon became obvious that even the plays and novels of the early period did not provide the specific social and political contexts necessary for dealing with the past. The question asked was often not so much "Why did no one manage to stop Hitler?" as "Why were we the ones to fall prey to this evil situation?" Turning the question this way put the experiences of the recent past into a particular pattern of thought. The German people were seen as the collective victim of a terrible fate, rather than as a group of morally responsible individuals. An entire historical epoch was reduced to merely one manifestation among many of the eternal struggle between good and evil; history came to be seen in terms of primal myth. As writers groped for structures and forms to express their experience of their own time, they adopted in a somewhat uncritical way this idea of history as a recurrent pattern. Equally at a loss to make sense of what had happened, the German reading public accepted the new myths presented in drama and fiction.

The earliest postwar literature was rooted in the writings of exiles, emigrants, and survivors of the concentration camps, often produced during the war and published either immediately in foreign countries or after the war in Germany. As in lyric poetry, the adequacy of traditional forms was again put to the test. And as in poetry, the coded language that had been used by anti-Nazi writers during the Third Reich seemed to supply the answer to a problem which was most acutely felt: that the enormity of what had been experienced could not possibly be encompassed by familiar literary structures. So the search began for equivalents, parallels, and paradigms; gradually the "slave language" was transformed into a new allegoric mode.

The religious pattern of guilt and redemption lent the first viable framework for this intractable material. Ernst Wiechert's *Forest of the Dead* (1946), a moving testimony to his four months' internment in Buchenwald in 1938, and Bernd von Heiseler's *The Reconciliation* (1953), an attempt at a more elaborated version of the Christian standpoint Wiechert had presented, are typical of this phase; Elisabeth Langgässer's novels *The Indelible Seal* (1946) and *The Quest (Märkische Argonautenfahrt*, 1950) are a more sophisticated version of the same schema.

Aside from Wiechert's relatively simplistic application of the Christian model, his use of nineteenth-century realism presents the major difficulty of his novel. The hero's model in the concentration camp, a man known as Father Kilb, is a petit bourgeois grocery store owner whose idyllic life has been brutally disrupted by his deportation. Much of Kilb's virtue lies in no more than this, the false accusations that make him, in the hero's eyes, a successor to Heinrich von Kleist's seeker after justice in the 1810 novella *Michael Kohlhaas;* the quality which radiates from Kilb like a holy aura is in large measure due to his embodiment of nineteenth-century values. Again and again, Wiechert harks back to standards long since gone and no longer entirely appropriate. The protagonist is inwardly purged and steeled by his Buchenwald experience, but his transformation hardly takes place on the same plane as the historical events it must confront.

The guilt-redemption scheme is given an added mythic dimension in Langgässer's *The Indelible Seal,* published in the same year as Wiechert's *Forest of the Dead.* Structured around models from the Jewish and Christian traditions, the novel strives to create a modern legend. Two saints in particular become examples for the central character, Belfontaine, and their lives are interwoven with his reflections in the course of travels from Germany to France and back. Through Belfontaine, the traditional figures of the Wandering Jew and the Eternal Pilgrim are ultimately united as the multiple levels of the narrative come together. Like Wiechert's, Langgässer's view of the recurrent struggle between good and evil is often simplistic, but she overlays it with a typological scheme reminiscent of the relationship between the Old and New Testaments. Langgässer's novel is thus a stepping-stone in the movement towards a mythic depiction of the Nazi era, a development that continued into the fifties. Her modern legend presents the Third Reich as the most cataclysmic of a series of historical catastrophes within the eternal struggle for salvation. In effect, the National Socialist regime is equated with the rule of Satan, and the characters become abstractions whose significance lies in their embodiment of eternal verities.[6] But the novel never quite reaches the level of sophistication attained by Thomas Mann's *Doctor Faustus,* the most masterful of the early mythic novels.

Langgässer's later work on a similar theme, *The Quest,* moves further than its predecessor, linking the religious framework with a mythological one and drawing a parallel between biblical theology and classical mythology. On the surface, it concerns the pilgrimage of seven characters to a Benedictine monastery immediately after the war. On the way, their recapitulation of personal experiences during the Third Reich begins to reveal common configurations behind their apparently dissimilar lives. For the pilgrims, the Argo of classical myth becomes a symbol of man's eternal journeying, and they see themselves as latter-day argonauts. Another image they use for their journey is that of descent into the underworld, suggested by repeated references to Eurydice and Persephone. Their quest is a search for the return of their souls from the realm of darkness. It takes them through the labyrinth of memory and the underworld of guilt; their Golden Fleece is the Christian grace they discover at Anastasiendorf. Just as the image of the voyage conflates different religious and mythic traditions, so the goal of their journeying becomes a mystically superimposed version of various real and mythic places. The upper and lower poles are formed by the contrast between the concentration camp, Theresienstadt, in the past, and the monastery, Anastasiendorf, in the present. Metaphorically, the two poles are the underworld and the Heavenly Jerusalem. Layer upon layer of parallel references become fused in the image of the city, especially the lost city of Troy, which is revealed as the archetype of all cities. Towards the end of the novel, the circular pattern of the city draws up into itself other circles upon which it is superimposed to form an immense symbolic spiral: the mystic rose upon which all is centered.

To be sure, the argonauts are not content to remain at the mystic center. Instead, they bear with them on their return to to the outside world the insights gained on their trip to the monastery. In this way the novel's abstractions are brought back to the level of down-to-earth reality. Reinforcing the return to the worldly is the appended tale of two "Children of Medea," orphaned in the winter of 1945 and prevented from perishing only by their involvement with a group of black marketeers.

Yet, although no specific resolutions to the problems of the argonauts are offered at the conclusion, the novel is not open-ended. The seven lives ultimately conform to the same concentric pattern as the architecture of past, present, and future, symbolized by the mystic rose design that seems to underlie the plan of Troy. For all its realistic detail and psychological finesse, the novel reduces history, in the last analysis, to the abstract patterning of myth. Even the potential for resistance, embodied in the figure of the young resistance fighter Irene, is ultimately subordinated to the mystic pattern.

Simultaneous with the mythic trend was a move towards parable and fable, largely the result of the Kafka renascence promulgated by Group 47, writers who deliberately set out to create a new tradition for postwar literature. Included in Group 47 were writers like Günter Grass and Uwe Johnson, who were to make a significant mark in the late fifties and sixties, as well as more restricted talents like Wolfdietrich Schnurre and Hans Erich Nossack.

One of the few full-length novels in the parabolic vein, Schnurre's *The Fate of Our Town* (1959), is made up of an elaborate mosaic of tiny metaphorical prose pieces. Here universalization is based not upon ancient myth but upon modern tropes. Hermann Kasack's *The City Beyond the River* (1947), the allegorical tale of a man's visit to the realm of the dead during the latter part of World War II, was doubtless one of Schnurre's models for *The Fate of Our Town*. While in both cases the central character assumes the role of archivist or chronicler, this implied historiographic view of reality is ultimately subsumed into the patterning of metaphor and allegory. Like Langgässer, Kasack believes in eternal recurrence, although it occurs here less as part of the actual structure than as part of the novel's reflective base.[7] His dependence on mysticism, represented by the figure of the Meister Magus and his pronouncements, lends an optimistic undercurrent to the pervading tone of despair, so that the European catastrophe, as he terms it, is viewed as part of a necessary process that will ultimately return Western culture to what he regards as its Asian origins.[8] In his parallel novel of a modern chronicler, Schnurre seems to take issue with Kasack's (and possibly also Langgässer's) mystic vision.

Like Langgässer, Schnurre constructs a realm where a number of different time periods interpenetrate and mutually illumine each other. Distinguishable, though not clearly separate from each other, are the present technological world and a vague kind of medieval society that presumably stands for the Third Reich. The spirit of ancient history is embodied in the dust-covered mummy Chrysanthema, who comes to life somewhat precariously in the narrator's household. The narrator himself is presented as a medieval scribe engaged in writing the history of his native town; in the act of writing he begins to reflect more seriously on the nature of his role as chronicler. These reflections mark an important step in the development of fiction about nazism. Unlike Kasack or Langgässer, Schnurre perceives no order in the events of recent history, nor does he wish to impose upon them the intrinsically unrelated order of myth. His complaint that he cannot find the right "epic flow" is not a modish exclamation on the absurdity of the world or the breakdown of the modern novel.[9] "Mankind would be innocent if the bookshelves of our minds were as neatly ordered as our novels," the chronicler cries in despair.[10] In other words, he recognizes a discrepancy not apparent to some other novelists of the period: that mythic structures may organize our chaotic impressions of history too schematically, evoking a response of powerlessness in the face of what appears to be a predetermined pattern.

Set in a city divided and besieged by powers from the east and west, *The Fate of Our Town* is a parable of postwar Berlin. One of its weaknesses lies in the mythologizing of the two major powers as the "sabre riders" from the east and the "army of atonement" from the west. The political criticism implied in these two images may be well taken, but when it is extended throughout the novel it obscures subtleties that need to be brought to light.

Paradoxically, the figure of the archivist turns out to be one of the least emancipatory in the whole book. The isolation enforced by his occupation is exacerbated by his involvement with three strange women, Xeres, Ludwiga, and Chrysanthema, who bear the main burden of the novel's metaphorical structure. Absorbed by these symbols, the narrator retreats further and further from reality (as indicated by his various peculiar love affairs: with a fish, or with a wave, for example) until he ends up in a monastery preparing to write the ultimate message to mankind. Resignation seems to be the only possible "solution" to his dilemma. But even this, while taken seriously by the narrator-scribe, is not viewed without irony by the author himself, who takes pains to make the reader aware of the cost it exacts. At the conclusion of the novel, the monk discovers, in an ancient, dusty room, pages from a book of revelations written by his predecessors long ago; all are illegible. But upon his return to his own cell, he realizes that he will never make use of this insight: "I know that I will remain silent, that I will forget, and that I will never record anything other than what the rules of my order demand of me."[11] The monk's solution is a deceptive way out, and the novel's conclusion must be read ironically.

One possible alternative is provided by a friend of the chronicler, Richard, a circus performer whose professional name is "Achmed, the Unsettling," a reference to similar epithets used about politically engaged writers like Brecht and Dürrenmatt. In this role, Richard stands for the artist who attempts to make people more conscious of their part in the fashioning of history. But alas, as the archivist discovers, "revolutions (in which Richard persists in believing) cannot be started in conjuror's tents."[12] It is symptomatic of this novel that Richard is seen almost entirely through the eyes of the narrator, who views him as a central, if problematic, figure. The difficulty, as Richard himself gradually comes to realize, lies in the fact that criticism of the status quo is useless unless there are forces that can be marshaled to change it. Art that tries to point out what is wrong with society sometimes has the opposite effect from that intended. "As the waves of laughter that surge around Richard when he appears as Achmed die down again, they wash away with them all the misgivings of the good citizens; unrelieved, and glad to have in Achmed an escape mechanism that helps them let off the steam from their consciences that has befogged their minds, they all throng relieved and free out of the hall after the performance."[13] Richard despairs of finding a way to stir the conscience of his public. "It is as if," he complains, "the truth were made of cotton, and if one offers it to people, they stuff it gratefully into their pillows so that they can rest more comfortably."[14] Revolutionary art has always had to contend with this central problem: that aesthetic form might prevent the work's disturbing message from being fully appreciated. There are ways of avoiding this difficulty, but the question remains whether Schnurre has found a solution. Even Richard is said, ironically, to possess an enviable strength of character that lets him remain in hiding from the authorities for long periods of time: "And who, of all those who ended up becoming guilty along with everyone else, would not have been grateful for the strength of character to descend into the sewers, like Richard, for so long a time?"[15] The fact that Richard uses the sewers as his hiding place indicates Schnurre's critical attitude toward inner emigration.

The poet Ignatius represents another possibility. In contrast to Richard, Ignatius believes that in times of political crisis it is virtually impossible to continue with the traditional role of the poet, that it is in a sense criminal merely to sing the praises of nature's beauty. "He saw no justification any more, he told a stunned group of followers, in tracing the spiraling flights of buzzards up into eternity, and the very idea of singing about the murmuring woods was almost a kind of betrayal."[16] Ignatius' view of poetry bears a remarkable similarity to Brecht's in his famous poem "Bad Times for Poetry," where he says that not nature but political and social problems drive him to his desk and the composition of verse. Ignatius' former devotees do not understand this point. Instead, they cast him out, removing his books from the libraries, beheading his statue in the park, and burning his works in nightly bonfires. Ignatius' decision to start anew with language by cleaning typewriter keys is not any more likely to be politically effective than were his earlier poetic effusions. The narrator-scribe sees the weaknesses of both would-be resisters through art, Richard and Ignatius, but he, too, is unable to find a resolution to the artist's dilemma.

The difficulties of reconstructing this literary mosaic clearly limit the effectiveness of *The Fate of Our Town*. More problematic, however, is the novel's elevation of concrete historical problems to a parabolic plane. By equating the problems of postwar Berlin with the problems of the Third Reich and simultaneously clothing them in medieval garb, Schnurre implies that the problems are perennial in nature. The author himself seems unaware of the insight that flickers briefly in his narrator's consciousness: that the kind of truth which emanates from a timeless and hermetic sphere can scarcely be useful for the here and now. The book's parabolic structure has led it to this dead end; whatever inkling the reader may have of its hidden obverse, the scribe himself cannot help but end in resignation. Like myths, parables reduce our views of history to essentially closed models of thought. Within these frames, free individual action is virtually prohibited.

The mythic view was not restricted to West Germany alone, but also predominated in Switzerland, whose German-language theater was highly influential in the fifties. Of course, Switzerland's essentially conservative humanism was an important factor in the way its writers came to see the history of Nazi Germany. Taking up mythic forms was for them a way of connecting their own literature with the main stream of European modernism; they failed to realize that the great works of the twentieth century had used myth for an entirely different purpose. Whereas the earlier part of the century had needed myth to give coherence to the fragmentation of modern experience, the fifties needed forms that could liberate people from rigidly fixed thought patterns. Swiss writers were in a different position from German writers, and their special type of political engagement tended to take up Brechtian models and essentially turn them in upon themselves. An important element of Brecht's program had been the use of open forms, reflecting his view that the world could be altered and that critical detachment could help individuals to escape the prison of social and psychological determinants. But the Swiss writers, attempting to carry Brecht's dramatic models one stage further, in actuality closed the door that Brecht had carefully left open.

Plays like Max Frisch's *The Firebugs* (1958) or *Andorra* (1961), overtly criticizing the complacent bourgeois mentality and its reluctance to resist prevailing mores, reveal upon closer examination how closed dramatic structures rule out the possibility of individual resistance. Paradoxically, *The Firebugs* attacked rigid systems of thought, while at the same time harking back to paradigmatic forms: the medieval *Everyman* and Greek tragedy. Admittedly, the play is intended as a parody of these models. It stresses repeatedly that fate is a concept more appropriate to drama than to life, but by conflating various paradigms that depend on this notion, the play ultimately gives credence to the idea of inevitability and universality.[17] A major difficulty is *The Firebugs'* intentional applicability to both prewar and postwar situations, including its implicit reference to the Communist overthrow of Czechoslovakia. The play's meaning broadens in scope as its relevance to specific historical issues narrows. Such simplifications are not really commensurate with the moral dilemmas of political reality.[18] Its farcical element, far from emancipating us from these models, as it is intended to do, trivializes and distracts from the issues at hand.

In Frisch's novel *Homo Faber* (1957), there is a similar dilemma. Though it seems to refer mainly to postwar problems, the novel deals in a continuous undercurrent with issues raised by the recent past. Here again, life is viewed as a modern variant of a classical model, in this case, the Oedipus story. Much is made of the question to what extent human beings are determined by some outside force—fate—or by their own actions; what the protagonist calls chance manifests itself exactly as if it were fate. Like *The Firebugs,* the novel suffers from a disparity between two modes of thought: the tragic and the ironic. Insofar as Faber is a modern Oedipus, what happens to him takes on the quality of fate, whether or not he regards it as a random chain of circumstances. Once sequences become repeatable, events can no longer seem like chance occurrences. By basing his tale upon myth, Frisch virtually eliminates the possibility that Faber might have been able to act otherwise. If Faber's blindness is less avoidable than Oedipus', he is still not genuinely free, but a prisoner of his own psychological makeup, and so the determinants of psychology become a modern equivalent for fate. The clash between myth and freedom appears irresolvable.[19]

Even where Frisch moves away from pre-established mythic patterns, as in *Andorra,* he sees the individual as hopelessly locked in to social determinants. The boy Andri, whose father conceals his illegitimacy by claiming that he is a Jewish refugee, is a moving example of how an individual can take on the role assigned to him by society. When the Andorrans finally succumb to the Nazis, they allow Andri to be taken away without protest. True to the period in which it was written, the play's main concern is the problem of identity; on this level, Andri's refusal to believe his father's revelation of the truth about his heritage is perfectly credible. The problem lies in the play's attempt to transform the relationship between Germans and Jews into a piece of general psychologizing in terms of the familiar identity crisis of the late fifties and early sixties. Similarly, Frisch's portrayal of the turncoat Andorrans, once so proud of how they had protected the supposed Jew, is both a criticism of their self-complacency and a tacit acceptance of social determinism. The drama becomes a paradigm of a modern Everyman and a modern Everypeople. By highlighting the psycho-social determinants of the action, Frisch precludes the Brechtian response: "but they should have acted differently." Instead, the viewer is more likely to respond, "Yes, that's just how it was." A related product of much the same time and much the same type of thought is *The Visit* (1956), by Frisch's compatriot Friedrich Dürrenmatt. Once again, a universalized modern parable is constructed around the idea that people can be easily swayed and that society's morals are less than high-minded. When Claire Zachanassian, returning after a long absence, offers her home town a substantial reward if it agrees to participate in her cruel plans for avenging a former lover, the people are quick to see their advantage. The rapidity with which they allow themselves to become murderers is relevant to the discussion of nazism, but it is overlaid by the fable's universal implications.

Indeed, Dürrenmatt's whole theory of drama revolves—in explicit debate with Brecht—around the concept of the anonymous individual who has no genuine freedom of action. By regarding Hitler and Stalin, not as individuals, but as state machines of carnage, Dürrenmatt argues that there can be no individual guilt in the modern world and, hence, no individual tragedy. Like those of Frisch, Dürrenmatt's plays in the early postwar years are based on classical Greek forms which become ingeniously inverted in their application to the modern predicament. In the modern world there may no longer be fate or the gods, but in their place is not so much individual moral responsibility as a chain of accident and coincidence. "Thus there is no threatening God, no justice, no fate as in the Fifth Symphony, but merely traffic accidents, dikes bursting because of faulty construction, explosions in atom bomb factories, caused by absentminded laboratory assistants."[20] The very grotesqueness of these accidents renders the individual helpless, overwhelmed by them in the same way as he was crushed in the classical Greek drama by fate. The laughter that ensues—and Dürrenmatt calls his plays comedies—is merely the laughter of desperation.[21]

Of Dürrenmatt's plays, perhaps the most relevant to the issue of individual responsibility are *Romulus the Great* (1948) and *The Physicists* (1962), although only the former has direct bearing on the Third Reich. Curiously, resistance is not depicted in *Romulus the Great* as action, but as a passivity that blocks the actions of others. By refusing to intervene, the emperor Romulus allows the Roman Empire to come to its inevitable decline. In the last analysis, though, the operative force is the power of the future. Whereas Romulus believes that he has passed judgment on Rome, he merely leaves it to its inevitable decline. His counterpart, the Germanic emperor Odoaker, implores Romulus to join forces with him to prevent his bloodthirsty nephew Theodoric from ushering in a new age of terror, but their belief in the inevitability of the future turns both emperors away from the path of political or military action. The individual is powerless: "You must submit to your fate. There is no other alternative."[22] The upshot of it all is that one cannot intervene in the course of history without in the end being crushed by fate. Cunningly, Dürrenmatt substitutes the word *reality* for *fate* in contexts that are to be taken without irony (Romulus declares, for example, that the emperors' grand designs for the future have been "corrected by reality"[23]), but the ultimate effect is to create the impression that things could not have turned out otherwise.

However much Dürrenmatt insists that reality is a random chain of accidents, events do seem to have some covert form of patterning in this play. The Roman Empire is suspiciously like the Third Reich, but Romulus is not Hitler; the anticipated bloody reign of Theodoric recalls the Third Reich while not being precisely identical with it. Yet despite these distinctions, the effectiveness of the play as a political statement depends on the similarities, not the differences, between the Roman Empire and our own age.

Active resistance is presented twice in *Romulus the Great*, each time in the form of parody: first on the night of the Ides of March, when the patriotic members of the Empire attempt to assassinate Romulus ("Et tu, cook?"[24]), and again when the royal messenger makes a last desperate attempt on the life of an emperor who has, unbeknown to him, already abdicated his office. The association of Caesar and Hitler could be a fruitful one, but Dürrenmatt does not even indirectly raise ethical issues connected with the assassination of dictators. And Theodoric, the dictator of the future, escapes entirely unscathed. Romulus' pessimistic view that the murder of one dictator would not prevent the rise of a thousand others neatly sidesteps the essential moral dilemma.[25] Moderate humaneness and an essentially fatalistic world view win the day.

Unwittingly, Dürrenmatt implies here through his absurdist stance that the individual has lost all power to determine his own fate. Modern civilization, with its generally amorphous structure, persistently thwarts man's attempt to change it. When Dürrenmatt discusses Brecht's contention that the world can be changed, his only rebuttal is a backhanded compliment to Brecht's technical expertise: "It is often simply the case that Brecht the creative writer sweeps Brecht the dramaturge along with him, a perfectly legitimate phenomenon that only becomes dangerous when it ceases to occur."[26] In the work of Brecht, the audience's reflections form, as it were, the invisible obverse of the play on the stage.[27] In Dürrenmatt, the positive model is actually demonstrated—in this case, in the figure of Romulus. Unfortunately, Frisch and Dürrenmatt, rather than Brecht, are the true representatives of this early phase in the rethinking of the Nazi past. They reflect and help to popularize notions of history in which freedom of action is precluded by the inevitable movement of events.

This entire group of Swiss and German writers of the late forties and fifties translates the events of the recent past into cosmic dimensions, stripping history of its roots in time and endowing it with eternal qualities. When Schnurre's narrator claims that he is the "servant of truth, not Chronos," he speaks for an entire generation of writers who saw the mass guilt of a particular nation at a particular time as the universal, ever-recurring guilt of all mankind.[28] To be sure, they are also aware that the chain must somehow be broken. Schnurre tried to do so by setting up a mosaic that had still to be pieced together, evidently hoping to stimulate a productive and critical response. His abstruseness interferes with this, however, and the reader of *The Fate of Our Town* is more likely to give up in despair. Langgässer and the Swiss writers, by contrast, do not lead outward from the patterns they set up but into the realm of myth and archetype.

In reflecting the view that resistance to Hitler had been virtually impossible, the closed forms thus confirmed, rather than questioned, the reader's belief in inevitability or historic recurrence. Thus the schema-response pattern is relatively static, adopting accepted opinions without provoking new ones. As reflections of a basically pessimistic view of the individual's role in history, these works fulfilled psychological needs but failed to refine political awareness.

Socialist Paradigms

Discontinuity from the prewar to the postwar period was an initial problem in the GDR, as in the Federal Republic, but here there was no talk of a zero hour.[29] Instead, an attempt was made almost from the outset to identify the emerging socialist state with the Communist resistance and to see in the underground resistance movement predecessors of those engaged in building up the new regime. This postulation of a fictitious continuity is problematic in the extreme. In the first instance, model patterns of behavior and thought were not directly transferable from the historical resistance to the socialist state. Moreover, this new vision of the past was at variance with the experience of most East

Germans, who had not been directly involved with the resistance against Hitler. The popular paradigm of an East German resistance heritage disregarded moral complexities and dilemmas that did not fit the socialist model. Like the myths and metaphors of its Western counterparts, it closed doors instead of opening them. While resistance had been desirable in the Third Reich, it was no longer so in the Democratic Republic, and the problem finally became so acute that the myth of continuity had to be abandoned. In the late fifties, just as West German literary forms were gradually becoming more open and flexible, East German critics called for a clean break with the past, thus all but eliminating the possibility of probing the issues it had raised. Whereas the reliance on resistance models had unwittingly served an escapist mentality, the new approach disregarded even more radically a psychological need to work through past experience.

The first phase of East German literature rested upon perceptions of historical reality gained from exile, rather than from first-hand experience of nazism. Emigrants to Mexico and Russia naturally found that their view of fascism in Germany was influenced by their experiences in their country of exile.[30] When this understanding of history was coupled with adherence to the strict requirements of socialist realism—the presentation of a model situation and a positive hero—the possibility of critical distancing became even more remote. Despite slight thaws in the official line in the mid-fifties and the early seventies, writers were urged to keep to traditional forms of narration, avoiding more innovative structures, which in the socialist view are only accessible to a literary elite. Against this background, opposition could be expressed only within the accepted paradigm; attempts to break out of the closed model, as in certain works of Anna Seghers, Johannes Bobrowski, and Christa Wolf, were greeted with suspicion.

Only occasionally was the unreality of the socialist paradigm brought to the fore. Stephan Hermlin's short story "Lieutenant Yorck von Wartenburg" (1946), an imaginary account of the last moments in the life of a member of the officers' conspiracy against Hitler, is a good example. Cooped up in his prison cell awaiting execution, Yorck von Wartenburg dreams of a "corrected" version of the unsuccessful assassination attempt of 20 July 1944. Told as if it were real, the dream continues until the penultimate moment, when the dreamer awakes to a terrible awareness of failure. Now at last separating dream and reality, he nonetheless clings to his vision as he dies. Hermlin's vignette should have drawn attention to the real nature of East German resistance myths: that their intended function lies precisely in their unreality, in their correction of what really happened, and in their projection of an ideal to be turned to in the future.

Unfortunately, the East German paradigm has been cast in the mold of a simplified realism which ignores this function of literature. In positing consonance between literary presentation and accepted views of reality, it minimizes the reader's awareness that fiction is rooted in ideology. In calling for agreement from its readers, it denies them their potential for political growth.

This increasing rigidity of the paradigm can be seen in the development of the East German tradition. Bodo Uhse, in *We Sons* (written in 1944 but not published until 1948), is still able to exploit the double optics of limited first-person narration. By pointing out the imperfections of his schoolboy protagonist's understanding of reality, he encourages the reader to develop a more complete vision. By setting his story in the year 1918, he calls upon the reader to think beyond the end of the novel by drawing parallels and making distinctions. And by making the positive hero an absent model (the boy's dead mentor Erxner), he creates a dialectic that demands our participation for its completion.

Similarly, Anna Seghers' early novel *Transit* (published during her exile in 1943) sets up a dialectic between her worker-protagonist and the uncompleted manuscript of which he accidentally gains possession. The blank page at the conclusion of the manuscript corresponds to the novel's orientation towards the future, in which the positive model is to be adapted creatively to a new set of circumstances.[31]

But the comparative subtlety of these more dialectical approaches is soon abandoned. Seghers herself, attempting again and again to soften the edges of the requisite socialist hero, often falls prey to the more typically West German extreme of irrationality and myth. As she broadens the scope of her canvas and tries to encompass the socio-political mechanisms of an entire era, as in *The Dead Stay Young* (1949), she balances precariously between the socialist paradigm and its mythic counterpart. Even her formal innovations, much as they resemble the multifaceted technique that Heinrich Böll was to handle with relative success in *Billiards at Half-Past Nine* (1959), fail to modify the overall impression that life falls into a single, vast pattern. In depicting people from different generations and from a range of social classes, Seghers was trying to create an effect similar to that of the frescos of Diego Rivera, whose work she had much admired during her Mexican exile.[32] Artfully arranged and politically expressive, such frescos were complex, but still easy to understand. In this respect they appealed to Anna Seghers' desire to address the non-elitist reader without sacrificing subtlety of form. But in supporting the fresco-like panorama of *The Dead Stay Young* with an underlying symbolic pattern (the generational parallels and the frequent use of leitmotifs), she invalidates her own attempt to perceive history as open-ended. Her conclusion consists of the suggestion that the resistance heritage be handed down through the generation as yet unborn; more appropriate would be an exhortation to rethink prevailing views of resistance.

These problems are not unexpected in a writer like Anna Seghers, originally from the middle class and thus bound to feel torn between innovative literary forms and the prescribed one-dimensional paradigms. But even proletarian writers like Willi Bredel, who were more familiar with social complexities, resolve the issue of continuity between the Third Reich and the postwar period by resorting to the socialist paradigm. Bredel's trilogy, *Relatives and Friends* (1941–53), rests almost entirely on the image of the family heritage as the bearer of the resistance tradition. And Bodo Uhse's unfinished late novel, *The Patriots* (1954), ostensibly a spy story, develops the paradigm through the use of symmetrical arrangements: constellations of characters, parallel or contrasting plots, counterpoint and connections within the underground network in which his characters move. All of these substitute for the mythic substratum of the West German novels and create their own version of closed literary structures. If we compare *The Patriots* with even such second-rate works of West German fiction as Hans Hellmut Kirst's trilogy *Zero Eight Fifteen* (1955), we can see what is missing. Both novels carry the appeal of an adventure story, but Kirst's adds an undercurrent of irony, an assumption that the reader knows better than the characters and can view them with a degree of detachment. By its very nature, socialist realism reduces the potential for ironic presentation. The type of novel that must be read against the grain, by constructing the inverse of the actual story told, is something of a rarity in East German fiction. A look at one exception, Eberhard Panitz' *Unsaintly Sophia* (1975), which begins at much the same point in time as *The Patriots* leaves off and deals, like Uhse's novel, with the Russian involvement in the German underground resistance, may cast some light on the status of ironic structures in East German fiction.

What Uhse had abandoned after *We Sons,* Panitz resurrects for a new purpose: the limited-point-of-view narrator. Everyone seems to know more about Sophia than the narrator, but, fascinated with snippets of information he grasps here and there, he feels impelled to carry on the quest for her identity. The surprise ending—that Sophia, a Russian agent parachuted into Germany toward the end of the war and subsequently mayor of the small town where the story takes place, is actually the mother of the narrator's wife—provides an ironic answer to the question of continuity. Like Christa Wolf's *The Quest for Christa T.* (1968), Panitz' novel places the burden of the detective work on the reader, who has to complete the picture of Sophia that constantly eludes the narrator. Whether her unorthodox way of governing the town is to be read as resistance or merely as human complexity re-

mains unresolved in the novel itself. But the book's two-level approach
to the past forms an incipient dialectic for the reader to complete.

The spy story resistance novel was not the only model to be used in
East Germany. The middle generation preferred to accept its own
views of the past and turn them to account through situational irony.
This differs from the open irony of Panitz' *Sophia*, since it depends
upon an accepted view of things in the present which forms the crite-
rion for evaluating the past. Franz Fühmann's work is perhaps the
best example of this method. His experience of nazism from within,
as a product of the German school system and as a soldier in Hitler's
army, coupled with his postwar conversion to communism while a
prisoner of war in Russia, equip him to be a spokesman for an entire
generation. His best short stories, such as "Comrades" (1955) or
"The Capitulation" (1958), depend almost entirely upon plot rever-
sals in which the other face of the Nazi view of reality is suddenly
revealed. Other works employ elements of dream, fairy tale, and
myth uncommon in East German writing. One of his most moving
small masterpieces, "Bohemia by the Sea" (1962), uses Shakespeare's
unintentional displacement of Bohemia to the seaside in *A Winter's
Tale* as a metaphor for an old woman's postwar displacement from
her inland home to a seaside town. The image from Shakespeare
becomes a suggestive, multilevel bond between her psyche and the
narrator's consciousness. More grandiose, but ultimately less convincing, is the use of myth in "King Oedipus" (1966), even though it
demonstrates the unmasking of Nazi ideology. But the tale depends
on an underlying belief in historical inevitability, whereby World War
II is understood as part of a transitional period that parallels the
transition from one form of society to another in Sophocles' *Oedipus
Rex*. When Fühmann lets his imagery sweep him away, he uses a kind
of nature myth not unrelated to the popular metaphors of nazism. His
"Barlach in Güstrow" (1963), the one piece which presents resistance
to nazism from within, suffers markedly from this fault. One cannot
help feeling that Barlach's resistance, his decision to stand firm despite the desecration of his sculptures, is rooted in what amounts to a
crypto-fascist mode of thought.

During this period, another group of middle generation writers had
begun to develop a new socialist paradigm that took into account
personal experience of nazism while also pointing beyond it. Their
literary models form a more direct counterpart to the resistance heritage novels than do the stories of Fühmann. Harking back to the
traditional German novel of development and education (*Bildungsroman*), this group tries to gain perspective on the past by viewing it in
terms of personal development. Erwin Strittmatter's *The Miracle
Worker* (1957), Dieter Noll's *The Adventures of Werner Holt* (1960–

63), and Erik Neutsch's *Peace in the East* (1974–78) are two-part novels with strong autobiographical elements. All three stress the problematic, even paradoxical, nature of the transition from nazism to socialism. But despite their greater complexities, the development novels can hardly be said to break out of the closed structures of programmatic thought. The close identification of author and protagonist divests the novels of the *Bildungsroman*'s original advantage: its ironic structure. Ultimately, the adventure-story pattern of the positive hero novels prevails here too; the novels show how a character abandons nazism and embraces socialism but do not explore the nature of ideology in general. Individual political and social development follows a consistent pattern, and one novel can almost be substituted for another, so unvarying is the underlying model. In Neutsch's series of novels, the pattern even begins to take on the status of myth, as young Achim, in a schoolboy poem written to his girlfriend after her recovery from an abortion, sentimentally invokes the story of Eurydice. The young woman's return to consciousness from a coma and Achim's ultimate enlightenment after political and sexual ignorance, error, and guilt take on the inevitability of the mythic return from the underworld. Despite this gesture toward myth, the development genre maintains its basic form, though relying rather heavily upon a more inward, psychological presentation.

In this regard, the East German novel lags conspicuously behind its counterpart in the West. Perhaps the most convincing testament to this is Uwe Johnson's second novel, *The Third Book about Achim* (1961), conceived against the foil of GDR theory but published two years after his move to the Federal Republic. Here the idea of history as a product of individual perceptions becomes a central theme of the novel. Realism and fiction are thematically linked in a story line that involves a journalist's attempt to write the definitive biography of Achim, an East German cycling champion. Achim's present life seems unintelligible from the journalist's Western point of view, and what he learns about the cyclist's past is simply not acceptable to the party officials who have commissioned the book and who prefer schematic views of continuity to the shifting complexities that Karsch discovers. Johnson's peculiar status allows him to create the unusual phenomenon of a West German response to an East German schema. Unlike its East German predecessors, *The Third Book about Achim* remains defiantly open-ended, constantly teasing and prodding the reader to complete the vision that the journalist has abandoned in despair. In pointing up this issue of subjective perception, Johnson, unlike his journalist Karsch, does not simply throw up his hands in horror or succumb to an unresolved plurality of interpretation. In using the subjective lens to distort historical material almost beyond recognition, he draws attention to the fact that a unified vision of reality is itself a fiction. Although his view of the contrast between East and West is somewhat simplistic, the novelist refrains from codifying them into unyielding models. The discrepancy between the relatively direct mirroring of accepted views one tends to expect from fiction and the puzzlingly elusive version of reality Johnson gives in this novel forces the reader to become more critical of common assumptions. *The Third Book about Achim,* one of the earliest attempts at reader activation in the postwar German novel, points the way to a new genre of reflection on nazism.

But Johnson is an unusual case. We shall see later, in Johannes Bobrowski and Christa Wolf, two other exceptions to the dominant socialist realism of GDR theory; but, in the main, East German novels continue to be locked into a set of relatively inflexible, predetermined patterns.

CHAPTER TWO

THE FLOWER OF EVIL
Thomas Mann's *Doctor Faustus*

One work, more complex and of more influence on subsequent literary developments, stands out among the mythic or paradigmatic novels of the early phase: Thomas Mann's *Doctor Faustus* (1947). Discussing the strange phenomenon of osmotic growths, crystals whose formations appear as an uncanny imitation of natural plant life, the narrator of *Doctor Faustus* makes a comment that could stand as the ironic signature of the book as a whole: "But one thing I will say: such weirdnesses are exclusively Nature's own affair, and particularly Nature arrogantly tempted by man. In the high-minded realms of the *humaniora* one is safe from such impish phenomena" (20).[1] Yet is the humanist really safe from the uncanny? In a more serious form, this is the chief issue of *Doctor Faustus,* and it is a question with profound ramifications for a reconsideration of the Nazi past. The concluding sentence posits that the humanities can provide a refuge from mischievous tricks of nature. But the real question, one that the narrator never explicitly poses, is whether the humanistic tradition can provide a platform adequate to the task of resistance against evil. The witty comment on osmotic growths in reality implies the opposite, that the humanities are no less liable to freakish outgrowths than the realm of natural science; and it is this hidden ambiguity of the scholarly and cultural tradition which the novel seeks to explore and expose. The narrator's shudder and the protagonist's laughter at the chemical freaks form a dualistic response that becomes increasingly less clear-cut as the novel proceeds. The stage is set for a multilayered analysis of a series of uncanny phenomena that begins apparently harmlessly with the osmotic growths and concludes much more ominously with the "flower of evil," the mad genius of its musician-protagonist, Adrian Leverkühn.

Thomas Mann's *Doctor Faustus* acquires its special place by virtue of its unusual handling of myth and allegory. That it does not quite escape the formal labyrinth it sets up is in part the result of its genesis during the war years and partly the result of Mann's very personal involvement with the material, which had concerned him in a different context at a much earlier period of his life.[2] The novel is distinguished

42

from related contemporary works by its use of irony and ambiguity. Its narrative innovations prepare the way for important successors of the two decades following, Günter Grass' *The Tin Drum* and Siegfried Lenz' *The German Lesson*. Thus, while not entirely characteristic of German literature in the late forties, *Doctor Faustus* nonetheless sets the tone for later novels on nazism and is the first link in a literary chain.

Unlike most of the other works under discussion, Mann's novel is unmistakably the product of exile, dependent upon views of nazism held by the German emigrants in California and determined by the political barrier between them and their compatriots who had remained in Germany during the war. Of course, during the first years of the war, many of the simple facts about nazism were not widely known in America, although Thomas Mann did the best he could to disseminate information that came to his attention by means of his essays and radio broadcasts. While Mann informed his listeners as early as 1942 of the extermination of Jews in Germany and Poland, in *Doctor Faustus* he allows for the information lag between Germany and America by having his narrator, Serenus Zeitblom, first learn of the concentration camps in 1945.[3] But the marked change in tone that takes place at this point in the novel is also attributable to Mann's own response to his homeland's increasingly apparent guilt during the later years of the war.. Like most of the postwar novelists, Mann's views of nazism were less influenced by historiography than by the press, in this case by the American Hearst press and the reactions of his German friends to its reports. In particular, his critical engagement with what became known as Vansittartism (after Gilbert Vansittart, whose total identification of all Germans with nazism had been extremely influential in Britain and the United States during the early forties)[4] played an important role in his attempt to construct an account of Germany and nazism that might avoid this simplistic categorization. His simultaneous debate with the polar opposite of Vansittartism, the argument, most prominently put by Bertolt Brecht, that there were in essence two Germanies, a good and a bad, acounts for both the subtleties and the problems of Mann's ambitiously constructed novel.[5] By layering ambiguity upon ambiguity, presenting the dualistic protagonist through the eyes of a no less dualistic narrator, Mann hoped to escape the pitfalls of overly schematic presentation; but he also created some formal obstacles that were difficult to overcome.

In terms of his analysis of the relation of nazism to the German tradition, Mann was in many ways ahead of his time, especially if one compares his novel with works of historiography that were approximately contemporaneous, such as those of Friedrich Meinecke or Gerhard Ritter.[6] What they and their more popularizing successors saw as a discontinuity of tradition was understood quite differently by Thomas Mann. Of crucial importance for Mann's more critical view of the tradition was his choice of a narrator representing the humanistic tradition in both its remarkable scope and its specific narrow-mindedness. This enabled him to present the flowering of German creative genius (symbolized by the protagonist) with a certain measure of scepticism, while simultaneously requiring that the more pedantic side of the tradition (symbolized by the narrator) also be seen by the reader with a distinctly critical eye. In thus representing the two sides of the cultural tradition, he was able to cover a wider field than would otherwise have been possible and to present it with greater subtlety than had hitherto been the case. In this respect Mann's analysis of the genesis of nazism must be seen less as a product of his time than as a pacesetter for future analysts, literary and otherwise.[7] That the topic of active resistance is only indirectly invoked in *Doctor Faustus* (through the discussions on free will and the political withdrawal of the narrator) is entirely consonant with public opinion at the time of the book's genesis, which tended to deemphasize the possibility and significance of resistance to Hitler from within Germany itself. It was not until the late forties that historians like Hans Rothfels began to remind the world of the resistance fighters of 20 July 1944, and only in the mid-fifties that others, such as Gerhard Ritter, again took up the question of resistance;[8] Mann is scarcely to be blamed for his emphasis on passivity and inner emigration. His partially sympathetic critique of the latter by means of the figure of Zeitblom is doubtless representative of a view held by many of the German exiles. Whatever influences may have helped form Thomas Mann's views of nazism, it is remarkable that he completely refrains from mentioning historiographic sources in *The Story of a Novel*, his painstaking record of the literary and philosophical influences upon the conception of *Doctor Faustus*.[9] This silence suggests that in Mann's eyes his presentation of nazism was much less a mere element of the montage than other aspects of the novel. Nor was it on the same level as the acknowledged reference to Schönberg, from whose musical theories Leverkühn's compositional principles are partially derived, or the unacknowledged but not too heavily disguised borrowings from the life of Nietzsche, which account for such details of the plot as Leverkühn's visit to the brothel and his subsequent infection with syphilis. Mann's depiction of nazism, in other words, is part and parcel of a developing conception inseparable from the work as a whole. In fact, *Doctor Faustus,* for all its reliance on extra-literary material, is a prime example of the way in which fiction does not simply mold preexisting views of history into a convenient shape but also creates them in the very process of its narrative presentation.

The material Mann takes as his starting point has no integral connection with politics, and a large measure of the novel's originality lies in the way in which Mann creates this connection. After all, *Doctor Faustus* purports to be the biography of an avant-garde composer as told by his schoolmaster friend; thus it seems to fall into a line of artist novels and novellas, taking up once again a theme that occupied Mann for most of his life. Mann had already undertaken a broadening of the artist theme into the realm of metaphysical speculation in *The Magic Mountain* (1924), but in *Doctor Faustus* he integrates the philosophical, theological, social, and political content much more skillfully. The university studies of his latter-day Faust provide one opportunity to present this material; the protagonist's later contacts with a variety of social spheres allow other types of thought to be given. But the real key to *Doctor Faustus* is the point of view from which it is narrated, that of a somewhat narrow-minded and pedantic bourgeois humanist.[10] In working out this scheme, Mann goes considerably beyond his chief model, E.T.A. Hoffmann's at once tragic and witty double novel *Tomcat Murr* (1820–22), the autobiography of a cat written with ink-stained claw on the back of manuscript pages containing the biography of his musician master. Though Hoffmann's philistine cat and mad musician find their counterparts in Mann's schoolteacher and composer, *Doctor Faustus* introduces greater continuity and a closer linkage between the two levels of the narrative. Apart from Adrian's letter from Leipzig, only one portion of *Doctor Faustus*, Mann's equivalent of Faust's pact with the devil, is given from a perspective other than that of the fictional biographer; this scene, perhaps the most difficult for the man of reason to narrate, is told in the form of a letter from the composer to his friend. Whereas in Hoffmann the relation between the two time planes is quixotic and confusing, Mann insures that the time span of the narration (the duration of World War II) forms an ominous counterpoint to the tale of Leverkühn's development and his collapse into madness in 1930. Apart from the outline of the revamped Faust myth, there is very little actual plot in this novel; it consists, rather, of an elaborate network of thoughts and opinions (mainly in the form of conversations or summaries of lectures and talks) and detailed descriptions of fictitious pieces of music and the theory that lies behind them. This ambitious interweaving of aesthetics, ethics, and politics makes *Doctor Faustus* a landmark in the attempt to come to terms with nazism.

If the central issue of Mann's novel is its double focus, this must be seen not merely in the dual time frame of protagonist and biographer but also in the simultaneous use of two literary forms, the mythic and the ironic. What is remarkable about this conception is the fact that, theoretically speaking, the two structures are in certain respects mutually exclusive, since irony tends to modify myth's dependence on recurrence and predestination. When successors of Thomas Mann like Elisabeth Langgässer took up the mythic structure alone, they thus were isolating only one pole of this delicately balanced novel. Indeed, it has not been uncommon for readers of *Doctor Faustus* to emphasize one structure at the expense of the other. Shortly after the book's appearance, Ernst Fischer in a now well-known essay reproached Mann for having created what Mann himself most wished to avoid: a new German "myth of fate."[11] Attempts to defend *Faustus* from this criticism tend to center on the ironic role of Zeitblom as narrator and, more importantly, on Mann's own self-distancing from the two positions. I shall take up the controversial question of Mann's stance a little later; for the moment, let us concentrate on the mythic layer of *Doctor Faustus* and its implications for the question of resistance to nazism. Naturally, the mythic cannot be really isolated, and it should be understood throughout this discussion that the ironic frame ultimately modifies my evaluation of the mythic stratum.

The basic myth depends on the identification of the composer Adrian Leverkühn with Faust. Unlike James Joyce, who uses Homeric myths as a hermetic underlay for his *Ulysses,* Mann provides the motivation for the conflation of Leverkühn and Faust within the plot of the novel itself. By chapter 25 at the latest, the reader comes to realize that Leverkühn sees himself as Faust; it is not a mere construction put upon the tale from outside. On the psychological level, Leverkühn's account in the letter to Zeitblom that constitutes the bulk of this chapter is a manifestation of this particular self-perception. At the same time, it is clear that the reader is not intended to discount the Faust identification as only a hallucination of Leverkühn's or as a mere conceit.[12] There is a sense in which we are meant to understand that Leverkühn *is* a modern Faust, beyond all cynicism or irony. It goes without saying that the metamorphosis of the Faust figure from the Renaissance to the present is an important component of the restructured myth. What once took the guise of magic now appears as a response to a certain cultural situation, a particular juncture in the history of aesthetics and politics. Underlying these transformations, however, is the hypothesis of a perennial recurrence in which basic myths reveal themselves again in new forms.

This has implications for the novel's symbolic demonstration, chiefly through the character of Leverkühn, of the genesis of nazism out of the German tradition. In the last analysis, it suggests a patterning of events with at least a certain measure of inevitability, or, perhaps more accurately, an inbuilt constraint upon thought that prevents events from being understood without recourse to mythic structuring.

In terms of Leverkühn's function as a symbol of Germany's involvement with evil, Mann's shift of the pact with the devil into the psychological sphere does more than merely modernize the Faust myth. In essence, it supplies a new level to the sense of inevitability implied by the recurrence of the myth itself. We are to understand that it is the nature of Leverkühn's (and Germany's) genius which gives rise to involvement with evil, that genius and evil are in a sense the two faces of one coin. Thus, a kind of causal connection is posited that makes more sense in mythic terms than it does in terms of history. But unlike some other mythic reflections on nazism, Mann's analysis of the relationship between the German tradition and Hitler's rise to power is very finely drawn. The mythic structure carries the broader outline, but not the specific details. The result is a paradoxical complex of social, cultural, and historical analyses on the one hand and schematic shaping of the material on the other. Mann was acutely aware of the problems mythic thinking brings with it, and he was obviously at some pains to mitigate them as much as possible by the inclusion of a considerable amount of specific detail. In terms of his theory of irony, myth and history are doubtless expected to balance each other, but the unresolved nature of his paradox remains a difficulty for the reader nonetheless.

Compounding the problem are the coincidental doublings that link various elements of the story, expanding the principle of recurrence beyond the purely mythic sphere. But how real these are remains ambiguous. To begin with, they exist to a large extent primarily in Leverkühn's perception of things, as when he calls the Schweigestills' dog by the same name as the dog on his father's farm or claims to have swum during his childhood in their nearby pond. Yet the likenesses between the Leverkühn and Schweigestill farms cannot be attributed entirely to Leverkühn's psychological makeup; Zeitblom, too, believes in them. Similarly, certain characters come in pairs: the translator Rüdiger Schildknapp has the same kind of eyes as Leverkühn, so that the two of them come to represent the two faces of creativity; Leverkühn has two intimate friends (*Duzfreunde*), Zeitblom and Rudi Schwerdtfeger, and two mother figures, his real mother Elisabeth Leverkühn and the mother substitute Else Schweigestill; and the prostitute who infects Leverkühn with syphilis has a parallel in the mysterious Frau von Tolna. The Rodde sisters, Clarissa and Ines, are polar opposites, and so on. Leverkühn incorporates a similar doubling in his musical compositions, as when, in his *Apocalipsis cum figuris*, the same sequence of notes that has appeared in the angelic children's chorus is repeated in the hellish laughter of a succeeding passage. And, finally, Leverkühn's last work, *The Lamentation of Dr. Faustus*, is a revocation of both the "Ode to Joy" in Beethoven's Ninth Symphony and the "Watch with me" of Gethsemane (490).[13] Moreover, this musical reconstruction of the Faust legend conflates it with the Orpheus myth, making the two figures seem like "brothers as invokers of the world of the shades" (488). Faust's descent into hell is re-created musically by Leverkühn as a simultaneous ballet and gallop "of fantastic rhythmic variety" (489).

In short, the whole composition is constructed around repetitions and echoes in contrasting configurations and inversions to create, as Zeitblom observes, a vast artistic paradox. Its final note, the high G of a cello, has a dual effect: "that tone . . . which was the voice of mourning, is so no more. It changes its meaning; it abides as a light in the night" (491). The idea of recurrence becomes imbued with ambiguity. Is there an underlying identity between apparently disparate phenomena, or is this a construction of the human mind? Again, Mann refrains from solving the puzzle.

In leaving the question open, Mann attempts to minimize his implication that man is essentially powerless in the face of recurring cycles of events. But can the individual extricate himself from what appears an inevitable pattern? The key incident that deals with this problem is Leverkühn's attempt to cure his syphilis while it is still in its early phase. Twice fate seems to be against him—the first doctor dies suddenly before completing the treatment and the second is carried off to prison on the occasion of Leverkühn's third visit—but Mann makes it clear that Leverkühn could have sought another doctor. It is Leverkühn's interpretation of this sequence of events as a sign of fate (later apparently confirmed by the devil's contention that it had actually been engineered by him) that determines his course of action. Significantly, Zeitblom tells the story without comment, yet one feels it would have been better if Leverkühn had somehow managed to resist his fate.

Altogether, the matter of Leverkühn's involvement with evil is fraught with problems that remain basically unresolved. While he allows himself to be infected with syphilis, his willingness to do so seems to stem less from the conscious mind than from the unconscious: it corresponds to a deep-seated need which the rational mind seems powerless to combat. Thus what appears to be voluntary action is, in fact, a kind of necessity, the fulfillment of psychological predestination, the price Leverkühn must pay for the full flowering of his genius. This intentional ambiguity echoes in miniature the working-out of this problem on other levels in the novel.[14]

Resistance to nazism is scarcely treated as such in *Doctor Faustus;* instead, a continuing discussion of free will and freedom in both the theological and the artistic domains sets the more specific historic problem into a general framework. The first mention of free will occurs in the reproduction of Schleppfuss' lectures on theology at the University of Halle. Of course, this colorful theologian is not accidentally named Schleppfuss, a name that suggests the folk image of the limping devil. This puts him into a somewhat questionable light, as does the story he tells about a young man whose impotence with women other than his betrothed was finally cured when he had his girlfriend burned at the stake as a witch. Nonetheless, it is Schlepp-fuss who introduces a crass version of the issues upon which the entire novel turns: the question whether evil is a necessary concomitant of the divine and how good and evil are related to each other. As Schleppfuss sees it, the real vindication of God consists in his ability to produce good from evil, a problem treated on another level in the novel through the allegory of Leverkühn's pact with the devil. One topic of Schleppfuss's lectures is the old question why God gave man free will; Zeitblom comments, "Freedom. How extraordinary the word sounded, in Schleppfuss's mouth!" (101). The word has a strange ring, as Zeitblom even then dimly perceived, because it is a freedom from which the virtuous must necessarily abstain: "Piety and virtue, then, consisted in making a good use, that is to say, no use at all, of the freedom which God had to grant the creature as such" (101). Freedom is merely the freedom to sin, Schleppfuss claims, and hence it is best to make no use of it. Zeitblom notes that the question of freedom was not a burning issue for the students who attended his lectures, but the very fact that he comments on it makes the reader reflect that, in neglecting to engage in Schleppfuss' debate, the students have been fatally short-sighted. In canceling out other definitions of freedom by presenting them in a scornful and disparaging tone, Schleppfuss in effect deprives the students of the opportunity to conceive of freedom in terms of positive action. Zeitblom expresses only mild disappointment that this involves a "diminution of the intensity of being" in the individual (101).

Leverkühn himself uses the word freedom in a different sense, embedding it in the context of artistic creativity and cultural tradition. Talking with Zeitblom about his musical mentor Wendell Kretzschmar, he describes him as the sort of person needed in an age when the idea of freedom exerts a negative, rather than a positive, influence upon talent. Leverkühn defines freedom as synonymous with subjectivity but recognizes at the same time another kind of freedom, one that expresses itself within the constraints of organized form and exploits aspects of subjectivity to create from them something objective.[15] This theory of the dialectic of freedom (193), the idea that a willing submission to order is intrinsically a kind of freedom, is what gives rise in Leverkühn's thinking to the whole concept of twelve-tone music. As he sees it, this is a form of music that frees itself from conventional harmony and counterpoint and willingly subjects itself to a higher, more objective order. Though sceptical of the new theory of music, Zeitblom readily perceives this metaphysical property of its organizing principles, comparing it with the magic square of Dürer's *Melencolia I,* in which all the rows of numbers have the same sum (192). Ironically the magic square is symbolic not of freedom but of fate.[16]

Leverkühn's theory of the new freedom in composition has other ramifications besides the hidden reference to the paradox of free will and fate. The conversation had begun with the idea that Kretzschmar was the most needed person in a decadent age. This point, which provides the framework for the discussion of music theory, is much more overtly political.[17] Leverkühn's criticism of his age stems from his belief that it has become too free. Modern freedom, he says, lies "like a mildew" upon talent and will ultimately lead to sterility. A startling idea, the conception of freedom as mildew! One cannot help feeling alarmed at this expression of the thought that artistic talent needs the supporting structure of organized, traditional forms in order to flourish. The idea of talent mildewed by freedom draws attention to the problematic nature of Leverkühn's theory. What is needed in the modern age, according to his view, is a new union of the archaic and the revolutionary such as he had already experienced in one form through the teaching of Wendell Kretzschmar. The new music he envisages will combine in similar fashion the archaic (the principles of inversion and variation) with the revolutionary (the introduction of the twelve-tone chromatic scale as its basis). Zeitblom's response is to understand it politically, as a kind of conservative revolution: he perceives a "restorative element in your Utopia" (193). This leaves the emphasis somewhat more one-sided than Leverkühn had anticipated. But Zeitblom, the pedantic rationalist for all his partial misunderstandings, sees a danger in the new theory of combining the "progressive and regressive" (193) and warns his friend that it could ultimately lead to the dissolution of reason in magic. Leverkühn, however, moves on a different plane where both aspects perenially hold the balance, like the scales in Dürer's picture. What interests him is the ambivalence or paradoxical nature of his new construct, which seems to him to mirror the ambiguity of life itself. And it is Leverkühn who has the last word in the discussion between the two friends, despite the reader's awareness that Zeitblom's doubts and scruples have never been adequately resolved. Is it enough to take equivocality as one's ideal? Are there not circumstances in which a belief in ambiguity can have dangerous consequences?

Only much later in the novel is there a different analysis of the archaic-revolutionary complex. In a debate within the Kridwiss circle, we witness the jostling of two forces that may be presumed to be operative in the community at large and that form the crux of Mann's understanding of the genesis of nazism. Again, we must consider his way of working with ambiguities. Baron von Riedesel is a straightforward example of the return to conservatism that characterized many of the nobility at this time; his counterpart Dr. Breisacher (ironically, and fully in accordance with Mann's thoroughgoing ambiguities, a Jew) is a disturbing example of the new archaic revolutionary giving voice to a "radical conservatism that no longer has anything aristocratic about it, but rather something revolutionary" (284). Here, as Zeitblom comments, is an instance where "the avant-garde coincides with the reactionary" and ordinary conservatism is outbid by the "frightfully clever playing of atavistic cards" (284). Of course, Breisacher's views are very different from those of Leverkühn, but Mann's critique of this particular kind of atavistic modernism casts a shadow over Leverkühn's restorative Utopia. Again, the debate applies what appear to be political terms to the sphere of aesthetics, in this case, the development of music from its earliest polyphonic forms. According to Breisacher's outrageously provocative views, the real decline of music and the beginnings of what he perceives as decadent modern forms lie in the very first movement away from the objective play with numbers that had characterized the earliest polyphony. Whereas a name like Bach signals the epitome of conservatism for the baron, Breisacher curiously assigns Bach to the phase of decline. His reasoning is fascinating to follow, especially if one bears in mind the magic square theory of music developed by Leverkühn several chapters earlier. Breisacher's criticism of Bach turns upon his interpretation of Bach's compositional principle, which he describes as conceiving of every note ambiguously and exchanging them enharmonically. The reader must recall that Leverkühn's first exploration of the various musical keys and their relation to one another had resulted in the discovery of enharmonic changes. In fact, ambiguity of one sort or another has long been part of his interest in music; one need only think of his earliest musical experience, singing canons with the milkmaid on his father's property, which had revealed to him the possibility of the same few measures functioning in turn as the first, second, and third parts of the round. A more progressive version of musical ambiguity can be found in the violin concerto he writes for Rudi Schwerdtfeger, which has no key signature and revolves around three different tonalities, the leading chord being a dissonant combination of triads from all three (409). And his *Apocalipsis cum figuris,* where the narrative warning is accompanied by pedal harmonies in an unrelated key (anticipating the structure of Zeitblom's biography), also contains a *responsorium* of two four-part choruses in contrary motion (357). His earlier decision to set certain poems of Blake and Brentano to music is another aspect of this concern with ambiguity. For Blake, the forces of good and evil are both preordained and inextricably intertwined; his cankered rose is another version of the flower of evil which manifests itself in Leverkühn's genius. Brentano's sensual fascination with evil is even more ambivalent than Blake's. Leverkühn's adaptations of Brentano provide the other face, as it were, of Schumann's musical settings of Eichendorff poems (Leverkühn becomes familiar with them through his mentor Kretzschmar), since Eichendorff, though equally fascinated by the ambivalence of good and evil, more often than not resolves it in moral terms. One of Eichendorff's best-known poems, "Zwielicht," is specifically mentioned as "that piece invoking all the romantic perils and threats to the soul, which ends with the uncannily moral warning: 'Hüte dich! Sei wach und munter!' " (77). Whereas Schumann prefers to set poems by Eichendorff to music, Leverkühn takes the less resolved ambivalences of Brentano as the basis for his compositional ambiguities.

All this seems perfectly in order until Breisacher's cynical analysis of the decline in the musical tradition. However much one dislikes the unpleasant and supercilious theorist, one cannot help seeing how questionable his views make the magical aspect of Leverkühn's fascination with music.[18] If the inventor of the well-tempered clavichord, the proponent of harmonic counterpoint, is the epitome of ambiguity, a creator of music that is neither fish nor fowl (as Breisacher cuttingly puts it [281]), then how much more so must be the music of the modern experimenter in equivocality, the creator of avant-garde tonalities organized by magic square designs. It is clear that Leverkühn takes the point, since he averts his eyes from Zeitblom's inquiring gaze. And Zeitblom himself, who perceives not only Breisacher's one-upmanship but also the dangerous aspect of his revolutionary atavism (his plea for a return to objective polyphony based on purely numerical organization and hence itself a kind of number magic), again remains significantly silent. Apologizing later for his failure to dispute the point with Breisacher, he observes that only recently has he realized how much leeway polite tolerance and forbearance have granted to the other side. Tacitly, he castigates himself for not having engaged in the intellectual resistance against proto-nazism.

Zeitblom's paradoxical position, his combination of insight and passivity, is in accord with his role as a representative of inner emigration. Unlike Mann himself, Zeitblom has remained in Germany during the Third Reich, though to be sure he has resigned from his teaching post to avoid overt involvement with the Nazi regime. His intense preoccupation with the fate of his friend, which he implicitly recognizes as in some way related to the rise of nazism, is indication enough of his belated feelings of guilt over the essential passivity of his role. At the same time, with schoolmasterly pedantry, he takes pride in his attempt to distance himself from political events and to write with detachment of a friend's life which actually calls forth his most intense responses. By depicting Zeitblom in this manner, Mann manages to present a critique of inner emigration at once telling and sympathetic.

Why does Mann choose as a narrator a figure so imperfectly capable of ironic distancing? In his usual ambiguous manner, the author tries not only to put the main thread of his story into question but to sustain an extremely delicate balance. The idea of employing a separate, individually characterized narrator was a technique that Mann had added to his inventory especially for the purposes of *Doctor Faustus*. In a practical sense Zeitblom, as his name indicates, is needed to embody the principle of time and to add a dimension lacking in the life of Leverkühn, who is mentally incompetent during the final decade covered in the novel.

Alongside this counterpoint of the Pan-European creative mind (Leverkühn) and the more narrow-minded scholar-teacher (Zeitblom), the two characters also embody an intrinsic paradox in terms of their class origins. This, too, was of crucial importance to Mann's understanding of German fascism. Leverkühn's family is of the older German type: financially well-off, they are the owners of a dignified farmhouse; they abjure modern, citified ways, preferring to follow simpler customs both in dress and thought. His father is well-informed on numerous aspects of natural science, and Leverkühn's university education, though not typical of the family as a whole, can yet be seen as a flowering of its traditional old-German potential.[19] Although Zeitblom's education is almost identical to that of Leverkühn and he functions in the novel as the representative par excellence of the educated upper middle class, he has, in fact, risen somewhat above his origins as the son of a small-town apothecary.[20] His inner emigration would be unthinkable were he not, in his own way, a man of letters, which helps bring to the surface a problem central to the conception of the novel: the question of the independence of the intellect. Just as Leverkühn's creativity, simultaneously progressive and regressive, is ironically typical of the epoch from which he hopes to emancipate himself, Zeitblom's intellectual position as a teacher of the humanities is at once distanced from and subtly bound up with the period in which he lives. It is not simply that Zeitblom is slow to comprehend the problematic nature of what he regards as inner resistance; his apparent acceptance of the Leverkühn-Faust connection also prevents him from taking on more than a rather benign protectorship towards his friend. Is the realm of the humanities really free from freakish phenomena? Zeitblom's traditional modes of thought prevent him from freeing himself from patterns of conceptualization, including the pattern of myth. This ambiguity of intellectual freedom explains Mann's selection of an imperfectly distanced narrator like Zeitblom.

Another aspect of the Leverkühn-Zeitblom relationship is its simultaneous polarity and identity, traceable on one level to the autobiographical component of the novel.[21] While Thomas Mann's underlying belief that the world is to be explained in terms of polarities interdependent and related at the core adds to the subtlety of the novel's conception, it also prevents him from presenting a more differentiated view of history. The unfolding of the two time levels, Leverkühn's experience and Zeitblom's account of it, is in the same way at once a counterpoint and a harmony. In terms of character, the two men are contraries, but Leverkühn's flowering and destruction parallel the flowering and destruction of the German tradition represented by his humanist friend. The paradox of individuality and identity remains ambiguous and unresolved.

There is another problem, however, that seems to have been less evident to Mann. This is the change in the presentation of Zeitblom in the course of the book. The exaggerated stylistic parody of the pedant in the first half of *Doctor Faustus* gradually yields to a more straightforward tone, at times verging upon a heartfelt cry of despair that can only be taken as a direct expression of the author's response to the concluding phases of World War II.[22] Unfortunately, this returns the novel to the very dilemma which the introduction of the caricatured narrator was intended to resolve: dependence on mythic structuring and on the notion that, under certain circumstances, good may go forth from evil. Without doubt this change in the function of Zeitblom has much to do with Mann's decision to end the novel tragically, again implying a kind of inevitability, the unalterable fate of genius within the world design.

The conclusion of the Leverkühn story is preceded by the moving account of the death of his little nephew, Nepomuk (known as Echo). Leverkühn views the child's death as the price he himself must pay for his purchase of genius through involvement with evil. The devil has sworn that Leverkühn will never again be able to enjoy love, and his one experience of an unusually sweet, pure love, felt for the child, is hence in Leverkühn's mind destined from the first to disaster. In this context, Nepomuk's death becomes a forewarning of the insanity and death that await Leverkühn. But there is also another context, to which Leverkühn merely alludes, that puts Nepomuk in a somewhat different light. This is the identification of little Echo with Shakespeare's Ariel. It is significant that the only Shakespearean plays that Leverkühn had previously set to music were the comedies, such as *Love's Labour's Lost,* not the tragedies or the problem plays. Now, for the first time, he is concerned with one of Shakespeare's late, ambivalent masterpieces. The reason for this preoccupation with *The Tempest* is relatively obvious. Despite Prospero's haunting abjuration of magic at the end, *The Tempest* provides an essentially positive resolution for each of its protagonists. Ferdinand and Miranda are to marry and return home with Prospero and the rest of the shipwrecked company; Ariel is set free from his bondage to the aging magician. On his nephew's deathbed, Leverkühn refers to Prospero's last words to Ariel, "Then to the elements / Be free, and fare thou well!" (*The Tempest,* 5.1.317–18). This suggests an interpretation of the child's death in which the positive outweighs the negative and the otherworldly Echo is saved from contamination by worldly evil.[23] But unlike Prospero, Leverkühn does not abjure his magic. Instead, his work on his final composition, *The Lamentation of Dr. Faustus,* is the creative expression of a profound mourning for Echo which in turn gives the lie to the positive side of his Ariel conception. The bittersweet ending of Shakespeare's play is modulated into a more darkly ambiguous presentation of the creative genius as a modern version of the magician Prospero.

In a different way, Leverkühn's own death is also ambiguous. Though not accompanied by the gruesome suffering that marks Nepomuk's death from meningitis, his end is nonetheless uncanny. Zeitblom's last view of him in sunken-eyed, virtually comatose repose on his bed creates the impression of an El Greco-like spirituality, as if Leverkühn had already freed himself "to the elements." As Zeitblom observes, Adrian Leverkühn's spirit lives on in his music, the ultimate flower of evil, which is at once a harbinger of nazism and a protest against it. Paradoxically, this music, by reason of his insanity, has lain dormant during almost the entire period of Nazi dominance and its rise to power.

Such ambiguities are only to be expected in a novel whose basic form depends upon equivocality. More significant is Mann's treatment of the Faust story, in which he reverts to the original medieval conception of the myth. Denying Goethe's addition of the salvation of Faust, Mann is also somewhat sceptical of Goethe's contention that evil is part of a higher design for good. Yet Zeitblom maintains that Leverkühn's music may become the source of a new flowering of the German cultural tradition, a kind of salvation for Germany, despite the damnation of the composer himself: "On your madness they will feed in health, and in them you will become healthy". (243). This final complexity has its roots in Zeitblom's (and Mann's) fathomless despair, and its lack of resolution is entirely consonant with the intellectual mood of the German exiles at the time of the novel's completion. Only as we look back at the novel, especially through the eyes of Mann's successors, do the difficulties of this kind of non-directed irony become apparent. In developing its own plot simultaneously with and against the grain, the novel leaves its readers in an agony of evaluation.[24] If we seek a resolution to the moral problems it poses, we will somehow have to escape the mesh of equivocality that constitutes the terms in which the novel is couched.[25] Within the framework of Mann's elaborate construct there is essentially no way out. Like the osmotic growths, the novel strives towards the light of an ever-elusive resolution.

CHAPTER THREE

THE REVOCATION OF MELANCHOLY

Günter Grass' *The Tin Drum*

When, in the late fifties, Günter Grass began to write what is now known as his Danzig trilogy (*The Tin Drum, Cat and Mouse,* and *Dog Years*), one might almost say that he was attempting to create the work that *Doctor Faustus* had turned out not to be.[1] Grass saw the weak spot in the mythic conception of history which underlay novels like *Doctor Faustus* and tried to construct a narrative that would reveal and amend some of these difficulties. The shift from Thomas Mann to Günter Grass thus marks an increasing awareness of certain problems inherent in the postwar attempt to come to terms with nazism. Of the three works in the Danzig trilogy, *The Tin Drum* is the best able to be read as an answer to *Doctor Faustus.*[2]

Connections between the two novels can be found in their mutual reference to Goethe's humanistic vision, as well as in their exploitation of Laurence Sterne's and E. T. A. Hoffman's playful fictional structures. But another unspoken connection between Mann and Grass might well be seen in Albrecht Dürer. Not until *From the Diary of a Snail,* with its appended essay on Dürer, does the connection become explicit in the works of Grass, but looking back from the perspective of this work, it is clear that Dürer had been implied all along. The crucial link is Dürer's engraving *Melencolia I,* for Mann the Renaissance counterpart to Adrian Leverkühn's music, for Grass the foil against which Hermann Zweifel's snail progress (in *Diary of a Snail*) is to be measured.

In *Doctor Faustus,* the magic square of the Dürer engraving expresses Leverkühn's idea of an all-encompassing symmetry in music. The composer has the picture hanging in a prominent position above his piano, and his friend Zeitblom comments, "I believe I never visited his room without giving a quick glance, slanting up or straight down and testing once more the invariable, incredible result."[3] In *The Tin Drum,* nazism seeps slowly into the Matzerath household and causes a significant change in the furnishings: the portrait of Beethoven is removed from its place of honor above the piano and replaced by a photograph of Hitler. But genius is not entirely banned from the living room, just moved to the opposite wall, and an uneasy relationship is set up: "So began the most sinister of all confrontations: Hitler and the genius, face to face and eye to eye. Neither of them was very happy about it" (116).[4] In a similar ominous confrontation in *Cat and Mouse,* Grass takes issue with another favorite combination of Thomas Mann, that of evil and humanism, when the reader's attention is drawn to an almost conspiratorial exchange of glances between the pictures of Hitler and the humanist Conradi in the school assembly hall.[5] These ironic placements of evil, genius, and humanism clarify Grass' criticism of Mann's suggestion that there may be a causal connection between evil and humanism rather than a perverted misuse of one tradition by the other.

In his 1971 anniversary lecture on Dürer, Grass defined two elements in Dürer's engraving as "stasis" and "progress," Saturn and Chronos. The running hourglass, the diligently scribbling cherub, and the rainbow in the background—these symbols of time, activity, and future hope form the subtle counterpoint to the more static images which predominate: brooding Melancholy herself, the supine dog, and the geometric forms. Not coincidentally, the hourglass is placed between the balanced scale and the magic square whose columns add up to thirty-four in all directions. Saturn, the god of geometry and numbers, is also the deity of lowering fate, and fate itself is seen as a magic square in which all sums come out the same.[6]

In Mann's novel, the invocation of a saturnine fate is bolstered by the conjuration of evil in the shape of the devil. But it is precisely with the myths of evil and fate that Grass takes issue in *The Tin Drum,* reinterpreting the clash between stasis and progress and the struggle of good with evil.

One of the most decisive shifts that has taken place between *Doctor Faustus* and *The Tin Drum* is in social class. While both novels concentrate primarily upon the middle classes, the milieu in Grass is shabbier, poorer, and altogether more mundane. Instead of upright peasant stock like the Leverkühns, the small shopkeeper class is the focus of *The Tin Drum,* and Grass knows how to draw these people down to the most telling detail. A comparison of the household settings in the two novels may clarify this distinction. The house where Leverkühn grows up is part of a moderate-sized property that has belonged to his family for several generations. The building is a comfortable-looking half-timbered house with a solid stone foundation; it forms a hollow square around a courtyard dominated by an ancient linden tree. On Sunday afternoons visitors are regaled with good country fare: brown bread and butter, honey, strawberries and cream. The scene is a paradigm of traditional German country life, and the narrator clearly regards it in a positive light. The birth of Grass' protagonist, Oskar Matzerath, takes place in quite different surroundings. Grass describes first not the living room of the ground floor apartment, but its long, bent corridor piled high with packages of laundry powder and the large kitchen half-full of canned goods, bags of flour, and boxes of oatmeal. We have moved from an era of health-giving country foods to one of commercially packaged groceries. The unattractive overflow of these foodstuffs from the shop into the apartment suggests the dominance of economics over comfort. The living room is a model of the tawdry taste one might expect of a lower-class family that has just worked its way into the middle class: a purple sofa contrasts glaringly with wine-colored wallpaper and a blue rug; a black and gold clock dominates the scene; an amazingly intricate black sideboard with wrought-iron decorated doors is topped by a crystal dish of fruit and a green cup won in the lottery. The crowning touch of cheap sentimental taste is found in the bedroom, with its yellow color scheme and sky blue four-poster bed. A white mirrored wardrobe, a toilet table, a marble-topped commode, and a brass lamp with pink china shades complete the decor, and a large framed picture of Mary Magdalene above the marriage bed adds just the right bourgeois touch with its squeamish reference to sexuality. Where Mann idealizes his country folk, Grass caricatures his petit bourgeois family.[7] The chaste rectitude of the farm architecture in *Doctor Faustus* contrasts markedly with the new emphasis on fancy possessions and cheap decorations in *The Tin Drum*.

This change in the social class upon which the novel centers is significant. In part it shows Grass' greater concern with social analysis. But it also shows a different understanding of the genesis of nazism. Instead of focusing on the emergence of nazism from what appears to be its antithesis, the German cultural tradition, Grass emphasizes its intimate connection with the upward-striving and increasingly commercialized working and lower middle classes in the towns and cities. His depiction draws upon a new awareness of the subtle guilt of those who had thought of themselves as basically innocent victims of nazism. Thus Grass moves the debate from cultural history to sociology. *The Tin Drum* is a vivid demonstration of how the desire for worldly goods, the debasement of taste, and ever-present peer pressures helped create an atmosphere in which nazism could flourish.

In this respect Grass follows, and perhaps anticipates, a trend in the perception of nazism that became evident in the late fifties and particularly in the sixties. As a new generation of scholars emerged, the earlier separation between politics and the social sciences gave way to a new approach that attempted to integrate the two. In addition, political science, with its more theoretical and less event-oriented methodology, began to establish itself as an accepted discipline in the German university system; Karl D. Bracher's first important book, *The Dissolution of the Weimar Republic* (1955), is one of the best-known products of this orientation. Within the discipline of history itself, the impact of industrialization on the class structure and its consequences for the developing German state became the object of intense study, as for example at the Heidelberg Institute for Social and Economic History led by Werner Conze.[8] However, since the really influential publications from this school did not appear until the sixties,[9] Grass can scarcely be seen as a direct outgrowth of the new historiographic method. Rather, the interest in social analysis he shows in *The Tin Drum* is part of a new understanding of socio-political forces in general.

In regard to the genesis of nazism, Grass engages more directly with an issue that had long dominated the scholarly debate: the problem of continuity or discontinuity in German history. Once again, he employs what may be seen as an ironic inversion of *Doctor Faustus*. Adrian Leverkühn's father is described as a typical old-fashioned German from the best tradition. Oskar's paternity is less clear-cut. His official father, the German Matzerath, is a particularly unattractive example of the small shopkeeper class, unintelligent, prone to violence, and ultimately a loyal member of the Nazi party, on whose badge he finally chokes to death. Oskar's putative father, Jan Bronski, is a stereotype of the reputedly ineffectual Pole, as illustrated by his participation in the hopeless defense of the Polish Post Office in Danzig (Bronski spends most of the time playing cards and building a card house with Oskar and a dying companion). The two polarities, German and Polish, tough and weak, combine with the uncertainty about Oskar's paternity to create a grotesque parody on Mann's elaborate dualisms. It implies that the rise of nazism is less clearly continuous with earlier developments in German cultural tradition than Mann had suggested in *Doctor Faustus*, and, despite its Polish setting, it throws the emphasis on a more characteristic example in terms of social class.

In Mann's novel the maternal heritage is restricted to Elsbeth Leverkühn, with her unpretentious country ways, her chaste restraint from exercising what must have been a fine singing voice, and her motherly care of Leverkühn during his final illness. Grass makes a good deal more of the mother-archetype, following it back to Oskar's grandmother and treating it, in contrast to the treatment of the two fathers, with considerable humor. The opening images of the novel conjure up an earthy figure with potato-colored skirts emblematic of Mother Poland herself. Like Leverkühn's parents, she bears a simple biblical name, Anna. The episode describing Oskar's conception, in which the firebrand Koljaiczek impregnates Anna under her multiple skirts before the unsuspecting eyes of the police, gives an ironic twist to the idea of family heritage, which Thomas Mann had treated with such gravity in *Doctor Faustus*. And the protective nature of the grandmother, so positive at the beginning of the novel, gradually becomes more questionable at the end. After the alarming Ring Finger episode, which results in Oskar's being sought as a murderer, Oskar must decide between a return to his fantasized grandfather in America and the shelter of his grandmother's skirts. But he correctly recognizes (as Leverkühn does not when he goes to live with his mother-substitute Else Schweigestill) that a return to the protective womb is no longer possible. Intervening episodes, such as Oskar's hiding under the table during card games played by his mother with his two "fathers," illustrate even more penetratingly the questionable nature of such an enterprise. His mother, Agnes, is perhaps the least motherly figure imaginable. Cheaply dressed and more concerned with her extramarital affair than with her family life, she has only sporadic moments of affection for little Oskar and completely rejects her second pregnancy. The scene in which she is forced to eat eels and that in which she dies as a result of stuffing herself with fish in an attempt to abort her child must be the most grotesquely repugnant in German literature—intentionally so, since it is her function as a mother in the traditional sense that must be put in question. The moral ambiguity of this counterweight to Elsbeth Leverkühn is perennially fixed in one of Oskar's old family photos: posed between the two men as for a card game, Agnes, unseen by her fellow players, holds a card towards the camera: "Who would not swear by the queen of hearts?" Oskar ironically comments (57).

In terms of education, Oskar is the direct opposite of Adrian Leverkühn. Whereas Adrian's genius is guided by traditional university study and his mentor, Wendell Kretzschmar, Oskar is self-taught and must painfully conceal his learning from those around him. Oskar's first day of school is emblematic of his relationship to book learning. He disrupts the class by drumming out the beat of the children's rhyme so chaotically sung by the unruly group of first-graders, but what the teacher regards as disorder, Oskar perceives as bringing order into things, teaching the children how to sing the song properly. During the recitation of the weekly schedule, he again drums out the beat of the syllables, underscoring the mechanical nature of the timetable which seems like "irrevocable fate" (81), and, at the same time, discovering the blissful trinity of the three-syllabled school subject, religion. And, finally, with a piercing double shriek, Oskar shatters the teacher's eyeglasses, effectively half-blinding the purveyor of knowledge and light. From that day on, his parents make no further effort to ensure his education, and Oskar is responsible for his own acquisition of elementary learning.

In the shabby surroundings of Gretchen Scheffler's doll-filled rooms, Oskar surreptitiously absorbs what he can and, more significantly, what he wishes to. His attitude throughout is highly unorthodox. He comments that, as a dwarf, he would have been quite satisfied with lowercase letters alone, thus indicating his desire to escape the formalized categories that characterize so much traditional education. That he simultaneously takes up Goethe and Rasputin as his reading primers and role models is on one level a parody of the two souls in Goethe's Faust (compare the two photos in the family album where Oskar is dressed up in Russian and Goethean costumes). At the same time it is also perhaps a more radical adaptation of the dualism seen in Thomas Mann's Adrian Leverkühn. The ingenious book that Oskar makes for himself by combining torn-out pages from Goethe and Rasputin again recalls Hoffmann's *Tomcat Murr,* that curious mixture of two separate texts. Even in the mental asylum, Oskar still reads his two favorite authors, vacillating "between the faith healer and the man of the Enlightenment, between the dark spirit who cast a spell on women and the luminous poet prince who was so fond of letting women cast a spell on him" (91).

While Mann's Faustus must be bound to the devil by a modernized version of the traditional pact, Oskar, who has inwardly abjured the renunciation of the devil spoken for him at his christening, belongs to the devil's party from the outset. Moreover, he stresses that he is in his own way a musician: "There are composers who write concerti for strings and percussion" (48); Oskar not only is a drummer but also, like a trained singer, can shatter glass with his voice. At his birth, a brown moth creates a veritable orgy of drumming against the naked ceiling lamp. These strange forms of music indirectly establish a connection with the composer Adrian Leverkühn. The significant difference lies in the way Grass de-mythicizes the Faustus figure. Where Mann inverts the Goethean tradition, Grass pointedly removes the last underpinnings of the myth from his character. The most important change is the elimination of the concept of genius. One of the more suspect themes of Mann's novel, in a political sense, is the ambivalent coupling of genius with evil. In *Doctor Faustus,* the innate quality of genius leads to the pact with the devil, who simply appears at the appropriate stage in Leverkühn's development as an incarnation of tendencies already present within him. For Oskar, choice is the operative element from the outset. He chooses not to renounce Satan just as he chooses not to grow up. Fate plays no role here, and what appears as accident is in reality willed. Even so, it does not turn out for the best. Oskar can use his drumming talent as he wishes, but ultimately he chooses to avoid making certain crucial distinctions. At first he becomes not a resistance fighter, but an anarchist; and after the war he chooses to become involved in the slick deception of the government-sponsored West Concert Bureau, which promotes collective repression of the past. If Adrian's actions are psychologically predetermined, Oskar consciously exercises his free will. This shift is indicative of a change in thinking that has taken place between the two generations of postwar German writers, and it reflects a new view of the culpability of the German people.

Adrian Leverkühn's pact with the devil is grotesquely mimicked in Oskar Matzerath's attempt to usurp the role of Christ. The story of Oskar's first confrontation with Jesus is framed by a flashback to his christening, thus ensuring the reader's recognition of his opposition to the Christian legend.[10] On a visit to the Church of the Sacred Heart with his mother, Oskar notes three different statues of Christ: the first, a stylized figure with an open, bleeding heart and blue eyes that Oskar regards as identical to those of his putative father Jan Bronski; the second, a Christ on the cross perceived by Oskar as a model gymnast ("athlete most amiable" [139]) and thus as somehow connected with the Berlin Olympics of the preceding year; and the third, the baby Jesus together with John the Baptist on Mary's knees, a Jesus who looks identical to Oskar himself. Oskar's attempt to compel the Christ child to use his drum is a failure, a miracle that does not take place. "Either he drums or he is not a real Jesus; if he doesn't drum now, Oskar is a realer Jesus than he is" (143). The tiny statue refuses to drum, and Oskar's demonstration of how it is done only brings down the wrath of his mother and the vicar. In the ensuing tantrum, in which a spitting and scratching Oskar kicks off a portion of the plaster halo, Satan comes to Oskar's aid, urging him to destroy with his penetrating tones three high stained glass windows in the apse of the church. Aiming straight for the dove representing the Holy Ghost, Oskar tries but fails to shatter the glass. Again the expected miracle does not take place. Jesus and Oskar, Christ and Anti-Christ, have failed equally.

In the succeeding chapters of the novel, Christian legend is inverted repeatedly. The ghastly interlude where Oskar's mother dies from gorging herself on fish occurs on Good Friday. Maria's son Kurt, whose true paternity, like Christ's and Oskar's, remains unclear, is compared with the statue of the infant Jesus in the church, which now, at the very moment when Oskar has ceased to hope for a miracle, suddenly begins to drum after all. Producing a medley of wartime hits, including "Lili Marlene" and all of Oskar's old favorites, it seems to rival Oskar's musicianship. To Oskar's disgust, the statue tries to turn the dwarf into a second Peter: "Thou are Oskar, the rock, and on this rock I will build my Church. Follow thou me!" (358). But Oskar, viciously breaking off one of the plaster toes, hisses back: "Say that again . . . and I'll scratch the paint off you!" (358). Once more Satan tempts him with the thought of shattering church windows, but by now Oskar has learned that he has no power over the divine. If, in subsequent chapters, Oskar regards himself as a follower of Christ, this can only be seen ironically. At the end of the chapter "Imitation of Christ," he says that the anarchistic Dusters are to become his apostles (359). This group of juvenile delinquents provides the appropriate companionship for one whose whole being now seems bent on destruction, as symbolized by the glass-shattering.

Oskar's career as Anti-Christ reaches a climax as the Dusters celebrate a Black Mass in the Church of the Sacred Heart, which has become the focal point of Oskar's satanic aspirations. At his first meeting with the Dusters, he demonstrates his ability to shatter glass, destroying the windows of a chocolate factory whose products are destined for the German air force. Characteristically, the end result is to save the factory from destruction during a bombing raid by eliminating the windows that would have reflected the moonlight and revealed its location. This suggests that Oskar's glass-shattering is an act of destruction for its own sake, not an act of support for either the Germans or the Allies. In a subliminal way, Oskar connects the Dusters with his firebug grandfather Koljaiczek, although he notes, "The Dusters were not firebugs" (374). Within the context of *The Tin Drum* (and prior to Max Frisch's very different use of the word in his 1959 play *The Firebugs*), *arsonist* suggests anarchist, and the paradigm of the anarchist is Oskar's rebellious grandfather, whose death by drowning in the course of a police chase is at times interpreted by Oskar as merely a clever way of "going underground" (*untertauchen*). Grandfather Koljaiczek may have had the potential to upset the system, but he failed to do so; Oskar has inherited from him the task of completing this undertaking. But the Dusters have no political interests, and their policy is simply to be against everything and everyone. "We have nothing to do with parties," declares one of their number. "Our fight is against our parents and all other grownups, regardless of what they may be for or against" (374). Oskar explicitly denies stories connecting the Dusters with resistance groups such as the Edelweiss Pirates from Cologne or the Polish partisans from Tuchlerheide and discredits even more thoroughly the hint of any relationship with the 20 July 1944 conspiracy. Their Black Mass is preceded by the removal and demolition of the central Christian decorations in the church: the Christmas scene with its little people and animals and Oskar's pseudo-twin, the little Christ child. Their original plan had been simply to rob and desecrate the statues in the church. But once they have removed the statue of Jesus and Oskar has climbed up into the vacated space, the idea of a Black Mass takes hold. Oskar comments on the serious intent behind the inversion of the religious ceremony: "not a silly parody, but a Mass which even at our trial was consistently referred to as a Mass, though a black one to be sure" (379). Betrayed by the girl Lucy Rennwand, the group allows itself to be taken without resistance by the police. Oskar calls their trial "the second trial of Jesus" (382); it ends, again, in an inversion of the Christ story, with a verdict of innocent. But Oskar, as we know, is by no means innocent.

The ultimate degradation of the Christ myth is reached at the point when Oskar, now hunchbacked and somewhat taller than in his earlier years, starts working as an artist's model in West Germany. Together with a young woman named Ulla, he poses for the painter known as Raskolnikoff because he always speaks of "crime and punishment, guilt and atonement" (472). The most famous product of these sittings, entitled *Madonna 49,* portrays Oskar in fetal position between Ulla's legs as a blasphemous modern variant of mother and child. Clearly, 1949 is no year for piety.

Another inversion of the underlying myths is Oskar's attempt at intercourse with Sister Dorothea, a nurse who rooms in the same house. Calling himself Satan, Oskar tries to make love to Dorothea through a small section of coconut fibre mat on which Dorothea is lying. This strange combination of self-flagellation and self-stimulation fails to have the desired effect, and Oskar finds himself disconcertingly impotent. But even though this is no satanically inspired interlude like Adrian Leverkühn's contact with the prostitute Esmeralda, it leads indirectly to Oskar's becoming a full-fledged musician. After his failure with Dorothea, Oskar is consoled by another fellow lodger, Klepp, who ultimately helps him to found a band known as the Rhine River Three. No longer a solitary anarchical drummer, Oskar now becomes part of a systematized attempt to teach the German people how to cry, held in a nightclub called the Onion Cellar. This is scarcely a positive turn of events, however, since those who frequent the Onion Cellar cry because they are chopping onions, not because they feel remorse over the German past.

The novel's last chapter, "Thirty," takes up again the inverted Christ myth in its allusion to Jesus' age at the time of his crucifixion. Tellingly, it opens with the word *flight* (577). In this attempt to escape from reality lies Oskar's final guilt. Planning to flee to America, where he imagines his supposedly drowned grandfather Koljaiczek may have made his fortune, Oskar makes it only as far as Paris. On an ascending escalator in the metro, he sees himself in turn as Dante rising from hell and Goethe (he should say Faust) returning from the Mothers, but this ascent leads him directly into the arms of the international police who are waiting to arrest him for his alleged involvement in the Ring Finger episode. Proclaiming himself as Jesus, he gives himself up without offering any resistance. His trial and subsequent commitment to the insane asylum follow; Oskar comments plaintively that if Jesus had been hunchbacked he could hardly have been crucified. Madness is

Oskar's salvation, as it was, in another sense, Adrian Leverkühn's before him. But is it a sufficient excuse for Oskar's sins? And is Oskar really mad?

In Thomas Mann's novel, it is the object of narration who finally becomes insane; in Grass' work, the narrator himself. The use of a narrator who stands somewhat outside events is common to both writers, and in both cases the narrator is to be regarded by the reader with a certain degree of scepticism. Limited-point-of-view narration of this kind is not new to the postwar novel, but its continued use in contexts of moral import is not insignificant. These narrators share the limitations of the individual unable to perceive historical events as a whole and, at the same time, draw our attention to this limitation and help us see beyond it.

Despite this similarity, the narrators Serenus Zeitblom and Oskar Matzerath are diametrically opposed, both as characters and in relation to the narrated events. Zeitblom is a continuation of the Dürer theme in the form of the humanistic tradition. Writing in the stiff and circumstantial language of the scholar, he reflects the mundane and hermit-like life he leads. Whereas Zeitblom, living in Germany, reports the gradually mounting German catastrophe as if from a great distance, Oskar, an eccentric outsider, is in the midst of events as they occur. Zeitblom's inner emigration is all too evident; Oskar's drumming is not a protest but an anarchistic response which ultimately degenerates into open-eyed and undeluded collaboration. By placing his narrator in the thick of things, Grass avoids one weakness of Mann's novel: its tendency to deal with the problems of the Third Reich only indirectly and through the medium of allegory.

Finally, in narrating his story, Oskar goes through a very different process from that of Zeitblom in the Faust novel. At no stage does there appear to be any real insight on Oskar's part, as there is in a limited way on the part of Zeitblom. The idea of working through guilt by writing about it (a principle which operates in Grass' next novel, *Cat and Mouse*) is patently inappropriate in Oskar's case. On the contrary, we know from the start that his writing will involve the violation of over a ream of "virgin paper" (16). At the end, faced with the ultimate confrontation with his guilt, Oskar runs out of words. There is nothing left but the evil figure of the Black Witch, the bogeywoman of nursery rhyme who turns out to be a good deal less harmless than other threatening figures of childhood. Oskar feels her frightening shadow over him; her presence is inescapable.

In terms of narrative structure, both novels use a scheme first devised by Laurence Sterne in *Tristram Shandy*, filtered for Mann through Hoffmann, modified for Grass by Cervantes and Rabelais. In view of its peculiarity, Tristram is obliged to give an account of the principle governing his book. "By this contrivance the machinery of my work is of a species by itself; two contrary motions are introduced into it, and reconciled, which were thought to be at variance with each other. In a word, my work is digressive, and it is progressive too,—and at the same time."[11] More ironic and less comic than Tristram Shandy, the style of Serenus Zeitblom may quite properly be described as digressive and progressive at the same time; Oskar, for his part, also finds occasion on his progression through recent history to give vent to his own brand of digression, substituting for Shandy's chapters on buttonholes and whiskers his prolix reflections on crosses or handwriting. But the dual principle of construction is more than one of mere digression and progression. In both works two lines of development exist simultaneously: in *Doctor Faustus*, the unfolding of Leverkühn's genius and the collapse of Germany; in *The Tin Drum*, Oskar's progress and the loss of Poland. In *Doctor Faustus*, Zeitblom represents the "opinions" to which Leverkühn provides the "life" (to employ the terms of *Tristram Shandy*'s subtitle); and because his opinions are so manifestly those of the educated bourgeoisie, he shows us a very particular perspective on this life. But the novel does not give any clues to the convergence point beyond the novel's ambiguous duality.[12] In returning to the rogue schema of his picaresque models, Grass discovered a more successful way of distancing himself from the opinions of his narrator. Where Mann sought simply to add a lighter touch to the dark events of his age through the character of Zeitblom, Grass takes a thoroughly comic approach. By making Oskar at the start a character who provokes our interest and calls forth our sympathy, Grass is able to manipulate the reader's reception of the narrative more readily than can Mann in *Doctor Faustus*.

The Tin Drum reverses the structure of *Doctor Faustus*. At first we identify with the outlandish dwarf observer who seems to shed such unsparing light on the other characters, but, in the course of the book, we gradually come to see through Oskar and are able to unmask him as the impostor he has become. Where *Doctor Faustus* asks to be read with a grain of salt, *The Tin Drum* is to be read in a much more radical sense against the grain. Its message is different from the story Oskar tells. Thomas Mann's somewhat questionable narrator has become in Günter Grass a thoroughly unreliable one. The fact that he is writing from an insane asylum would seem to provide an early clue to Oskar's deficiencies,[13] but at first we are not inclined to pay this too much heed. Instead, we are constantly invited to identify with Oskar's viewpoint, although to do so would end, as he does, in the deceptive establishment of the West Concert Bureau. Thus, as we are caught up in Oskar's life, we also progressively detach ourselves from it, looking back more and more sceptically at what appeared to be his auspicious beginnings as one who refused to be integrated into Nazi society. This dual viewpoint is re-created in the novel by Oskar's alternating use of the first and third persons, only superficially the result of his childlike mind. Just as the narrator's view from the madhouse creates a constant double focus, so the reader's vacillating awareness of Oskar then and now gives a more critical dimension to the story. This is the one aspect of the novel that Volker Schlöndorff's film fails to capture, and it is thus not accidental that the movie breaks off at the end of the war, before Oskar's ultimate perversion. Schlöndorff's elimination of the double optics can be only partly counteracted by the film's greater stress on the questionable nature of Oskar's early protests, such as the exaggeratedly schmaltzy Viennese waltz in the rostrum scene.[14] Schlöndorff's understanding of the novel goes beyond the reading of those who emphasize the positive side of Oskar's character, his rebellious and independent spirit and the protesting nature of his drumming. But it does not indicate clearly enough the detachment that Grass has tried to build up between character and reader. Like the virtual image behind a reflection in a mirror, the real meaning of *The Tin Drum* must be reconstructed by the reader, since it is in fact the obverse of the view presented by Oskar the narrator.[15] Grass' mobilizing of the reader's critical faculties is more pronounced than Mann's in *Doctor Faustus,* of which it has been said that "there is no critical thought which the book does not think about itself."[16]

To put it another way, *Doctor Faustus,* although complex, asks the reader to fill in only a few gaps; instead of provoking criticism, it creates a "fortress" against it.[17] While the whole point of *Faustus* lies in the ambivalent relations between author and narrator, *The Tin Drum* uses a more dialectical method, at first persuading the reader to sympathize with Oskar, only to see him completely exposed at the end. That Oskar's final deformation comes so unexpectedly and seems so shocking reveals how uncritically one has been reading up to that point, a salutary effect for the novel's intended audience, the postwar German public.

In selecting the name of a butterfly, *Hetaera esmeralda,* as the appellation Leverkühn gives to the prostitute who infects him with syphilis, Mann has been said to be returning to the primitive and archaic.[18] But the insect world thereby invoked is a far cry from either Kafka's "Ungeziefer" or Joyce's "Earwicker." *Hetaera esmeralda,* associated by name with emeralds, is a thing of beauty, a gauzy and transparent being which dwells in the sanctuary of leafy foliage. In its simultaneous capacity as butterfly and prostitute, this image unites within itself the double aspect of the flower of evil concept that underlies Mann's novel. If we compare it with the brownish moth that drums against the lights at Oskar's birth, we can once again see the nature of the shift that has taken place between the two novels. Overshadowing the light, the moth brings a warning to Oskar which he apprehends but chooses to understand in his own way. In contrast to the sexual union between Adrian and Esmeralda, the moth's attempted union with the light bulbs is revealed from the first as vain and death-directed (in the German text, the digression on the verb *to drum* ends with the words *to drum to death*). Most important, however, are the qualities which Oskar assigns to his representative of the insect world, which is, as he explains, most decidedly not one of those great and gloriously beautiful moths to be found in darkest Africa, but merely one of appropriate East European proportions, "that medium-sized powdery-brown moth of the hour of my birth" (48). The grand allegory has shrunk to more modest dimensions; if it is less aesthetic, it is more suited to the vantage point from which Oskar writes.

Grass' attempt to de-mythicize nazism does not stop with *The Tin Drum*. It continues in subtle details through the Danzig trilogy and into the *Diary of a Snail*. When Grass opens his novel *Dog Years* with an elaborate word play on the many and various compounds of *Deich*, preluded by some fanciful juggling with the names *Brauchsel* and *Weichsel*, the crucial word *Deichsel* is conspicuously absent. In *Doctor Faustus*, we discover that *Deixel* is one of a number of medieval variants for *devil*,[19] so we can deduce that in *Dog Years* it is the devil who is pointedly not mentioned by name. In Grass' lecture "On Stasis in Progress: Variations on Albrecht Dürer's Engraving *Melencolia I*" (the 1971 anniversary lecture appended to *Diary of a Snail*), there is another significant omission. For all the references to the great representatives of our age, to Marx and Freud, to Marcuse and Rosa Luxemburg, the reference to Grass' predecessor in the realm of fiction is patently missing. Or, rather, he is relegated to that sphere of oblique reference accessible only to those familiar with the works of Thomas Mann. Doubtless Adrian Leverkühn is the prime example of what is meant when Grass says: "True, where melancholy has taken demonic forms, it has been accepted as a professional quirk of genius," or "melancholy as the privilege of an elite who pass their time in sophisticated inactivity, and arrogance as its conservative expression."[20] We are reminded of the devil's charge against parody in *Doctor Faustus:* "It might be fun, if it were not so melancholy in its aristocratic nihilism."[21]

Grass points out in the Dürer lecture that melancholy is essentially a function of belief in stasis; it is a response to the assumption that the course of history is not really open to change: "The voice of melancholy can always be heard when conditions are thought to be unchangeable and when stasis is defended as a kind of melancholy heritage."[22] When resistance seems virtually impossible, melancholy becomes a substitute for action. Grass' critique of melancholy thus pinpoints the failures of the mythic perception of history, with its emphasis on the eternal recurrence of events and the unchangeability of the human predicament. But Grass also points out that melancholy is no other than the obverse of Utopia: "For wherever progress is frustrated by premature aims or utopian flights from reality, wherever its advances are so slight as to be ludicrous, the conservative who 'knew it all along' triumphs."[23]

Melancholy is thus the expression of a deterministic view that comes into force when utopian visions seem vain, giving rise to their inverse: apocalyptic visions. Dürer's *Melencolia*, with her foreboding magic table, becomes in Grass' imagination a common factory worker at a conveyor belt, alienated from herself and from a natural progress of time. "No dire astrological constellation, no predetermined, inscrutable fate," Grass comments, since in his view workers have it within their power to change their condition.[24] As *Doctor Faustus* progresses, Dürer's *Melencolia* becomes transmuted into Keats': "Ay, in the very temple of Delight / Veiled Melancholy has her sovran shrine" ("Ode on Melancholy"). This, too, finds its inversion in Grass' lecture in the image of the grass widow who, with the help of a rubber device from a mail-order firm, succumbs to the empty pleasure of masturbation. Grass is highly critical of Mann's association of beauty and evil: "When benighted genius proclaimed the rule of barbarism and the monstrous forces of the irrational were unleashed, this melancholy, interpreted as creative madness, could count on the applause of aesthetes and the sacred awe of the public at large."[25] At the same time, Grass also criticizes his juniors, whose wistful resignation he regards as just as dangerous as the creative madness of a Doctor Faustus: "Saturn has released his children from history."[26] Thus the attack moves in two directions: against a deterministic view of history and an ahistoric flight from reality. Although these views were not formulated until 1971, we can see in retrospect that both aspects were present in *The Tin Drum*, which attacks the concept of fate and questions the urge to flight.

Representative of two phases and two poles of modern German literature, *Doctor Faustus* and *The Tin Drum* provide a measure of the culture's "snail progress" in its reflection on its own past. If Thomas Mann has been viewed somewhat harshly here, let us not forget Grass' comment: "Only those who know and respect stasis in progress . . . , who have experienced the dark side of utopia, can evaluate progress."[27] In the last analysis, the two novels can only be measured against presuppositions current at the time of their genesis. But conversely, the impulses they generate in us, the way in which we create, in an act of reception itself historically determined, the virtual image that carries us beyond the surface of the novels themselves—this, too, is a trail the reader leaves behind, another kind of "stasis in progress."[28]

CHAPTER FOUR
CHOICE AND COMMITMENT
Alfred Andersch's *Zanzibar*

Contemplating Ernst Barlach's sculpture *Reading Seminarian,* the disillusioned young Communist Gregor comments, "He is lighter than we are, light as a bird. He looks like someone who would close the book at any time and get up and do something quite different" (40).[1] In Andersch's novel *Zanzibar,* the little wooden figure becomes a paradigm of critical reading. Gregor observes the statue more closely than the others, noting that the monk is different from him and his Communist friends. "He wasn't absorbed. He wasn't even devoted to his reading. What was he doing really? He was reading, simply. He was reading attentively. He was reading accurately. He was reading with the greatest concentration. But he was reading critically" (40). How can the monk read religious texts and not give himself up to them? How can he be part of a system of beliefs and still remain inwardly free? It is a question Gregor cannot yet answer for himself. And it is one that becomes the central issue of the novel in a number of different variations.

As one of the earliest works to deal thematically with the problem of critical reading and to link it explicitly with the question of individual freedom, *Zanzibar or the Final Reason* (1957) deserves a niche of its own in the canon of postwar German literature. If the novel appears to be less well regarded in recent years, this is perhaps due to its lightly woven texture and its adventure-story format, which certainly cannot compete with the denser and more inclusive works of Mann, Grass, or Böll.[2] But Andersch, in part because of his decidedly leftist standpoint and in part because of his own personal experience, is able to deal more specifically with moral responsibility than many of his contemporaries. *Zanzibar* forms an intriguing contrast with the two major novels that appeared only two years later: Günter Grass' *The Tin Drum* and Heinrich Böll's *Billiards at Half-Past Nine* (1959). Like Grass, Andersch believes in the possibility of individual choice and rejects the pessimistic determinism that had dominated so much of the early postwar fiction about nazism; like Böll, he is concerned with the individual psychology of his characters at crucial moments of insight and decision. But he approaches these problems from a vantage point outside the

70

predominantly bourgeois world in which Grass and Böll situate their stories, and he handles moral discriminations more subtly than Böll, more sympathetically than Grass. In terms of techniques, *Zanzibar* is the first novel about nazism to use multiple-point-of-view, thus functioning as a formal precursor to Böll's *Billiards at Half-Past Nine,* where a more complex version of this technique is developed. Finally, Andersch's novel, with its basically straightforward narration in which the passages of interior monologue are clearly assigned to the individual characters, deliberately addresses a broader public than do the more heavily literary novels of his contemporaries.[3] The greater accessibility of his novels means a greater likelihood that they will be understood, but Andersch does not play to the complacency of his audience; he strives to make his readers actively think through the characters' moral dilemmas, to turn his readers into people who can read attentively without losing themselves, people who can "close the book and get up and do something."

In *Zanzibar or the Final Reason,* five characters come together in the space of about a day, and through their accidental involvement with each other separately resolve for themselves the problem of individual freedom in a fascist society. The way in which this theme is developed owes much to Andersch's own experience. His activities as a Communist Youth leader in 1933 had led to two brief internments in Dachau; and disillusioned with the Communist party's inability to carry out effective resistance against nazism, he decided to leave the party. But later, as a member of the German army, Andersch was finally able to realize his idea of individual freedom; he crossed the lines in 1944 and gave himself up to the Americans. It was the beginning of a long political commitment that was to continue after the war through essays, radio broadcasts, and the editorship of the journals *Der Ruf* and *Texte und Zeichen.*

Of the five characters in *Zanzibar,* Gregor has the closest resemblance to Andersch himself, and he bears the burden of the novel's most significant reflective passages. A member of the Young Communists, Gregor has been sent to a small north German seaside town, Rerik, to instruct its remaining Communists in the new system of organization prescribed by central headquarters: the cell of five, whose identity shall remain unknown to all other Communist cells. Gregor's role as an emissary from headquarters is an awkward one, however. Disheartened by the Communist's unsuccessful struggle against Hitler, Gregor is at the point of deserting from the party and escaping to Scandinavia. His new task catches him in the crucial moment of choice. Although he would like to abandon the task, he decides instead to exploit it by using the small seaport to escape, hoping to wrest his personal freedom from an imposed situation by turning an official duty into a self-interested action. But in the end it becomes something more.

Knudsen, the old fisherman who represents the last outpost of the Communist party in Rerik, is also about to abandon his old allegiance. Left in the lurch by the ex-Communists in the town and anxious about the fate of his mentally disturbed wife, Bertha, Knudsen can ill afford to continue running risks for the party. He has reached a point where basic survival is all he cares about, and this can only be assured by lying low and keeping on with his work as a fisherman. By including Knudsen in his assortment of characters, Andersch shows his interest in the lower classes, who receive scant attention in other West German novels of this period. At the same time, his treatment of Knudsen is more complex and problematic than that of orthodox socialist literature, with its tendency to idealize the proletarian resistance to nazism. The inner doubts of the two Communists, Knudsen and Gregor, are seen by Andersch as strengths which enable them to develop their own individuality and independence to the full. What matters is not a particular political position, but the freedom to act independently of ideology, to keep oneself from being swallowed up by systems imposed from without. Gregor asks of the young monk whether he can wear his robe and still be free; the question is equally pressing for the fisherman, but Knudsen at first lacks the subtlety to conceive of a two-track solution. Only as he becomes involved in the action does he enact, without fully realizing its implications, his own inner emancipation.

Pastor Helander serves as a reinforcing contrast to Gregor. He has the same doubts about the system of thought to which he adheres and the same commitment to individual action beyond the confines of dogma. The Barlach statue, about to be confiscated by the Nazis, becomes a symbol that motivates him to perform his own small act of resistance. Protected up to this point by his loss of a leg in World War I, Helander has survived political scrutiny, but the Nazi dominance has shaken his belief in the goodness of God and in the fundamentals of his religion. In the course of the novel he moves towards a more existentialist viewpoint that provides him with an intellectual freedom at the moment of his death.

Less maturely reflective, the two remaining characters represent opposing poles on the scale of innocence. Judith Levin, the young Jewish woman whose paralyzed mother has committed suicide in order to free her daughter to emigrate, is a somewhat two-dimensional model of the protected girl suddenly forced to fend for herself. As the plot unfolds, she must jettison her stereotyped views and acquire a more realistic attitude (that she holds the rudder during the final escape by night is indicative of her new role). The boy, never identified by name, is a more symbolic figure of innocence. Daydreaming of himself as a kind of latter-day Huckleberry Finn, the boy embodies the urge of all five characters simply to flee. His gradual progress towards understanding and his final act of sacrifice are a heightened version of the process undergone by the others as they form themselves into an *ad hoc,* independent "cell of five" more meaningful than any organization imposed on them from above.

Resistance, then, in its most generalized form, is for Andersch a moral act that derives its motivation from an inner enlightenment independent of preexisting systems of thought. For the four characters who become in some sense resisters (Judith does not count here, since she is simply forced to leave the country), meaningful action involves self-sacrifice on one level or another. In the grip of an epiphany, Helander lets himself be shot by the Nazis; Gregor renounces flight because Knudsen refuses to smuggle out Judith and the statue if Gregor goes with them; Knudsen himself gives up the idea of flight to return to his mentally ill wife, who might otherwise be taken off to a concentration camp; and the boy abandons his plan to remain in Sweden after he and the fisherman have brought Judith and the statue to safety there, so as not to cast on Knudsen the suspicion that he had taken his boat beyond German waters. Yet, although they have given up their dreams of freedom in the literal sense, in helping to save Judith and the statue they have gained a kind of inner freedom. Idealized though it is, this is the first literary portrayal of inner freedom that leads to concrete action, thus going beyond the preservation of personal integrity practiced by the inner emigrants. What Arno Schmidt called, in an early review of the novel, "a lesson in . . . flight as protest"[4] must thus be understood to mean flight not from a concrete situation but from imposed systems of thought.

But Andersch's idea of personal freedom is not as universal as this may make it sound. In some ways the most dated figure in the book is Pastor Helander, who reveals most clearly how much Andersch's working out of the personal freedom motif in *Zanzibar* owes to the general atmosphere of the fifties. Helander's reflections would be unthinkable without the existentialism then newly popular, which gives his brand of inner revelation its own particular flavor. His empty church becomes symptomatic for him, not of the Nazi takeover, but of the *deus absconditus.* "The town, the church and the parsonage had become a dead, echoless space since the Others had come into power. No, not since the Others had come but since God had withdrawn. The Lord doesn't think it necessary to be here, thought the pastor in bitter scorn" (89). Helander's anguish and aloneness are not rooted in political realities but in a state of existential despair from which he still hopes to be able to make his leap of faith. Once Gregor has taken the wooden statue with him, Helander feels free to go to the hospital and have his painful wound attended to, but just as he is about to call a taxi, he suddenly conceives a kind of martyrdom for himself. "He thought, 'If I don't pick up the receiver, God may perhaps not be so far away as I think. Perhaps then he'll be quite near' " (92–93). His martyrdom is fulfilled the following day when the Nazis discover the missing statue, but it is fulfilled in a peculiar way. His first response to the arrival of the Nazi authorities is anger towards the absent God, thinking "that one should castigate a God who did not stand by his people" (142). In a blind attempt to punish God, he decides to shoot the four Nazis, thus breaking the spell of despair that seems to lie on him and disrupting the apparent paralysis of his world. In accordance with existentialist belief, the moment of decision and personal action is also the moment at which one is most intensely alive, and so it is that Helander, shooting the first two Nazis from the doorway of his room, is borne away on a wave of euphoria. In his imagination he has already transformed the window behind him into the brick wall of his church; now he suddenly apprehends that the "writing on the wall" which he has so long awaited must at last appear to him. Totally transfigured, Helander turns to what is for him no longer a window on the world but a window to God. "He turned around and looked at the wall, and as he was reading the writing he scarcely felt the fire penetrating him, he thought only, I'm alive, as the hot little fires burned him. They hit him all over" (145). The passage is so given up to Helander's vision—the appearance of the writing on the wall, the experience of intense being, and the transfiguring sensation of fire—that we must almost force ourselves to accept the other reality, Helander's death at the hands of the Nazis. But the important thing is that Helander has broken through conventional ideas of life and death and attained a highly personal revelation that defies the categories of traditional religion.

The personal decisions of the others, though not so heavily embedded in existentialist theory, nonetheless owe much to its general conceptual framework. Andersch's portrayal of their motivation does not accurately reflect the possibilities that would have been open to them at the time. Rather, it seems to be the result of his own reevaluation of such moral dilemmas from the viewpoint of the fifties.

Andersch underscores the principle of individual escape from accepted systems of thought by the use of metaphors of space. As long as the boy remains caught up in his Mark Twain idealism, he can be found sitting in sheltered places, under the overhanging branches of a willow or in the attic of an old tannery. These secret spaces are his refuge, but they are also a kind of mental restriction, as we gradually come to see. As long as he remains tied to his adventure-story way of thought, he remains ignorant of the political system around him; only slowly does he come to recognize the revulsion that led to his father's death (or suicide) at sea. His reevaluation of the utopian image Zanzibar occurs only at the very conclusion of the novel when, after an evening of freedom in the Scandinavian woods, he perceives a better ideal in the moral decision to support Knudsen by returning. Through this act of commitment, he realizes a new kind of inner freedom, one no longer confined to a fantasy world.

Two other sets of imagery cast their own strange glow over the world of *Zanzibar:* the red towers of Rerik and the golden shield of Tarasovka. Judith's mother, who had spent her honeymoon in Rerik, had often told her daughter of the wonderful towers. " 'They're not towers,' she had always said. 'They're monsters, marvelous red monsters you can stroke' " (18). But to Judith, the red monsters appear lowering and evil. They stand indifferent and uncaring, cold like the ice blue sea of what for her is a "dead" town (18). Gregor sees them in a different way, though not as any less threatening. He knows the towers are empty—the Nazis are not using them to control the harbor—but he still feels watched by them and constrained by their presence. "He sensed that it would be difficult to desert beneath their gaze." Similarly, he senses their evil influence on his work for the party, feeling that he must totally re-think his position "in a town where there are towers like that" (21). As old watchtowers they symbolize watchfulness, and they arouse in Gregor the fine antennae of self-awareness and self-judgment. Not until after his sacrifice, when he has left Judith on the boat with the statue, the boy, and Knudsen, does Gregor see the towers in different proportions. Returning across a sandbar from the island, Gregor looks back at them from a distance: "From this perspective they were not heavy red monsters any more, but pale little blocks in the grey light of morning, fine square posts, blue-grey at the edge of the harbor" (134). The sun begins to rise in the background, showing a scarlet stripe across an otherwise colorless expanse. Gregor is returning to reality, to the greyness of dawn and a threatening rainfall. The world is drained of color and devoid of shadows; Gregor feels it is ready to be tested again. It is this mood of detachment and critical judgment that enables him to see the towers of Rerik for the first time in an unromantic light. But he can only do so because he has gained the inner distance in which to step back from the external situation.

Tarasovka, with its surrounding golden sea, is Gregor's equivalent of the boy's dream of Zanzibar. Gregor remembers it as part of a successful maneuvre during his time in the Russian army. What had impressed him was not the conquest itself but the shining expanse of the Black Sea lying like a golden shield around the grey huts of the town. Gregor's preference for beauty over military victory marks the beginning of his desertion from communism: Tarasovka is for him a symbol of a personal vision that supersedes party dogma and cancels it out.

Overpoweringly vivid, the red towers and the golden shield stand like beacons in a novel otherwise poor in images. They draw attention to the central importance of individual vision, making the reader aware that the same thing can be perceived differently by different people or by the same person under different circumstances. And in a novel whose basic plot structure revolves around external action, they signal the inner developments also taking place.[5]

Indeed, it might be maintained that the only symbols possible for Andersch are those whose meaning does not remain fixed. In a 1955 review of Ernst Jünger's *The Gordian Knot,* Andersch criticizes his use of eternal symbols: "The symbols here are meant to be signs of the eternal in the flux of appearance. But, one might think, if reality reveals its eternal, unchangeable aspect in the symbol, why would one want to change it, then?"[6] It is Andersch's emphasis on the changeability of the world that precludes the use of symbols to illustrate eternal verities. If symbols are to be used at all, Andersch argues that they must carry with them the consciousness of their restriction to a particular view at a particular time. The changing towers of Rerik are Andersch's attempt to demonstrate this principle.

The plot structure of *Zanzibar* would be rather uninspiring were it not for two innovations that Andersch introduces into an apparently straightforward scheme. First is his inversion of the adventure-story model, and second his use of multiple-point-of-view. His handling of both of these is significant for the development of the postwar German novel.

In structuring his tale as a modification of the Mark Twain model, Andersch revokes an important modern myth. Unlike the Faust myth, this is not one of fate and inevitability; on the contrary, it is a myth of untrammelled individual freedom. But it lacks the awareness of human responsibility that Andersch believes so essential. In a totalitarian regime it is not enough simply to escape the oppressiveness of society by drifting off on a raft in a return to the natural state. The boy must learn that the exotic lands and romantic experiences which call him so insistently are not a valid reason for flight.

Andersch treats this with great tact, refraining from explicitly analyzing the boy's change of heart at the end. The reason for it has been given, to be sure, in Judith's moral exhortation to the boy during their escape; but despite the novel's otherwise heavy reliance on interior monologue, we have no access to the boy's thoughts at the end. In the final paragraphs we move almost imperceptibly from his thoughts ("only when Knudsen is gone will I be really free") to his observations ("the boy saw that the cutter was still moored there. . . . The boy could see Knudsen sitting on board; he was sitting on a water barrel smoking") and finally to a totally external view of the boy ("the boy did not cast another glance back at the woods as he stepped onto the wharf. He walked leisurely towards the boat as if nothing had happened" [147]). The surprise reversal takes place so quickly that we are not even sure at first that it has happened. And yet the ending is unequivocal: the boy has decided in favor of Knudsen. What is important here is that this is left for the reader to put together; we are compelled to linger a little over the book's conclusion, to re-create in our own minds the justification for the boy's action. Similarly, the myth of Huckleberry Finn and the exotic ideal of Zanzibar are not explicitly abandoned; the idea that they are no longer apposite is merely hinted at, left for the reader to complete in thought. The novel is not really open-ended, but its conclusion is sufficiently laconic to provoke a related effect. Thus it can be seen as an early attempt to move beyond the mythic structures that had dominated in West German literature up to this point.

Perhaps even more significant is the multiple narrative perspective. While not really very avant-garde (we are never in any doubt, for example, about actual events or people's responses to them, as we sometimes are in novels like Faulkner's *The Sound and the Fury*), the technique is nonetheless relatively new to the postwar German novel. The five characters are not there simply to represent a social or political spectrum, nor to show a variety of different views, but rather to demonstrate Andersch's belief in the importance of individuality.[7] Their various decisions are reached separately, by an inner process peculiar to each individual; the relegation of their thoughts and those segments of the action pertaining to them to more or less separate narrative blocks is intended to emphasize this aspect. Although the "Young Monk Campaign" and the "Jewish Girl Campaign" (as Gregor calls them) cannot take place without the participation of all five, the characters are not united by anything other than the needs of the situation. They never become a concerted political group. But despite these attempts to prevent the novel from falling too neatly into patterns, the multiple-point-of-view technique as Andersch uses it here fails to present a genuine plurality of vision.[8] In the last analysis all the characters, though starting from different positions, come to the same conclusion: a new belief in the need for questioning and criticism. This suggests that multiple perspective as such is not necessarily a guarantee of open-ended narration. Although Andersch motivates the reader to draw inferences and make comparisons, the expected conclusions are

already suggested by the similarity of the characters' moral development. There are no serious gaps for us to fill; there is no missing
Heracles for us to imagine.

In the fictional exploration of the Nazi past, multiple-point-of-view
novels, as we shall see in Böll's *Billiards at Half-Past Nine,* take up an
uneasy position in the movement from closed to open structures. To be
sure, Andersch's interweaving of five different viewpoints is more
thought-provoking than the basically straightforward models of socialist realism, but, since the viewpoints in no way reflect ironically upon
each other, we are only required to follow the flow of the parallel
strands to the end. Andersch's particular handling of a technique that
could have been used more subtly is once again indicative of prevailing
attitudes in the late fifties: the conclusion suggested by Andersch, the
concept of individual action, was still not one automatically accepted
by his German readers, most of whom felt that nazism had robbed
them of their individuality. Despite the increasingly insistent call for a
more critical spirit, most people still needed concrete examples of the
form that this critique was to take. Andersch's method is a nice solution to his dilemma; that of the socialist writer addressing a basically
non-socialist public; but it fails to fulfill its own aim of inspiring critical
reading.

This intention is articulated in the novel by a new evaluation of the
role of art. The little Barlach statue, designated as degenerate by the
Nazis, becomes symbolic of the power art can exert. For Gregor and
the boy it gives rise to a new understanding of the function of reading.
Thinking back to his training at the Lenin Academy in Moscow, Gregor remembers his total absorption in books: " 'We didn't see the bell
tower of Weliki outside the window, I'm willing to swear on it,'
thought Gregor, 'we were so absorbed' "(39). Later we learn that
Gregor's lack of awareness may have contributed to his Russian girlfriend's death, the official liquidation of a brilliant young woman who
had not been cautious enough to conceal her affair with the young
German. "He had already learned in Moscow what he most needed
later on in Germany: watchfulness" (106). But this new caution was
only the first step towards the lesson he learns from the sculpture: the
ability to be simultaneously attentive and detached. The boy learns this
lesson less directly and never articulates it himself. His previous reading matter is virtually the opposite of Gregor's Communist textbooks
at the academy; apart from *Tom Sawyer,* the boy reads *Treasure Island, Moby Dick, Oliver Twist,* a book about Captain Scott's last
journey, and various novels by Karl May (76). His absorption in these
books, with their idealistic image of an individual pitting himself
against society and nature, seems at first no less complete than Gre-

gor's absorption in his studies at the Lenin Academy had been. But in the course of his reflections, he gradually becomes aware of the discrepancy between these adventure tales of a bygone era and the needs of the present day. Not that he sees the present in political terms, however. His conversation with Judith on the boat the night of their escape sows the seeds of new perceptions.

> "He looks like someone who reads all kinds of books, doesn't he?"
> "He just reads the Bible," said the boy. "That's why they put him up in the church."
> "In the church, yes, there he read the Bible. But did you see him just now in the boat?"
> "Yes."
> "He was reading a totally different book then, don't you think?"
> "What kind of book?"
> "Any kind," said Judith. "He reads everything he wants to. And because he reads anything he wants to, he was going to be locked up. And that's why he has to go somewhere where he can read as much as he wants."
> "I read everything I want to, too," said the boy.
> "You'd better not tell anyone!" commented Judith (135–36).

By unwittingly identifying the boy and the statue, Judith puts the boy's reading into a political light. And the adventure stories, though primarily escapism for the boy, do present a counter-ideology which can be interpreted as a kind of rebellion against nazism. They form a space set off from reality where the boy can measure himself by standards other than those of his society, where he can dream himself free from its constraints and deceptions. And, yet, in returning with Knudsen after his brief time in the woods, the boy appears to have learned that the stories must be read differently. In the present world, the adventure tales cannot simply be reenacted. When he finally steps down the pier to the waiting boat, it is almost as if the boy, after living his Huckleberry Finn adventure, had at last closed the book, got up, and done something different. If the books have taught him the value of independence, he has now learned something more: that independence can only be won in a genuine confrontation with reality.

In this way Andersch creates *in nuce,* through the image of the reading monk, a model of his hopes for literature. We may identify with literature only if we are also prepared to detach ourselves from it, to step back and deliberate on it as Gregor deliberates on the statue. Looking back again to the beginning, we understand more clearly the Dylan Thomas quotation with which the novel opens and which makes of *Zanzibar* a Janus-faced link between the horrors of the past and the hopes for the future:

And death shall have no dominion.
Under the windings of the sea
They lying long shall not lie windily;
Twisting on racks when sinews give way,
Strapped to a wheel, yet they shall not break;
Faith in their hands shall snap in two,
And the unicorn evils run them through;
Split all ends up they shan't crack;
And death shall have no dominion.[9]

This epitaph, in a masterful translation by Andersch, makes of *Zanzibar* a monument to those who died at Nazi hands and a forward-looking tribute to the endurance of human constancy. The slender novel *Zanzibar* stands out as one of the earliest works to urge the consciousness-building potential of art and to call for individual engagement in the struggle to come to terms with the past.

Polemicizing against the then fashionable theory of "artistic autonomy" which, he claimed, is unable to account for truly great works of fiction, Andersch once defined the perfect work of art as "a successful escape from the blindness of pure self-sufficient form."[10] By calling on its readers to take up the young monk's challenge, *Zanzibar* takes one small step out of the magic circle of autonomous art. Andersch's later novel, *Winterspelt* (1974), was to break even more radically out of accepted molds, but it was also to call into question *Zanzibar*'s optimism about the pragmatic possibility of resistance.

CHAPTER FIVE

THE BEWITCHED CASTLE
Heinrich Böll's *Billiards at Half-Past Nine*

Unlike Andersch's *Zanzibar,* where the interior monologues essentially coincide with the chronological time blocks of plot, Böll's *Billiards at Half-Past Nine* (1959) weaves them into an elaborate tapestry of twentieth-century history. In contrast to the mythic novels of the period, however, *Billiards* does not simply impose various epochs upon one another but shows them as a progression where each point becomes an evaluative reference for every other. Although it is more schematic than *The Tin Drum,* which appeared in the same year, *Billiards at Half-Past Nine* is an equally fascinating, if equivocal, attempt to move away from mythic patterning and to use modernist techniques to portray the Nazi period. Its main concern is the relationship between the unresolved past and the social problems of the present, a theme that had preoccupied Böll in his earlier short stories and that was to be taken up again later in *Views of a Clown* (1963) and *Group Portrait with Lady* (1971). In many ways, Böll is more forthright than Grass in his appeal to his readers to take a moral stance towards the characters and events portrayed in his novel; however, by providing the value code in which to do this, he partially undermines the subtle vision his socio-psychological analysis has created. The transitional thinking of the late fifties could not be more clearly demonstrated.

Presenting their reflections on the past as they prepare to celebrate their grandfather's eightieth birthday, the members of the Fähmel family are set off against each other. In a series of interwoven monologues, three generations relive in memory the Wilhelminian empire, the Third Reich, and the economic miracle of postwar Germany. Dominating the novel are the grandparents, the architect Heinrich and his wife Johanna Fähmel, and one of their sons, Robert, who forms a mysterious and at first inaccessible core to the narrated events. The impending birthday celebrations lead Robert to reflect on his own role during the Third Reich. He recalls at some length his connections with a group of innocents called the lambs in opposition to the Nazis, whom he calls the beasts. This association would seem to absolve him of guilt were it not complicated by his unexplained bombing during World War II of a monastery originally built by his father.

The central characters, Robert, his parents, and his daughter Ruth, are problematic and not easy to evaluate, but an important clue is given by means of the mysterious figure of Alfred Schrella. We first hear of him as the one person who has access to Robert Fähmel during his private billiard sessions at the Hotel Prinz Heinrich. Only gradually do we learn that Schrella had been suspected of involvement in an attempted attack on a gym teacher during the Third Reich; that he had managed to escape from the police, first to Holland and then to England. In the seventh chapter of the novel, Schrella returns to Germany, where he is apprehended at the border and temporarily imprisoned. Of himself, he says, "then the way to keep me harmless was to lock me up, whereas today the way to keep me harmless is to set me free" (175).[1] In what way could Schrella still be dangerous in 1958, so long after the end of the war? Part of the answer lies in his previous alliance with Ferdi Progulske, the young man who tried to bomb the teacher; he represents proof that protest against the Nazi system, at least in such a minor form, had been possible and did in fact occur. Were the police chief Nettlinger to keep Schrella in jail, he would draw attention to his own involvement with the gym teacher and hence with nazism altogether; should the case come to trial, Schrella would undoubtedly recount tales of the torture perpetrated by Nettlinger and Wackiera on those schoolboys who chose not to go along with the Nazi groups.

But there is also another sense in which Schrella is a threat to postwar German society, though he himself cannot be expected to perceive this. He is unable to make his own political point of view clear to others, even when he tells the story of his escape from Germany. First he threatened a Dutch politician who had said that all Germans should be killed, and later he threatened an English politician who said something similar. On both occasions, he realized that his motivation was misunderstood: "thus one gets locked up because of a misunderstanding, and because of a misunderstanding one is set free," he comments (174). He has not been sufficiently articulate in expressing his moral views, and the real point of his protest has been lost. Even now, on his return to Germany, he makes no attempt to turn his case into a *cause célèbre* and thus expose Nettlinger's role during the Third Reich. Instead, he lunches with Nettlinger and exploits the apparent reconciliation to create an unpleasant scene which the police chief regards as a form of revenge: in the elegant dining room of the Hotel Prinz Heinrich, Schrella eats his salmon with his fingers, requests a picnic carton for his chicken, and leaves the hotel without finishing the meal. To Nettlinger, this behavior in such proper surroundings is the ultimate form of insult:

"All right," he said, "you want to get back at me. I can understand that. But do you have to do it this way?"

"Would you prefer me to kill you?"

Nettlinger made no reply (186).

But to Schrella the act is not one of revenge. He explains simply, "I just have to get out of here," although he adds, "I'd have kicked myself for the rest of my life if I'd let that chicken go back" (186). Perhaps this lack of interest in Nettlinger's reaction is indeed the ultimate insult; but because of the personal level on which it takes place and the discreet milieu which conceals it from public view, it remains ineffective as a protest against the continued existence of Nettlinger and his kind in postwar Germany. All it does is to assuage Schrella's personal sense of justice. The politely formal tone in which the two enemies converse throughout this scene indicates Schrella's retreat from further political engagement. His main business in returning to "this hospitable city" (presumably Cologne) is to clear his name from the criminal list, not to expose crimes committed during the Nazi era.

Enclosed spaces recur throughout this novel as indicators of retreat from engagement, symbols of an inner emigration that continues even after the end of the war.[2] The hotel dining room is one such enclosed space; so is its billiard room, as well as Robert Fähmel's office in the Modestgasse and the lunatic asylum in which Johanna Fähmel is incarcerated. With the exception of the scenes involving the grandchildren, Joseph and Ruth, who are shown on the highway and in the woods, almost all of the action of the narrated present (a single day in the year 1958) takes place in enclosed spaces. Significantly, Johanna's pistol shot, the penultimate action in the novel, is fired from a balcony of the hotel; but the final scene, the cutting of Heinrich Fähmel's eightieth birthday cake, takes place again indoors. Almost all of the characters have gained insights as a result of their experiences during the Third Reich and World War II, but they are still not prepared to bring them into the open. Even the understanding which the members of the family develop for each other in the course of this particular day cannot be expressed in words, only through symbolic gestures which retain a certain saving measure of ambiguity. Just as the action takes place in interior spaces, so the family's reevaluation of each other is not permitted to become overt or articulated.

Yet few of the characters are really taciturn types. Robert and Johanna are the narrators of several lengthy flashbacks; through them we are given the moral coordinates with which to evaluate the other actors in the story. These are the categories of lamb and beast so often criticized for their division of the novel's characters into a simplistic scheme of good and evil.[3] The Nazis are described here as those who have tasted the "sacrament of the beast"; a large group of their opponents is referred to as lambs. But it is worthwhile examining these categories more closely. The beasts are fairly clear: Nettlinger, Wackiera, Otto Fähmel, Heinrich Fähmel, Junior, and, finally, Gretz the butcher, whose blood-dripping boar hanging outside the shop is a symbol of the continuance of Nazi attitudes into the present day. The lambs are a more restricted group: in the past, there were Ferdi Progulske and his friends, as well as Edith Schrella; in the present, there is the hotel boy Hugo and the young woman Marianne (the latter on two occasions addressed as "lambkin"). Alfred Schrella expressly distances himself from this group, although he shares their opposition to nazism; and Robert, although he had vowed not to taste of the sacrament of the beast, is designated by Ferdi as a shepherd, not a lamb ("Shepherds," he said, "there are some shepherds who don't forsake the flock" [p. 42]).

Quite early in the novel, Böll provides an important clue to the evaluation of the lambs by introducing a ludicrous figure called the sheep lady, leader of a mystic group that sees the salvation of the world in "sheep's wool, sheep's leather, sheep's milk—and . . . knitting" (45). Not only does the pseudo-religion of this group appear questionable but also the purity of its motivation. Both the leader and her disciples are clothed in shaggy, filthy sheepskins; they use sheep dung as perfume and incense; their bare feet are dirty and callused. The revulsion evoked by the external form of their religion reflects upon fanatical belief in general, an issue that becomes acute again in the case of Edith Schrella. These disciples of the sheep religion are not lambs in the sense in which the term is used throughout the novel, but by representing something close to the lunatic fringe of religious believers, they draw our attention to the possibility of different shadings and gradations amongst the lambs proper.

Of all the lambs, Hugo throws the most light on the meaning of this concept. Unlike the others, it is not his political views which place him in this category, but simply his innocence, his retarded, still largely childish mentality. His uncomplicated mind makes him the perfect listener for Robert's billiard-room monologues, which reveal so much to the reader but appear to bring no new insights to Robert himself. That Hugo is unable to pass judgment on Robert's story serves to heighten, rather than counteract, the isolation that Robert has imposed upon himself. When he adopts Hugo at the end, it is more out of nostalgia for his own lost innocence than out of any real feelings for the boy.[4] Hugo reminds him of Edith and also provides him with the perfect inheritor of Heinrich Fähmel's farm properties, which Robert does not care to work. Thus the family will return to its origins, innocent again, but without having really purged itself.

Edith Schrella, later the wife of Robert Fähmel, is another such innocent. Heinrich Fähmel describes her as "the only truly gentle lamb of a person I ever saw" (91) and comments especially on her piety: "She was so deep in the Bible she could make fun of it all, in a Biblical way. During the air raids she used to laugh with her children" (92). Robert himself knows little about her, though he surmises later that she had probably never finished elementary school. What she does well, she seems to do primarily out of instinct; such, for example, is her relationship to her two children at an age when she herself is little more than a child. Johanna finds her religion too unorthodox. "Forgive me, but I've never liked sectarians," and later we discover that Edith does indeed pore over sectarian tracts.[5] More serious is Johanna's accusation that Edith is too passive in regard to God's will for man: "The Lord has done this, the Lord has done that, the Lord has given, the Lord has taken away. The Lord, the Lord!" (122). When she is finally killed by shrapnel, Edith becomes in a way a sacrificial lamb for the family, but her role all along has never been much more than symbolic. For Robert, the apartment where they live after their marriage is never more than a doll's house and Edith "a little blonde standing there in her red dressing gown" (132) who cannot even make tea properly. For her sake, he continues to renew his vows not to partake of the sacrament of the beast, yet she does not really have any influence over him. While he claims that he would never have married another, one senses that she is more a figment of his imagination than a concrete reality. She represents only a passive resistance to nazism, and her motivation, insofar as it does not stem from sectarian religion, remains basically opaque.

If Hugo is retarded and Edith simple-minded, then that other innocent, Ferdi Progulske, is a youthful fool. "He was no archangel, just an angel, his name was Ferdi. He was blond and fool enough to think he could use firecrackers against the ones who'd eaten the Host of the Beast" (120). Ferdi, too, has something of the sectarian about him, and as we discover from Johanna, "he didn't drink tea or wine, beer, coffee or cognac, just put his mouth to the water tap and laughed" (120). Her judgment on his action reveals its futility, yet it is at least an active resistance, and he rightly deserves to be named alongside that darker angel, Schrella, with his fierce and unbending moral code.

Marianne, Joseph's fiancée, is the last of the series of lambs. Unlike the others, she is not simple-minded. Her problem is that she has still not come to terms with her past. The shocking story of her family's suicide pact, made presumably to escape Russian retaliation after the capitulation of Germany, is told almost entirely from the perspective of the child she then was. Her father, presumably an officer in the SS, shot himself through the mouth; her mother hanged her younger brother; but Marianne was saved through the intervention of a kindly stranger who helped her flee across Germany and ultimately took her into his family. Marianne tells how she grew up with her foster parents and was converted to the Christian faith. "But we'll very soon make a little child of Christ out of our little heathen-child, out of our good little lamb," as the priest rather patronizingly puts it (205–6). When her mother is released from prison and comes to fetch her, Marianne argues that her mother's participation in the suicide pact has invalidated the natural claim of mother to daughter. When asked if she intends to be "harder than God in his judgment," Marianne responds, "I'm not God, and that's why I can't· be as forgiving as He is" (207). Christian religion teaches forgiveness, but to forgive in this instance would be a task too great for any human being, as Marianne points out. The mother's question and the daughter's reply illustrate an unbridgeable gap that has opened in postwar German society. Understandably, Marianne prefers to cut herself off from her past rather than to confront it; in her own mind she belongs to her foster family and is comforted when Joseph calls her by their name. Her inability to resolve the moral impasse created by the issue of forgiveness is characteristic of the postwar situation. More than this, traditional religion seems powerless to mend the break in the natural chain of continuity. As a thoughtful Catholic, Böll is aware of a certain glibness in the Church's handling of the problem. When Marianne argues that the terrible deed should deprive her mother of custodial rights, Böll has the priest answer in a slickly pragmatic tone, "You're a smart little thing. Remember that argument" (207). There is no comment on these various attempts to grapple with moral issues. Böll simply presents the problem in dialogue form, mediated by Marianne's narration.

Marianne's relationship to her natural family forms a telling counterpoint to Joseph's relationship to his. Whereas she refuses to have any sympathy with the motivation of her Nazi mother, he unwittingly misinterprets the actions of his resister father. Together with Ruth, who has long known of her father's deed and accepted it with nonchalant, even disinterested composure, Joseph and Marianne form a multifaceted picture of Germany's younger generation and its attitude to the past. But while Marianne has some right to resent the intrusion of the past, Joseph is the captive of a more selfish point of view. Even now, he fails to comprehend why his grandmother had given away good food and clothing to the poor during the war, thus preventing her own children from enjoying these luxuries. And the conversation between Joseph and Marianne reveals that, though superficially grown up, these children are in effect still not "big enough for that kind of bigness" (200).

The same criticism can be applied to Joseph's sense of outrage when he discovers that his father is responsible for the destruction of the abbey erected by his grandfather. His difficulty in accepting his father's action stems from his basically ahistorical standpoint: his view that cultural monuments should be preserved at all cost. But for Robert, the architectural importance of the abbey was secondary, as was his sense of family achievement. Böll makes it clear that the demolition is not to be seen as the result of a father complex (136). Some of this information is known only to the reader, not to Joseph. In particular, Robert's account of his conversation about the bombing with a young representative of the Allies casts considerable light on his motivation. Nonetheless, it is hard to understand how Joseph can remain so un-comprehending. Memories well up in Robert that he does not reveal to his interrogator, memories, for example, of the perversion of religion under nazism (the celebration of the summer solstice by monks from the abbey), memories which he sums up in the unspoken phrase, "be-cause they had not shepherded the lambs" (159). But we are not simply to understand that his destruction of the abbey was intended as an act of revenge on the church for not having protected Edith, Ferdi, and their kind. The destruction of the abbey seems to have been a deliberate attempt at resistance under the guise of cooperation with a lunatic general under whom Robert was serving. Unaware that in an age of air warfare there was no longer any need for creating a field of fire through which the Germans could defend Cologne, the general was easily persuaded that the abbey had to be destroyed. But in re-moving this large physical obstacle, Robert evidently had quite differ-ent motives. Presumably he hoped to accelerate the Allies' advance into Germany, and thus the ultimate conclusion of the war. Ironically, while the demolition did in fact hasten the Allies' approach, the war was only three days from its close in any event.

Complicating this interpretation, however, is the narrative technique by means of which the events are presented. Since Böll does not tell the story from an omniscient viewpoint, the reader must constantly weigh the various monologues against each other. This makes it par-ticularly difficult to evaluate Robert's action. That Robert is the one responsible for blowing up the abbey is known only to a small number of people, of whom one (Ruth) does not seriously reflect on it at all; another (Joseph) is by reason of his historical position incapable of understanding it; a third (Heinrich), while capable of deducing Rob-ert's motivation and perhaps inwardly aware of it, prefers in his all-per-vading discretion not even to articulate it in his most private thoughts. And Robert himself, whose interior monologues provide a good deal of information about his character, is unwilling to engage in the kind of self-examination which would divulge his true motivation. After all, even by the most favorable account, his resistance (if such it is) must be adjudged belated, misguided, and ultimately futile.

There is another way of evaluating Robert's action, and that is by reference to the other attempts at resistance presented in the novel. One of these, Ferdi Progulske's attack on the gym teacher, has set the whole train of events in motion; the other, Johanna Fähmel's attempt to murder a respectable citizen, is the one that brings them to an uneasy conclusion. Mad though she is reputed to be, it is Johanna who provides the closest thing to a valid framework within which the events of the past can be evaluated. But as a resister, she, too, is flawed.

Of all the characters in *Billiards at Half-Past Nine,* Johanna is from the outset the most independent of mind.[6] It is she who refers to Wilhelm II as the imperial fool, uttering what everyone has long thought but has not dared to say. Naturally, the case is hushed up and her boldness attributed to her pregnancy and her distress over the recent deaths of her two brothers and her young daughter. Even at this stage, protest is given the stamp of madness, and the snide suggestion is made that Johanna is merely the stereotype of the illogical woman. Yet her husband, Heinrich, knows otherwise: "All along I knew I should have been saying, 'I agree with my wife, absolutely.' I knew that irony wasn't enough, and never would be" (83). Thus, Heinrich spins himself into a protective cocoon of irony, an attitude that enables him to preserve his inner self-image while at the same time externally accommodating himself to society. This may not be so reprehensible in the reign of Kaiser Wilhelm II, but when he maintains his ironic stance into the Third Reich, it becomes more than questionable. Yet, however forthrightly his wife, for her part, confronts the political situation, she admires Heinrich precisely for his irony. This at least sets him apart from others and makes her feel that they agree in spirit, if not in the expression of that spirit. As she sees him, he is her "little David" setting out to kill the giant with his hidden weapon, "secret laughter" (118). And she is distressed when he finally loses that laughter and can no longer "walk roughshod over an emperor with every step."[7] Significantly, the reason she gives for his loss of irony is not the growing seriousness of the political situation, but his own gradual absorption into the prevailing system, the fact that he begins to take himself more and more seriously. The introduction of this concept has the effect of relativizing Johanna. The focus here is not so much on Heinrich himself as on Johanna's view of him. Her criticism of the no longer ironic Heinrich is not that his behavior is inappropriate, but that he has ceased to be true to his inner self. In spite of her own consistent moral code, she does not really think in political terms, for precisely by admiring Heinrich's irony, she has permitted him to dissociate himself from the present.

Johanna herself follows more stringent principles. And if she ceases to criticize the ruling powers publicly, she at least sees to it that her

own family does not derive any unfair advantage from its more privi-
leged position. Thus during the war, she does not allow her children
and grandchildren to accept gifts of food and clothing from the monastery, and she persuades Edith to support her in keeping to this idealistic course. The only concession she makes is to plead for amnesty for
Robert after the Ferdi Progulske affair. Even this is not entirely an
exception, since it is in fact her forthrightness that forces an old friend
of hers, the important official Dr. Emil Dröscher, to capitulate. "My
God, should we all hang ourselves?" asks Dröscher, whereupon she
replies: "All of *you*, yes" (128). Once again she puts into words what
others do not dare express: in this case, the culpability of the Nazi
officials.

But there is another aspect to Johanna which places her courage in a
somewhat different perspective. This is the element of youthful enthusiasm which dominates at least her pre-asylum days. "I wasn't quite
twenty-two when the Abbey was consecrated. I'd only finished reading
Love and Intrigue a little while before. I still had a little girlish laughter
left in my throat" (124). The girlish laughter gradually disappears, but
Love and Intrigue continues to play a role in determining her motivation. The heroine Luise's pious innocence is presumably the kind of
model that leads Johanna to align herself—to some extent against her
own more forthright character—with such lambs as Edith, who regard
their predicament as preordained and unavoidable. Unable to understand why she is attracted to Edith, Johanna has mixed feelings about
her. Rationally, she perceives that Edith acts as she does out of a sense
of piety, not out of reflection or insight. Emotionally, the Luise model
exerts its pull on her, as she sees Schiller's heroine as a precursor of
the lambs. Furthermore, *Love and Intrigue* might seem to imply, at
least to the youthful mind, that in the face of absolutism there is no
way out for the individual. Whatever Luise might do to preserve her
innocence, it would work against her in the last analysis: "criminal,
whichever way I turn."[8] Böll implies here that this tragic view of the
individual's predicament is inflated and wrong, since it might suggest
inaction rather than action. Applied to the conditions of the Third
Reich, this conclusion would be unfortunate. Johanna has perhaps
been unduly influenced by Schiller's Luise. She concentrates on pre-
serving her own moral innocence instead of on changing the status
quo; but, in the very act of doing so, she loses her innocence in a more
general sense. When she accuses others of foolishness, she unknow-
ingly accuses herself as well. "Children, the Lord was certainly pleased
with your foolishness. But you might at least have killed him" (122).
She means Nettlinger, but she might just as well mean Hitler. And if
she does outgrow the *Love and Intrigue* phase, she fails to pass on
whatever wisdom she has gained from this transition. Not only Edith

but Ruth as well (at least in Heinrich's imagination) are shown reading the play (149, 92). Johanna fails to break this fatal continuity.

Her long years in the "bewitched castle," as she calls the insane asylum, have constituted for her a period of "inner emigration" (151) in which she has retreated from the external conflict. When she finally decides to act, it is already too late. Just as Robert failed to act until the war was virtually over, so his mother refrains from action until thirteen years later. As she originally conceives it, however, her act of resistance does have a certain meaning: she intends to kill the chief of police, Nettlinger, as a protest against the fact that a number of former Nazis hold important state positions. But at the last minute she alters her plan. The idea behind her attempt on the life of a prominent politician is to eradicate what she regards as the murderer of her grandson, in other words, a representative of the bourgeois attitudes that prevent Joseph and his generation from developing true independence of spirit.

In a sense, there is some logic to this change of plan. Johanna herself says that to kill Nettlinger now would be to shoot "into the museum";[9] dimly she sees that it is not simply the persistence of former Nazis within the system, but more generally the urge to conformism that is deadening the younger generation's capacity for critical thought. But, as it turns out, Johanna's aim is poor, and the politician is not seriously injured. And, since the shooting is regarded as the act of a madwoman, she has again missed her opportunity to make a meaningful protest.

The conclusion of the novel adds a further dimension to the problem of symbolic protest. When a cake modeled after the abbey is carried in at the birthday party, Heinrich's first impulse is to smash with his fists this reminder of his own complicity in the system he abhors. But, in the end, all he does is to slice off the tip of the tower and pass it to his son on a plate. The scene has been criticized for its obtrusive symbolism[10]—but isn't this, after all, the whole point? The sense of futility we feel at Heinrich's systematic demolition of the hated model of the abbey carries over to our perception of Johanna's futile shooting. What difference can a mere gesture possibly make?

Johanna is a thoroughly complex figure. The criteria by which she measures actions—forthrightness, consistency with self, relevance to the historical situation—correspond closely to the book's hidden value system. As a would-be resister, she shares center stage with Robert, and as the single character capable of fully articulating the psychology of her motivation, she provides a perspective that would otherwise be lacking.[11] But there is an ambiguity inherent in her apparently superior vantage point. This is her restriction to the bewitched castle, the insane asylum which she perceives ironically as a place of inner emigration.[12]

Significantly, her inner emigration does not cease with the end of the war; although she could presumably choose to justify her previous behavior and prove her sanity, Johanna remains in the sanatorium for thirteen more years and doubtless returns to it after her attack on the politician. In this way, the figure of Johanna furnishes a critique of early postwar German society, with its reluctance to become politically engaged. Her image of her incarceration as in a bewitched castle brings to light the contradictions in her character. However much she believes in active resistance, she nevertheless sees her own fate as determined from without. It does not occur to her that only she can break the spell on her magic castle. Instead, there is a sense in which she actually enjoys living in this timeless realm. "I don't want to know what time it is," she says at one point (139), and a little later: "I'm not blind, just crazy and perfectly well able to read the date on the calendar down the hall. It's September 6, 1958" (145). By making her vantage point a timeless one, she over-generalizes the problem of the past: "You know," she explains, "that sacraments have the terrible quality of not being subject to the finite" (143), and her final solution, the attempted murder of a pillar of society, attacks the present problem not at its roots, the younger generation itself, but indirectly, through those presumed responsible for the younger people's attitudes. This criticism, however, must be advanced from outside the framework of the novel itself, as it appears that Böll himself at least partially shares Johanna's viewpoint.

It is not accidental that the novel is set in the late fifties, for it shows that the Germans, even at this relatively late point, had failed to arrive at a satisfactory resolution to the conflict between social determinism and the moral mandate for resistance. The lamb-beast scheme implies that there always are and always will be beasts and lambs, thus removing the issue from its specific historic anchoring; the portrayal of the lambs suggests that the innocent are almost inevitably bound to become helpless victims;[13] and the image of the bewitched castle carries with it the connotation that its inhabitants are under the ban of a force they cannot control. Even when individuals try to escape these forces, as Robert and Johanna do, they find themselves trapped in their own culturally determined psychology. Böll's attempt to provide the kind of detail, individuality, and differentiation his predecessors had often neglected is ultimately thwarted by his reliance on schematic structures not far different from the allegories and myths of earlier novels. The religious framework of the two "sacraments" and the fairy-tale image of the enchanted castle return *Billiards* to an earlier conceptual mode which its contemporary, *The Tin Drum*, has clearly left behind.

Böll's choice of a metaphorical conclusion that is more of a gesture than a statement has caused some misunderstandings. Some readers

see the book as basically supportive of conventional values and over-
look the more critical role of Robert and Johanna. By ending with the
unarticulated insights of his namesake, Heinrich, Böll takes a more
moderate line than the two would-be resisters. The novel is clearly
about values, but where does its value-center lie?

To be sure, this kind of novel is not told from the sort of perspective
which makes the search for a single center of values particularly profit-
able. The interweaving of different points of view, the heavy reliance
on interior monologue and narration by individual characters themselves, and the juxtaposition of various time levels and frames of reference remove the focus from any single individual. At the same time,
they also reduce the function of the objective narrator, who makes his
appearance only to slip almost unobserved into the perspective of one
of the characters (the sheep lady scene is shown largely through the
eyes of Hugo, for example). And at certain points, when no perceptible narrative voice is present, Böll allows conversation between his
characters to proceed essentially without comment (as in the scene
between Nettlinger and Schrella in the hotel). Just as the moral balance is not to be found in a single protagonist, so also there is no
clearly guiding narrator to take us through this ethical labyrinth.

Such, at least, appears to have been Böll's intention. But even here
there is a *caveat*. The perspectivistic technique, as used here, does not
entirely absolve Böll of the charge often leveled at him: that of having
prejudged his characters.[14] One difficulty of this novel lies in what
might seem to be its most positive technical feature, the use of certain
figures outside the family itself to furnish a perspective beyond that of
those immediately involved in the action. In particular, the introduction of the secretary Leonore is evidently the result of Böll's attempt to
avoid one problem of the traditional multi-perspective novel, its reduc-
tion of events to subjectivity. The thesis that all is subjective conflicts
with the claim that one can make moral judgments of events, and this
clearly is what Böll wishes to do. On the positive side, Leonore is the
"normal" figure whose tangential connections with the family enable
her to act in many ways as the proverbial impartial observer. She is
present both at the beginning and at the end, a fact which would tend
to support this view of her function. On the other hand, once we have
come to see Robert's true motivation, it is difficult to imagine that
someone as bland and unprofiled as Leonore could possibly understand him. Indeed, Leonore's affections lean throughout towards old
Heinrich Fähmel, and she is never made privy to the revelation which
so drastically changes the lives of the others. Yet is through her eyes
that Robert and Heinrich are first presented to us and with her categories of judgment that we first evaluate them. In a similar fashion, Böll
uses the old porter Jochen to give some of the crucial background

information on the Fähmel family and on Heinrich in particular, and we are constrained to take over this material in the categories Jochen uses. Leonore is somewhat insubstantial, Jochen a strange mixture of characteristics ("something of a father-confessor, of a confidential secretary, of a pimp" [20]). Only gradually, by juxtaposing these passages with the other points of view, do we come to realize Leonore's and Jochen's limitations.

Except where the principal characters speak or think directly, Böll's narrator weaves in and out of various perspectives. The prejudgments implied by the lamb-beast scheme and by the introduction of the protagonists through the eyes of figures on the periphery are overlaid and relativized by these uneasy shifts in focus, but they still remain partially in force. Thus Heinrich, for example, is more human and interesting than his morally more admirable son.

Multiple perspective can be used to point towards a specific empty center which the reader is intended to fill out, but when the juxtaposed perspectives are themselves ambiguous and complex, they cannot readily be played off against each other in this fashion. As in the work of Andersch, it is not so much the technique itself as the way it is used that reveals its author's underlying attitude to history. Both novelists are responding, in their different ways, to a perception of the Nazi period that had begun to emerge only in the late fifties, taking the place of the previous emphasis on mass conditioning and mass guilt. The new focus was on the individual and his or her complex enmeshment in a situation determined by social class and religious or ethical beliefs. But while Andersch's arrangement of the several viewpoints in his novel indicates his continued allegiance to a socialist standpoint, Böll's more complex organization of the various perspectives suggests a deeper sense of moral insecurity only partially masked by the lamb-beast polarity. As analysis of the Third Reich penetrated further into the elusive interaction of individual psychology and social structures, the ethical problems appeared increasingly ambiguous and irresolvable, and the multiply refracted images of the past failed to come together in a clearly recognizable focus. In this respect Böll speaks for a wider range of contemporary readers than does Grass, whose insistence on free will in *The Tin Drum* represents a more radical view than Böll's in *Billiards at Half-Past Nine*. A more important distinction between the two novels might be seen as Grass's essentially political, Böll's essentially moral, response to the new sociology. That two such different responses could appear almost simultaneously says less about the individuals Grass and Böll than it does about the Federal Republic, where the political and the psychological view of individual responsibility were still hopelessly out of step.

The prismatic narration of *Billiards at Half-Past Nine* thus leaves it precariously balanced between the mythic and the ironic, the schematic and the ambiguous, the prejudged characters and the open-ended form. The final scene of the novel takes place, significantly, in an interior setting and proves with a characteristic gesture that even knowledge is powerless to break down completely the walls of the bewitched castle.

CHAPTER SIX

RESISTANCE AND RESIGNATION
Günter Grass' *Cat and Mouse*

Günter Grass' anarchist turned collaborator, Oskar Matzerath of *The Tin Drum,* provides the evaluative context in which his successor, Joachim Mahlke of the short novel *Cat and Mouse* (1961), can best be seen. Oskar knows he cannot be absolved of guilt on the basis of his apparent protest during the early part of his life, and he explicitly denies that he has been a resistance fighter. The problem of resistance and collaboration is a tricky one, and it is all too easy to claim in retrospect a role one did not actually have. Of resistance, Oskar says: "The word 'resistance' has become very fashionable. We hear of the 'spirit of resistance,' of 'resistance circles.' There is even talk of an 'inward resistance,' a 'psychic emigration.' Not to mention those courageous and uncompromising souls who call themselves Resistance Fighters, men of the Resistance, because they were fined during the war for not blacking out their bedroom windows properly."[1] If the terms *resistance* and *inner emigration* are to mean anything, he says, we must be careful how we apply them. Oskar's unmasking should be seen as a warning that Grass' characters cannot be evaluated on the strength of their first appearance.[2] Similarly, Joachim Mahlke is not what he at first appears to be; he represents the obverse of the resistance-collaboration issue as shown by the character of Oskar Matzerath. In focusing on this problem through the use of characters whose motivation is complex and who are never seen objectively, Grass re-creates in fictional form a problem that repeatedly surfaced during the war crimes trials: the issue of just how to draw the dividing line between collaboration plain and simple and collaboration used as a cover for resistance. Since it was a problem that was still being thrashed out in individual cases before the Federal Republic courts, Grass could well expect his readers to be familiar with it.

Only much later does Grass present us with a less ambiguous example of resistance, in a small vignette in *Local Anaesthetic* (1969). One of its principal characters is the schoolboy Philip Scherbaum, whose very questionable attempt at resistance is his scheme to demonstrate the effects of napalm by burning a dog on the streets of Berlin.

95

But he cites as his exemplar a more viable resister: young Helmuth Hübener, executed in 1942 for distributing anti-Nazi pamphlets and broadcasting forbidden messages. This model is worth noting, since Helmuth Hübener's age (sixteen when he first began his resistance efforts) and the years during which his acts took place (the early forties) bear a close resemblance to the crucial dates of *Cat and Mouse.* Joachim Mahlke is fifteen when the actual plot of the story begins to unfold; the stages of the war referred to situate the action in the forties. Scherbaum contrasts Hübener's actions with those of the anarchistic Dusters with whom Oskar was associated in *The Tin Drum,* a group to which Philip's teacher Starusch also belonged: "Compared to that your teen-age gang was nothing."[3] In Oskar and Hübener we see two extremes: protest that does not amount to real resistance and a meaningful, genuinely heroic struggle against nazism. In Joachim Mahlke we shall see yet another variant.

If certain readers have let themselves be taken in by Oskar, underplaying the questionable aspect of his protest, the deception is even more widespread in *Cat and Mouse.* Here a morally upright and religious youth seems to be drawn almost against his will into the Nazi movement, apparently becoming a psychological cripple in the process. In fact, however, the book is structured around a series of images that form a covert network of references to inner emigration, resistance, and collaboration. Once we recognize these, we begin to penetrate beneath the surface of the story and discover its hidden meaning.

Significantly, the tale is not told by the protagonist but by Mahlke's friend Pilenz as he looks back on their schooldays and their military experiences during World War II. Pilenz' evasive attempts to conceal his complicity both in nazism and the victimization of Mahlke make the narration involved and circuitous. The title *Cat and Mouse* derives from the book's opening scene, in which Pilenz sets a cat at Mahlke's throat, with its prominent, mouse-like Adam's apple. Thus begins a chain of events in which Mahlke determines to prove himself and expunge the ridicule of his classmates. His public image of himself as a strange but legendary figure culminates in the stealing of a Knight's Cross medal from a submarine commander who had given a patriotic speech in the school auditorium. But later, when he has at last won the same award on his own, he fails to return from an army leave and mysteriously disappears into his favorite hideout, the radio cabin of a sunken minesweeper.

The difficult style and complex structure of *Cat and Mouse* has sometimes led criticism to extremes,[4] and only in the last few years have more balanced views of the book begun to emerge. Even so, they span a range that might well cause the reader to despair. The protagonist Mahlke has been seen as virtually identical with the Nazi state, or, less drastically, as an outsider who is at the same time a product and prime example of it.[5] On the other end of the spectrum is the perception of him as a young man engaged in an unsuccessful struggle for freedom from nazism.[6] But Mahlke, as we shall see, is engaged in more than a personal struggle: his aim is a somewhat more public form of protest against the Nazi regime and its ideals.

For some time now it has been a critical commonplace to describe Pilenz, the teller of Mahlke's story, as an "equivocating narrator."[7] His motivation is apparent: driven by a sense of guilt, he attempts through the narration of his friend's story to come to terms with his own past. The act of writing is to purge him of this guilt by enabling certain repressed aspects of the story to surface, thus permitting him to perceive his own role in it more clearly. But he omits significant parts of the action. How much he conceals not only from himself but also from the reader has not been fully grasped. The more obvious acts of concealment, such as his failure to be explicit about his role as persecutor in the opening cat-and-mouse scene (an omission so gauche that it is unlikely to deceive anyone), serve as decoys to distract the reader from more drastic omissions. Pilenz has provided us with a clever jigsaw puzzle with a few carefully selected missing pieces, but even when we supply these pieces we still have an inaccurate view of things. Why does Pilenz continue to falsify the record even after Mahlke's death? The reason lies not only in Pilenz' psychological makeup or in his ambivalent relationship to his friend but also in his own previous involvement with nazism. It is for this reason that he continues to play a cat-and-mouse game with the reader, who is thus compelled to read between the lines of his account. Only when we extricate ourselves from Pilenz' cleverly constructed net can we emancipate ourselves from his misrepresentations. The book's central image of swimming to freedom can be applied on three levels: to Mahlke, in the past events narrated by Pilenz; to Pilenz, through the act of narration; and to the reader, whose critical understanding of the book is to provide a clearer view of the problem of collaboration. That so few readers have been able to attain this critical perspective is a stunning proof of Grass' thesis that the judgment of the public has not been fundamentally changed by the events of the Third Reich and World War II.

Pilenz has stacked the cards carefully against the reader. We know, or think we know, just what he has left out: the inner soul of Mahlke (37);[8] the name Hitler;[9] the name Knight's Cross; and the true identity of the cat. We fall into his trap when we deduce from these omissions that Mahlke, despite appearances, is really a product of the Nazi era, that the mouse turns out in the end to be a cat. There is another way to fill out his gaps, and I think that it is a more coherent one. To reconstruct what Pilenz refuses to tell us directly, we must first establish some of his less obvious concealments. What he fails to present are, on the one hand, the positive side of Mahlke's moral and religious beliefs and, on the other, the extent of his own identification and collaboration with the Nazi regime.

Let us first look at Mahlke's motivation. Pilenz would like us to think that his setting the cat at Mahlke's throat is merely a catalyst that brings out into the open a psychological complex already present. The other schoolboys' naive psychologizing also assumes an emotional problem: "Maybe it's got something to do with his father's death" (35). It does, indeed, have something to do with his father's death, but Mahlke is not merely a child who, like so many others in this period, has been psychologically damaged by the loss of his father.[10] A more illuminating clue to Mahlke's motivation is given by the photograph in the hallway of his house:

> The whole width of the photograph was taken up with a rather modern-looking locomotive with tender, belonging to the Polish railways—the letters PKP could be clearly distinguished in two places. In front of the engine stood two men, tiny but imposing, with folded arms. The Great Mahlke said: "My father and Labuda the fireman, shortly before they were killed in an accident near Dirschau in '34. But my father managed to prevent the whole train from being wrecked; they awarded him a medal posthumously" (131).

Others have already noted that this sacrifice on his father's part has instilled in Mahlke a desire to emulate him, and that his father's post-humously awarded medal corresponds to the Knight's Cross which Mahlke later wishes to win. But other important details have been overlooked: the association of Mahlke's father with the Polish railway and hence with Poland itself; the description of driver and stoker as "tiny but imposing," conveying the idea that ordinary people can still have some control over destiny; and the date of the accident, 1934, one year after Hitler's takeover in Germany but before the annexation of Poland. Even more important are the words: "My father managed to prevent the whole train from being wrecked" (131). This is a small-scale version of that other sacrifice Mahlke constantly invokes, the sacrifice of Christ for mankind. Mahlke's mental erasure of the infant in the picture of the Madonna and his imagined sexual relations with Mary, which explicitly assign to him the role of God, indicate that it is redemption of the world, or at least of Poland, that Mahlke sees as his true goal. Pilenz' erasure of the blackboard caricature of Mahlke as Redeemer is only superficially a protective gesture; in reality, it is symptomatic of his attempt to conceal from the reader the seriousness of the Redeemer concept. If this notion is an inflated one, it is not to be seen merely as an example of yet another perversion to which the times have driven a hapless young person; it is inflated because the very idea that a single individual can avert total catastrophe, as Mahlke's father did, is made almost unthinkable by the pervasive oppression of nazism. Yet if we accept the idea that Mahlke's aim, to "redeem the world," is not meant entirely ironically, we can trace the different steps of his development more clearly. That Mahlke may be something of a saint is shown by Pilenz' repeated description of his reputation as "legendary" (34). And there are several other indications that Mahlke has set out to become the savior of Poland.

In addition to his father and the Redeemer, two other models become important for Mahlke. One of these is the Polish patriot Pilsudski, a long-standing member of the Polish socialist party, an advocate of Polish independence, and head of state almost continuously from 1919 until his death in 1935. Among the symbolic bric-a-brac of Mahlke's room, Pilsudksi's portrait occupies a prominent position. Like Mahlke's father, though on quite a different level, Pilsudski had averted catastrophe through his skillful strategy against Soviet Russia in 1920; the incident is known in Polish history as the miracle of the Vistula. This incident and Pilsudski's legendary fame are not quite so clear-cut, however, when we recall his later, more dictatorial rule of Poland. But Pilsudski's picture is soon joined by the amulet showing the Black Madonna of Czestochowa retrieved by Mahlke from the minesweeper. The Black Madonna is thought to be a likeness of the Polish queen Richeza, who, together with her husband Mieceslav, began the conversion of Poland to Christianity. The altar picture of the Black Madonna at Czestochowa resembles portraits of Richeza in the slash marks on her face, reputedly sustained during the heathen uprisings. Later, Czestochowa was the site of another miraculous event in Polish history, the resistance of the convent before the Swedish attack in 1655. One of the defenders of the convent was said to be a woman in a blue cloak, a coincidence which resulted in the declaration of the Virgin Mary as honorary queen of Poland. To us, this may seem like a minor detail from a far-off time, but in fact the episode still lives in the memory of Polish Catholics, as witnessed by the pilgrimage of one million Poles to Czestochowa in 1956 for the three hundredth anniversary of the consecration of Poland to the Virgin. Pilsudski and the Madonna, two legends ancient and modern, join with the family legend of Mahlke's father to form the motivation of the boy's attempt to carry off a miraculous defense of Poland.

At first, in the part of the story preceding the fictional beginning, Mahlke has been an odd man out, a shy, sickly child who scarcely participates in school life, who does not belong to the group, and who presents written excuses so that he does not have to take gym, that keystone of Nazi morale. When Mahlke at last wins his waterwings,

Pilenz shows this as the act by which he "swims to freedom" and finds his true self. But it seems more likely that neither the sickly child nor the "Great Mahlke" is in fact Joachim's true self. Both may simply be disguises for an identity in which his sense of purpose derives from his father's code of ethics, that part of Joachim which remains hidden from Pilenz until the end of the book. Joachim Mahlke seems to possess an unspoken insight into his historical situation which stems from his personal sense of justice, and it is clear throughout that he attempts to preserve his own moral code.

There are three stages in Mahlke's attempt to put his plan for redemption into practice: in terms appropriate to the Nazi period, we may call them inner emigration, resistance, and resignation.

His earlier, sickly child role represents an attempt to stand aside from events, to absolve himself of responsibility for them by refusing to participate in them. But it is effective on an individual level only, in that it saves him from personal guilt while allowing the rest of the world to go its own way. In order to fulfill his father's heritage, an aim symbolized by his wearing his father's clothes, he must go further than that.

Once he learns to swim, he has earned the passport to respect from his peers. This he needs if his later actions are to bear any weight with them. And it also enables him to take on a dual role, which Pilenz interprets as part of his basic ambivalence, part of his paradoxical psychological makeup. The narrated events take on a different character, however, if we regard this role not as ambivalence but duplicity. The flamboyant role-playing is a mask that permits him to maintain his own views in private while ostensibly joining in with his schoolmates. Like the mask of a clown, Mahlke's mask conceals a different personality, and when Mahlke announces at school that he wants to be a clown when he grows up, Pilenz comments that no one laughed in the classroom—"and I myself was frightened" (19). It is made abundantly clear, both here and elsewhere, that Mahlke approaches everything in deadly earnest and is not one to joke (though Pilenz tries unconvincingly to persuade himself of this possibility: "Was all this praying and worshiping in jest? . . . You had a strange sense of humor, if any" [25]). Mahlke's clown role is a problem critics have not satisfactorily resolved; in general, they tend to equate it with his Führer-like position in the schoolboy group. Evidently we have become so accustomed to Chaplin's version of Hitler (Chaplin is mentioned in connection with Mahlke's clown act [54]) that it seems as if this depiction of Hitler were not so much a parody as part and parcel of the real man.[11] This is a dangerous perversion of thought, and if we follow it we fail to see the real cohesion between Mahlke's Redeemer and clown roles. It is more likely that his clown aspect indicates both the mockery of society by which he attempts to become Poland's savior and the ultimate futility of this ambition.

Mahlke's inner emigration is symbolized by his transformation of the radio cabin in the minesweeper into a personal realm that is simultaneously a shrine to the Virgin Mary, the patron saint of Poland. The half-submerged inner space is the objective correlative of inner emigration. Moreover, the barge itself is not of German but of Polish origin, and it is a Polish Madonna medal that Mahlke retrieves from the interior of the ship. Just as the school principal, incidentally also a high official in the Nazi party, forbids him to wear the Polish medal openly at school, so his retreat into the submerged Polish radio cabin must remain out of range of his friends' observation. Mahlke's Polish loyalty remains unobserved and intact. When everyone else, including the Catholic priest Gusewski, changes his Polish name to a more Germanic-sounding one, Mahlke persistently refrains from following suit, even though his name, ending as it does in -*ke*, falls into the group of name types mentioned by Pilenz as sounding Polish and hence possibly eligible for alteration: "But the fashion of Germanizing Polish-sounding names ending in *ki* or *ke* or *a*—like Formella—was taken up by lots of people in those days: Lewandowski became Lengnisch; Mr. Olczewski, our butcher, had himself metamorphosed into a Mr. Ohlwein; Jürgen Kupka's parents wanted to take the East Prussian name of Kupkat" (120–21). Significantly, Pilenz here gives examples for the endings -*ki* and -*a*, but not for the ending on Mahlke's name, -*ke*. Of course, -*ke* can just as well be Germanic as Slavic, but in fact the name Mahlke (the only name of a major character that can be verified in a name lexicon) is of Eastern European or Slavic provenance, ironically with the meaning "the small one."[12] Its omission from Pilenz' list of examples would thus seem to indicate another guilty silence on the part of the narrator. Pilenz compares the name changing to that in which Saul became Paul upon his conversion to Christianity; the conversion is now ironically inverted. The motif is used later by Grass in his poem "The Dolphin," an attack on the political stance of Peter Weiss. The poet's reaction to the "convert at the microphone" bears a startling resemblance to that of Mahlke at the young lieutenant's lecture:

> I leaped!—
> . . . . .
> When asked to believe it, to believe,
> Anxiety soured my laughter:
> I secured my escape,
> Dived and swam to freedom.[13]

Similarly, Mahlke does not participate in the boyish laughter about warfare, an attitude symbolized by his refusal to wave to passing (German) warships. Nor does he applaud when the lieutenant speaks at the school; instead, he betrays obvious signs of anxiety. And when the lieutenant's successor, the submarine commander, also comes to speak, Mahlke at first plans not to attend. But Pilenz, hoping to convert him to the Nazi cause, sees his advantage and drags him along: "Flairing [sic] some possible gain in prestige for myself, I took him by the sleeve" (85). The imagery here, not reproduced in the English, is of submarines ("Ich witterte für mich Oberwasser"), and we will need to remember that *U-Boat* had the double meaning of submarine and a person who has gone underground. At the lecture, Mahlke, like an enemy submarine, senses (wrongly) that he has been recognized. While the principal makes his introductory remarks, the submarine commander, visibly at a loss without his periscope, attempts in vain to take a sighting: "his gaze roams free without cross-wires and dancing horizon, until Joachim Mahlke feels singled out" (87), but again, the "U-Boat" Mahlke escapes attention.

In the framework of Mahlke's duplicity—his inner Polish self and his external participation in the Germanized culture around him, his submerged and private realm inside the boat and his apparent membership in the group above decks—his Adam's apple takes on a new significance. Its connection with physical, especially sexual, prowess leads us to associate it falsely with the ideals of nazism; it has also been interpreted as symbolic of man's original sin.[14] The latter is an unfortunate coupling, for the implied equation of the German acceptance of nazism with original sin fails to account for the extreme forms the Nazi crimes assumed. Grass cannot have had such a cheap argument in mind. Rather, the Adam's apple represents an inner heroism based on humane idealism.[15] The superior moral code which drives Mahlke is related to his physical development, and his hanging of various baubles around his neck is not mere psychological compensation but an attempt to distract attention from his more adult view of the political situation. He is not physically abnormal but physically more mature (as he later recognizes himself); similarly, his psychology only seems abnormal in the midst of the prevailing mental perversion that has affected the other boys his age. The medals, screwdrivers, and pompoms are all ironic disguises for this accelerated maturity. Like his other disguise, the comically old-fashioned clothing of his father, these trappings are incongruous and blatantly opposed to Nazi ideals. Catholicism, central to Polish culture, was merely tolerated, but not accepted by the Nazis; the screwdriver that Mahlke retrieves from the boat is made in Sheffield, i.e., an enemy product; and the pompoms Mahlke introduces as a substitute for neckties are outlawed by school principal Klohse as effeminate and non-German. In this sense, then, it can be understood how his prominent Adam's apple becomes both his "motor" and his "brake" (110), the driving force that motivates him in his attempt to redeem the world and the restraint of superior moral judgment that prevents him from being swept along with the spirit of the times.

As for things German, Mahlke shows clearly what he thinks of them. Those objects retrieved from the minesweeper which are of German manufacture are not used as disguises or decoys, but are turned into symbols of absurd uselessness: the phonograph, which he plays at first with an empty turntable,[16] and the fire extinguisher ("Minimax" is today still the brand of most German fire extinguishers), with which he pointlessly "extinguishes" the glass-green sea (10).

A new stage begins when the speeches of the two former pupils in the school auditorium make it clear to Mahlke that inner emigration is not enough. As he sees the perversion of the spirit all around him—the gym-class atmosphere of the chapel, the hallowed "sacristy" of the gymnasium, the school's abandonment of the humanistic principles of its founder, the lieutenant commander's aestheticizing and romanticizing of warfare—he realizes that he cannot remain within his hermetically sealed inner sanctuary. Gradually he evolves as a would-be resistance fighter.

This new phase involves a certain amount of exposure, which Mahlke tries to keep to a minimum. The duplicity of Mahlke's inner emigration phase has led him to become superficially involved with certain aspects of Nazi life. As his individuality and moral sense begin to assert themselves, he requires a degree of shelter. As he grows older and has to move from the younger boys' Jungvolk to the older boys' Hitlerjugend, he loses his rank as a leader, in essence a demotion for his refusal to lead his Jungvolk troop in the Sunday exercises prescribed as a Nazi substitute for churchgoing. This is paralleled by his demotion from the humanistic high school, the Conradinum, to the inferior Horst-Wessel-Oberschule. In the first case, it is said that people like Mahlke could "go underground" more easily in the new surroundings; in the second, that not much publicity was given to the reason for his demotion. Mahlke has left the limelight, and at first it appears that he is embarking on a second inner emigration. Yet when he enlists in the military he joins not the submarines, as we might expect, but the tanks. The tank is an appropriate image for his present state of mind: an enclosed space from which the actual fighting is carried out, it nevertheless necessitates an occasional expedition outside the tank to plug up an open bolt hole. That he is now prepared to risk danger through exposure, even if minimal, shows how far Mahlke has progressed, although it also indicates how much further he might have ventured.

Mahlke's theft of the Knight's Cross is his first genuine attempt at an act of resistance. Because Pilenz is the narrator, we do not see the one scene that is crucial to the whole exploit and essential to an interpretation of the whole book: Mahlke's confession to Klohse. Yet it seems clear that had Mahlke presented the theft as a mere schoolboy prank, he would probably have escaped such severe censure from his principal. In the omitted scene he must have revealed the deeper reason behind his theft, but this appeal to Klohse's moral sense doubtless fails. Mahlke's aim then presumably becomes to win the Knight's Cross himself so that he can denounce the Nazi system publicly at his old school. In one of his political essays, Grass gives his own criticism of the Knight's Cross bearers:

> Today there exists an organization of Knight's Cross bearers which gathers together from time to time the surviving, in other words, a minority, of those specialists in bravery. There would be little to say against this if the organization did not promulgate the thesis that this military bravery had been meaningful. Now, it can be proven that millions of German soldiers died senselessly, that is to say, in vain. Millions of soldiers who believed that through their bravery they were defending *Führer, Volk, und Vaterland,* indeed, that they were spreading the just cause of Germany throughout the whole world, these millions of soldiers—this, too, has been proven—were serving organized crime.[17]

What follows these general remarks has a special relevance to *Cat and Mouse:*

> But where, I often wonder, is there a Knight's Cross bearer who has salvaged the remains of his military bravery in his postwar civilian life and who can speak out more or less like this: "Yes, I have realized that my military achievement was meaningless. Without knowing it or willing it, I helped criminals who needed time and space to organize and carry out their murder of six million people. I was wounded four times. I lost a leg. When the weather changes it hurts and reminds me. I refuse to wear honors that were bestowed so that behind our backs murderers and their accomplices, to whom we had all given power, could multiply and carry out their crimes.[18]

Doubtless this is the speech Mahlke never makes. His goal must have been to return to his school as a Knight's Cross bearer and to speak the truth, as the two earlier speakers had failed to do. But since he has given himself away in his first confession to Klohse, the principal prevents him from speaking at the Conradinum. Pilenz, the anxious witness to all this, tries to arrange another locus for the speech, but if Mahlke's speech is to have any effect, it must be given at the Conradinum, the symbolic representative of the humanistic spirit now perverted under nazism.

In the light of this passage from Grass' essay we understand the conclusion of the book more clearly. Having finally been persuaded that Mahlke's view was the right one, Pilenz now hopes that his friend will reappear and speak out at the meeting of Knight's Cross bearers against the senselessness of the award, but Pilenz is alone in his belated recognition that even in postwar Germany there is an unfulfilled need for the continued survival of the resistance spirit. "You refused to surface" (178).

It is illuminating to read this passage in connection with Hans Hellmut Kirst's best-selling trilogy *Zero Eight Fifteen*. In the last volume Kirst includes as a parodistic postscript a fictitious speech made at a gathering of Knight's Cross bearers. The speaker, a character named Hauptmann a.D. Schulz, claims that he and his comrades still believe that their actions during World War II constituted a just war, that even after the war there were no soldiers who were ashamed of their uniforms, and that in their view honor and respect are due the medal winners: "they have protected the Western World from its decline."[19] Following Schulz' rousing conclusion: "We shall continue their work!" the audience breaks out into lively applause; the narrator comments: "no one present protested."[20] In view of the popularity of Kirst's novels during the fifties, it is quite conceivable that Grass may have had this parody in mind when he developed the idea of Mahlke's protest speech.

Mahlke's volunteering for military duty is to be seen as a crucial part of his resistance that allows him to carry on his subversion of the system. Similarly, his affair with the commander's wife is actually a way of mocking the army by cuckolding the captain. That Mahlke has no intrinsic interest in sex has already been made clear; however, he uses the myth that has grown up around him for purposes of his own. Before his final descent into the underwater cabin, he claims that he slept with Tulla Pokriefke and that his involvement with her is why he has deserted the army, but both Mahlke and Pilenz know that he cannot have been with her, since she did not work on the tramline on which he returned that night (112). In both of these cases, there is a flagrant duplicity: his claim to be building a rabbit hutch for the commander as a pretext for the supposed affair with his wife; involvement with Tulla as an excuse for deserting the army.

A similar type of subversion is shown in the history of the Polish minesweeper, which is recounted in some detail. Pilenz tells us that this was one of three Polish boats that had been recovered from the catastrophic battle in the Bay of Danzig; the Germans were able to return into service (and bestow new German names on) two of these, but the third sank before it could be towed away. It was later rumored, Pilenz adds, that a Polish officer and his mate who were operating the boat under German command had flooded it "in accordance with the well-known Scapa Flow recipe" (38). The reference here is to an incident in the aftermath of World War I, when German ships, having been escorted in 1918 to Scapa Flow and kept under observation by the victorious British fleet, were finally scuttled and sunk the following year by their skeleton crews. The Scapa Flow incident was well known, as Pilenz says, and together with the history of the minesweeper it provides Mahlke with a model of patriotism under cover of apparent cooperation. Significantly, the bronze plaque with the boat's Polish name, "Rybitwa," is the first item Joachim recovers from the wreck. The sea battle in which the ship was involved immediately preceded the annexation of Danzig to the German Reich, as Grass explains in a different context; in *The Tin Drum* the peninsula Hela (from which the Rybitwa was being towed before it was scuttled) is described as "the last nest of resistance."[21]

A microcosmic representation of Mahlke's double role in the war is seen in the letter he writes to his mother and aunt, which the aunt asks Pilenz to explain to her. Pilenz does not do so, however, and the reader is left to work it out alone. Two things puzzle Mahlke's aunt: the discrepancy between the "squiggly line drawings" and the "neat Sütterlin script" (139) and the variation in the number of tanks Mahlke has destroyed as reported in his different letters. The second difficulty is easily disposed of: the number of tanks adds up to forty-one, one more than the number required to receive the Knight's Cross; the relatively small number reported at one point in the correspondence is due to a temporary removal from the front line which Mahlke suffered after he revealed his visions of the Virgin to the other soldiers. The first problem is more significant. On its more obvious level, the discrepancy between the neat handwriting and the childish drawings reflects the contrast that runs throughout the book between the seriousness of the war and the sense of childish adventure with which the schoolboys invest it. On another level, however, it indicates Mahlke's own dualism. From *The Tin Drum* we learn how Grass views Sütterlin script, a style of handwriting invented around the turn of the century and taught in schools during the Third Reich. In both its German and Roman forms, it displays upright, as opposed to slanting, lines and no contrast between thick and thin strokes. This is the writing that adorns the blackboard on Oskar's first and only day of school, and Oskar points out both the teacher's inept and debased version of the script and his own view of its intrinsic meaning and most appropriate use.

> This testimonial to a new stage in life was recorded in Sütterlin script that crept across the blackboard with malignant angularity. However, the loops were not right, too soft and rounded. The fact is that Sütterlin script is especially indicated for succinct, striking statements, slogans for instance. And there are also certain documents which, though I admit I

have never seen them, I can only visualize in Sütterlin script. I have in mind vaccination certificates, sport scrolls, and handwritten death sentences. Even then, I knew what to make of the Sütterlin script though I couldn't read it: the double loop of the Sütterlin M, with which the inscription began, smelled of hemp in my nostrils, an insidious reminder of the hangman.[22]

By using the Sütterlin script Joachim associates his letter with the official pronouncements of the Nazis, but at the same time he indicates by means of the childish drawings the absurdity of the war they are waging. His own duality becomes apparent in his inversion of meaning and expression: the Nazi script is used to express humane concerns: his inquiries after the health of his mother and aunt, his request that masses be said for his father and that prayers be said to St. Jude Thaddeus. The appeal to St. Jude, one of the last apostles of Jesus, who, with Simon the Zealot, suffered martyrdom in Persia, is not insignificant, since St. Jude is the patron saint of desperate causes. Mahlke's prayers, in other words, have made a progression from Mary to Jude that indicates his growing sense of the hopelessness of the Polish cause. The final portion of Joachim's letter is misrepresented to us by Pilenz, who describes it as "some pale landscape painting," when in fact it contains an account of the poverty Mahlke has seen while on duty and the recognition that the war is not helping to ameliorate it. "You can't imagine how run-down everything is here, how wretched the people are and all the many children. No electricity or running water. Sometimes I begin to wonder what it's all for, but I suppose it has to be" (141). Having won the Knight's Cross, Mahlke at last hopes to return to the Conradinum and expose the senselessness of this award earned in a senseless war. His projected speech is sketched out in part during his final row out to the barge. At first this speech is "little more than a chattering of teeth, but then he had them under control" (181). When we look more closely at the scraps of sentences Mahlke throws out, however, we can see something of the intention behind it. Using techniques learned from his two predecessors, the other Knight's Cross bearers who had spoken at the school, Mahlke had intended to begin by capturing the audience's attention with technical details: "Would have started in with explanations, the sights, armor-piercing shells, Maybach engines, and so on" (179). Then he had planned to invoke the example of his father, and at last to proceed to an account of his visions of Mary and the shooting of the tanks. The Virgin, whose apparition is regarded by Mahlke as proof that there is such a thing as transcendence, is associated, not with the Germans, but with those fighting against them. Mahlke describes her in military terms: "She came in from the left and headed for a clump of woods at convoy speed, twenty miles an hour. Just had to keep her in my sights" (180–81). In this indirect way, Mahlke indicates the perversion wrought by war. Characteristically, the speech is interrupted before it reaches a rhetorically convincing conclusion, and we are left wondering whether Mahlke would have actually taken the final step, the rejection of the Knight's Cross. That he had at least originally intended to abjure the award is made clear by an earlier remark. When he returned to the Conradinum in the hope of persuading Klohse to let him speak there, he said to Pilenz, "All the problems concerned with the award will be touched upon and dealt with in my speech."[23]

The final stage in Mahlke's development is that of resignation. Forbidden to deliver his speech at the Conradinum, he rejects the idea of giving it before the Dusters, much as Philip Scherbaum rejects this anarchistic group in *Local Anaesthetic*. Mahlke's hopes are finally crushed when he realizes that he is just another great hero to the younger boys who swarm after him for his autograph. There seems to be no way for him to dispel the illusion he has created to disguise his undercover resistance plans. At the end of the book, Mahlke goes down again to the underwater cabin, returning to his spiritual homeland but abandoning the attempt at resistance which the cabin had originally symbolized.

One interpretation of Mahlke's death is that it is a suicide, a self-sacrifice without a resurrection, but, as has also been recognized, one can just as well say that he is, in effect, murdered by Pilenz, who prevented him from taking with him the can opener he needs if he is to survive for any length of time in the underwater cabin. When we look back, we can see that Pilenz has always betrayed Mahlke. Typical is Pilenz' statement that Mahlke "always had an audience. . . . he had the Virgin Mary behind or before him" (61). But besides the Virgin, there is also always another audience: Pilenz himself, who keeps Mahlke constantly under surveillance. The recurrent image of the cat's glassy eyes shows that Pilenz, however great his admiration for Mahlke, is also in some sense a spy. "As often as I served at the altar, even during the gradual prayers I did my best, for various reasons, to keep an eye on you" (22). Pilenz as good as admits to having given evidence against their teacher Brunies before the latter was carried off to the concentration camp Stutthof, officially because he had eaten Vitamin C tablets meant for the schoolchildren, but in actuality because he was a Freemason. Father Gusewski, the priest who changed his name to Gusewing, appears to have been a key contact for Pilenz, since in his conversations with Gusewski, during which he feigns concern over Mahlke's Mariolatry, Pilenz also gleans information about Mahlke's doings during his absence. And, at the end, Pilenz deceives Mahlke about the necessity of his disappearing by telling him, untruthfully, that the police have already taken his mother for questioning. Despite his overt attempts to help Mahlke at various stages, he is secretly pleased when they do not work out. When Klohse forbids Mahlke to speak at the school, Pilenz comments (using the pervasive submarine imagery): "Nasty little triumph! Once again I enjoyed my moment of superiority" (*bekam ich Oberwasser*) (159). After he has abandoned Mahlke at the end he comments, "the weather seemed to be on the mend" (126). Only after the war, as a result of much self-torment and long talks with Pater Alban, does Pilenz view things differently; now at least he wishes Mahlke could return and speak out.

Grass' jacket illustration shows the extent to which Mahlke's attempted resistance has failed and indicates the connection between Mahlke and Pilenz. To be sure, the swastika has been erased from the Knight's Cross, thus restoring it to its original form as a Maltese Cross, a symbol of humaneness.[24] But the cat, not the mouse, is wearing the cross. What can this mean? We must assume that just as Pilenz had formerly scratched out Mahlke's name in the Labor Service latrines, so he has now scratched out the swastika from the medal, thus performing the act Mahlke did not live to accomplish. The cat still looks wary, but through his writing Pilenz has expiated his guilt and earned a medal of his own.

The parallelism between Mahlke's progress as he "gains his water-wings" by freeing himself from nazism and Pilenz' progress as he writes the book has been observed before.[25] In recounting the incident where Mahlke plays with the stolen medal on the minesweeper, Pilenz comments, "I was no longer swimming away from Tulla, but swimming toward Mahlke, and it is toward you that I write" (106). As in the image of transcendence which Mahlke invokes in his projected speech, two parallel lines—Mahlke and Pilenz—ultimately come together. This is indicated by the images of the cat and the snowy owl. The cat represents Pilenz, both in the opening scene on the playing field and in the scene with the stuffed cat in the school showcase. Mahlke has been associated with the snowy owl, a stuffed specimen of which had been left him by his father. It reflects both his center-parted hair and his "suffering, meekly resolute look, as of a redeemer plagued by inner toothache" (28). Just as Mahlke cannot dive to his underwater cabin in the winter, so the snowy owl must migrate southward in winter from its Arctic homeland. Both the cat and the owl hunt mice; both are described as glassy-eyed. Both Mahlke and Pilenz may have started out hunting different prey, but at the end their quarry is the same: the Nazi spirit in its wartime and postwar forms.

There is a further dimension to Grass' design for the jacket of the book, however. It was inspired, as Grass later informed an interviewer, by a cover picture of an issue of the German news magazine *Der Spiegel*.[26] In 1961, just as *Cat and Mouse* must have been going to press, Erich Mende had been elected as head of the FDP and was chosen by the *Spiegel* as the subject of a cover story.[27] The photo shows Mende in formal attire; beneath his white bow tie hangs a prominent Knight's Cross in which, in accordance with postwar regulations, the swastika has been replaced by a three-fold oak leaf. In this denazified form, it was perfectly legitimate to wear the Knight's Cross after the war, but, as the article informs us, Mende was one of the first to do so in a public situation. The *Spiegel* gives a sketch of Mende's life, from his prowess at school (first in his class right up to senior year) to the awards of the Iron Cross Second and First Class and finally the Knight's Cross (the latter for saving the life of German citizens in Narew, just outside Warsaw). A passage that cannot fail to have attracted Grass' attention draws, with inimitable *Spiegel* irony, a comparison between Erich Mende and Willy Brandt: "Mende's Knight's Cross is an honor whose worth can be professionally evaluated by all the bearers of the Iron Cross Second Class, an honor that was obtained in their own sphere of life. Willy Brandt's actions as a resistance fighter can at best evoke respect from generous people, but they remain for the majority of German citizens part of an unfamiliar sphere, more adventurous than political."[28] The parallel to *Cat and Mouse* must have delighted Grass. Had he not, after all, depicted in Pilenz' family, where the brother received the posthumous award of the Iron Cross II and the mother leads a sentimentally bourgeois (if also morally questionable) life, just the type of German who after the war would have appreciated FDP leader Mende more than SPD leader Brandt? Mende's failure to speak out against the regime that awarded him his Knight's Cross indicates, for Grass, a survival into the postwar era of that regime's insidious mode of thought.

This is why, for Pilenz, there is no "good ending" (188); the cat-and-mouse game continues into the present.

Of what value, then, has been Mahlke's abortive attempt at resistance? If it is difficult for us to reach an accurate evaluation of Mahlke's deeds, perhaps a clue may be found in Grass' poem "Pan Kiehot" and its prose equivalent in *The Tin Drum*. Here the Polish resistance to the attacking Germans is seen as a valiant but pitiful attempt at self-assertion, and their commander in the battle that ended with the annexation of Danzig is depicted as a Polish Don Quixote. "A pure-blooded Pole, a noble, mournful figure," he leads the counterattack under the delusion that his men are fighting not steel tanks but "mere windmills or sheep."[29] But his foolhardy behavior leads all the more certainly to disaster, and the Poles suffer drastic losses. The poetic version concludes in bitter irony at the self-delusion of the Poles, who consider themselves so clever that they can conquer with ease those "clumsy animals," the German tanks:

Then cleverly they broke, clumsily they kissed
—I know not whether sheep or mills or tanks—
They kissed the hand of Pan Kiehot;
He felt ashamed, he blushed for cleverness;
I find no better word; the Poles are clever.[30]

This tragically miscalculating talent, then, is the Polish tradition that Mahlke is carrying on in his very much less active form of resistance. Had he been able to speak out against nazism, he might indeed have been a resistance fighter; cut short, his actions remain in the realm of self-delusion. Like Pan Kiehot, Mahlke becomes an embodiment of the ineffectual Polish resistance, over which Grass, himself a Pole, appears to shake his head in sad bewilderment.

Yet despite the resignation implied by its ending, *Cat and Mouse* is, in the last analysis, a more effective model for the fictional treatment of nazism than its successor in the Danzig trilogy, *Dog Years*. In *Dog Years,* the double narrator structure is doubtless intended to set up a clearer dialectic than that of *Cat and Mouse,* as Matern's lies and false masks are played off against Amsel's more detached perceptions. But this is a case where two negatives do not make a positive, and the ironic juxtaposition of the two perspectives leaves the reader with too little guidance. *Cat and Mouse* is based on a subtler interplay: the friendship and antagonism between narrator and protagonist. Pilenz' concluding call for Mahlke's resurrection and thus for the resurrection of the resistance spirit urges us to carry the dialectic of *Cat and Mouse* beyond the end of the novel. This suggests that there is a continuing need to reassess the past. Like the Heracles of the Pergamene Altar, the true Mahlke remains hidden, waiting for us to search him out. The vicious image of an eternal cat-and-mouse game is thus turned into its opposite, the reader's ever-renewed attempt to summon up the missing hero.

CHAPTER SEVEN

ART AND CRIMINALITY
Siegfried Lenz' *The German Lesson*

By placing narration itself at the focus of *Cat and Mouse,* Grass was also probing by implication the function of literature in the confrontation with the past. Siegfried Lenz takes up this theme again in *The German Lesson,* whose "unreliable narrator," Siggi Jepsen, is a literary relative of both Pilenz and Mahlke. Siggi Jepsen starts out somewhat younger than Joachim Mahlke and concludes his story as he reaches the age of maturity. Like Pilenz, he uses writing to absolve his conscience and to come to terms (insofar as he can) with his experiences during the Third Reich. Confined after the war to a home for delinquent boys, Siggi is forced to write, as a punishment, a composition titled "The Joys of Duty," an essay that keeps on growing and becomes the novel itself. A second focus of *The German Lesson* is the Expressionist artist Nansen, whose role during the Third Reich represents both the potential and the weaknesses of a belief in the political effectiveness of art. Siggi's self-appointed childhood task has been to save Nansen's paintings, pronounced degenerate by the Nazis, from confiscation by the village policeman, Siggi's father. Through Siggi's strained relations with his family and his attempted support of the painter, Lenz focuses on the problematic issue of art as resistance.

Both the narrator and his artist friend are shown to fall short of their own ideals. To understand this, we must recall the position of Expressionism under the Nazi regime. Many opponents of nazism had hoped that the "destructive" element of Expressionism, which had so effectively broken down aesthetic conventions, might also be put to use politically as part of the resistance effort. But, in this case, aesthetics and politics were not identical. The revolutionary artistic aims of the Expressionists were coupled with less revolutionary political views, to the point where certain of them had even been accused of being unwitting contributors to the development of fascism in Germany. This paradox was fought out in the famous debate on Expressionism of 1937–38 in the exile journal *Das Wort,* and it is picked up in a different way by Lenz in *The German Lesson.* Alfred Kurella, who had at first exaggerated the case for a proto-fascist element in Expressionism, nonetheless summed up the ambivalence of the movement in his famous essay

"Last Word." Expressionism, he says, may be humanistic in intention, but this is a different kind of humanism from that which we have in mind when we speak of the struggle against fascism and against Hitler.[1]

The issue here is a crucial one, and it is worth asking how it is seen in postwar Germany and whether, furthermore, it is perceived as an issue at all beyond purely academic circles. It seems to me that Siegfried Lenz, in his novel *The German Lesson,* has provided his readers in the Federal Republic of Germany with a model by means of which the issue can be approached, as well as indicating, and criticizing, the categories within which people of various political leanings do in fact view Expressionism and its relation to nazism today.

The extreme coordinates are provided by the basically conservative narrator, Siggi, and his brother's radical friend, the young artist Hansi. Towards the end of the novel the two become engaged in a heated discussion following a visit to the Hamburg retrospective of the painter Max Ludwig Nansen, a figure who is, in most essential features, the fictional counterpart of Emil Nolde. When Hansi speaks against Nansen, Siggi is shocked; after all, he reasons, should not one who was persecuted by the Nazis be for that reason alone worthy of our admiration ("Doesn't that speak for him?" [439])?[2] We must ask with Siggi what it is that the new radicals find lacking in Expressionism and how they can dare to criticize its political stance. The answer is provided in the first instance by Hansi's own work, a series of pictures entitled *Revolt of the Dolls.* Here Hansi depicts rag dolls in aggressive and anarchistic actions: climbing factory chimneys, derailing trains, blowing up bridges and towers, digging a grave for Konrad Adenauer, and destroying that symbol of bourgeois comfort a stuffed armchair with a pair of scissors (438). Hansi belongs to a generation of artists that believes that art must convey an overt political message and for which the most appropriate message is a revolutionary or even an anarchistic one. For him it is not enough that Nansen was persecuted by the Nazis; Nansen's opposition to nazism should have been expressed more directly, forthrightly, and even aggressively.

In characterizing Nansen, Hansi introduces two concepts that are the exact opposite of his own artistic credo, yet he couples them, paradoxically, with the word *political.* " 'Now you just listen to me,' Hansi said. 'Your friend Nansen is the very type I regard as a disaster: back-to-the-land and all that, visionary, and political' " (438). Hansi is saying here that although it was impugned during the Third Reich, this kind of Expressionism shares certain attitudes prevalent under nazism. Most obvious here is the concept of "back-to-the-land," but equally important is the prophetic quality the artist feels he possesses. In this context, the word *political* becomes a kind of sneer. Of the three, it is the visionary aspect that Hansi regards as most peculiarly German: the artist's work is "all very Germanic," he explains in his casually sarcastic tone. He sees Nansen as a "cosmic window-dresser" whose implicit theme is the "quest for man's primal condition" (435). Even in Siggi himself, who has, as Hansi suspects, been a model for some of Nansen's paintings, the young radical perceives a likeness to some of the peasant types so beloved of Nazi art. "Of course I saw you at the show this morning, and you know what I thought the moment I set eyes on you? I thought: There's a born model for Nansen—for certain pictures, of course—say *Young Man Bringing in the Hay*" (437). Unfortunately, this view has just been seemingly supported by Nansen himself. By appearing at the retrospective in an immaculate gentleman farmer's outfit, he suggests that he does, in fact, belong somehow more to the past than the present. But no doubt this is just a mocking gesture towards his public.

How typical is Hansi of the public at the exhibition? To clarify this, Lenz gives us a fairly detailed summary of the introductory remarks made by the (fictitious) Hamburg critic Hans-Dieter Hübscher at the opening of the show. Two points are made in the lecture, and the painter is said more than once not to have objected to them. In terms of theme, Hübscher notes Nansen's "quest for man's primal condition"; in terms of form, he comments on the "enduring pictorial elements, plane, color, light and pattern" (426). So eternal are these qualities, in fact, that comparison can even be made to Rembrandt. Concluding, Hübscher says: "This work bears testimony to the fact that the sonority of color can transform an intuitively glimpsed meaning into pure paint" (427). His characterization of Nansen's work is couched throughout in terms of technique, the concept of artistic content subtly played down by the expression "an intuitively glimpsed meaning." Not only is the interplay of light and color the most important aspect of these paintings in Hübscher's eyes, it is presented as being a universal and eternal artistic problem, and the question whether Nansen's solution to the problem relates to his particular historical position is not raised at all. Nansen is visibly relieved to see this dimension eliminated from discussion, since consideration of his political stance during the Third Reich might tend to compromise him. The novel thus suggests that it is not appropriate simply to admire the formal features of Expressionist paintings such as those of Nolde while continuing to ignore the artist's politics.

It is helpful to compare this fictional speech with an actual speech given by Walter Jens on the one hundredth anniversary of Nolde's birth. Jens' speech is sympathetic to Nolde and brings no political criticism to bear upon him. In contrast to the one-sided paeon of praise given by Hans-Dieter Hübscher (whose very name reminds us of a German political figure and leads us to expect a different approach),

Jens brings out the ambivalence and the paradoxical nature of Nolde's position:

> A German painter, who, centuries after Dürer, wished to introduce a second German renaissance, became the deadly enemy of the National Socialists; the man from the country, who all his life inveighed against the "sweet sin of interracial marriage"; the opponent of those "impudent spruced-up rascals" who, he believed, were turning the temple of art into a brothel; the man for whom democracy was as much to be scorned as science, intellect, criticism, and book-learning; . . . this Nolde . . . never thought for an instant of making his private peace with the big bosses. Instead of conforming, he let things hinge upon a secret duel.[3]

Possibly Lenz heard this speech, which at least opened the door to a more complex view of Nolde's political position during the Third Reich. Jens makes the point that Nolde, while decried by the Nazis, nevertheless shared their views about the prototypically Germanic and the necessity of portraying this in modern art. Despite the Nazi prohibition on his painting, he shared the Nazis' ideas on democracy and intellectuals. This perception of Nolde's ambiguity was evidently unfamiliar to those readers of *The German Lesson* who made the book a best-seller. Such readers seem to have identified as the positive features of *The German Lesson* its story of a family divided under nazism and its evocative descriptions of familiar North German landscapes and of what they take to be re-creations of the spirit of Nolde's vision of this landscape. That Lenz' real intention is actually closer to the view presented in Jens' speech, that in some ways it goes further than Jens in its critique of Nolde, will become clear as we look more closely at the novel. Whereas Jens is still somewhat evasive on the basic political issues, Lenz is more explicit, although his personal views are not identical with those of that objectionable young anarchist Hansi.

Lenz' analysis of Expressionism in its connection with nazism is not particularly original. It has been pointed out that Expressionism and nazism share a common origin in the Youth Movement of the pre-World War I years, an anti-intellectual movement that preached escape from the ills of industrial civilization through a kind of nature mysticism.[4] Nazism exploited these ideals in its "blood and soil" mythology, whereas Expressionism filtered them into a different kind of anti-materialism and a more general enthusiasm for nature. Lenz conveys some of the common elements of the two movements in his evocative descriptions of nature and life in an isolated northern community, as well as in Nansen's painting of Hilke semi-naked on the beach. All of this suggests a corrective to the popular view of a clear-cut antagonism between the supposedly decadent art movement and its Nazi detractors.

More important than this, however, is Lenz' portrayal in Nansen of a character who is both Nolde and something more than Nolde. In this way, Lenz brings into relief the issue of resistance and would-be resistance. The question underlying this novel is: in what way might protest against nazism have found expression in art? Obviously, such a question can hardly have a simple answer. The reader must recognize that there is a distinction between the character Nansen and the real painter Nolde. By making Nansen slightly different from Nolde, Lenz indicates an ideal of artistic resistance which Nolde, in Lenz' judgment, failed to realize. Just as the protagonist of Grass' *Cat and Mouse* has not been recognized as a would-be resister, so, too, the element of true resistance in Lenz' Nansen has gone undetected by most of his readers.

This emphasis on Nansen may come as a surprise, since the novel seems to be concerned less with the painter than with Siggi and his family. Yet, if the novel's major theme is the permanent disruption of family relationships by Nazi ideology and the strictures of the Nazi regime, why are Nansen's paintings described in such intricate detail and at such great length?[5] However central the young narrator is to the novel, the clue to the book's value system lies in the descriptions of his friend's paintings. It is not mere indulgence in an aesthetically appealing subject that leads Lenz to present Nansen so fully.

What we learn about Nansen is, of course, affected by the fact that it is seen through the eyes of Siggi, then a child of ten. Later, its substance is corroborated by the psychiatrist Mackenroth, who also introduces information that corresponds with known facts about Nolde's life under nazism. That Nolde was the chief model for the character of Nansen has been recognized since the book first appeared; from the similarities and divergences between the fictional and the real artist, we come to understand Siegfried Lenz' criticism of Nolde.[6] At first, we learn that Nansen had joined a nationalist movement in the late 1920s but had resigned when he discovered that the central leadership was made up of homosexuals (147). While this is not a genuine political decision, at least it means he leaves the party. In contrast, Nolde, although a Danish citizen, joined the Nazi party quite early and did not voluntarily resign from it. When Nansen is invited to become director of the State Academy of Art, he sends off a damning telegram: "Gratefully acknowledge honor. Suffering from color allergy. Brown diagnosed as source of trouble. Regrets. Yours faithfully Nansen painter" (165). When Nolde was requested in May 1933 to resign from the Prussian Academy of Art because his paintings were considered decadent, he refused, saying that he found his membership quite in order.[7] Although their external actions differ in some respects, the prime aim of both Nansen and Nolde in taking up the feud with nazism was not politics, but the preservation of their paintings and the chance to continue painting. But Nansen's resistance to nazism goes further than Nolde's; the former provides a means for evaluating the latter. Nolde's protest was not directed against Nazi ideology, only against its judgment of his art.

Lenz recognizes in Nolde a basic ambiguity, which he brings to the surface in the character of Nansen.[8] After the war, the fictional painter works on a self-portrait that shows him as a face divided into two halves. Of course, the ambiguity has existed all along, unperceived by the painter, and even now the recognition comes slowly to him. He has difficulty in arriving at a clearly fixed image of himself: "it keeps on changing too fast, I can't resolve the contradiction in paint." The basic color opposition that informs the rest of his work also underlies the divided self-portrait: "the left half of the face was a strengthless reddish-grey, the right half greenish-yellow." This idea of two selves is a simplification, he knows, and, as such, a falsification; at the same time it reveals something about him that he would rather hide, even from himself. "Nothing was unequivocal," Siggi observes (334), and Nansen tries to justify this effect in terms of artistic principles: "The form must waver; everything must waver; light just doesn't behave well enough."[9] Furthermore, he is disturbed by the statement such a picture so obviously makes: "Content isn't what you should get out of a picture," he says. "But then, what?" (335).

Even earlier, Nansen's inner dualism is evident in his creation of an imaginary companion, Balthasar, the invisible disputant with whom he conducts his most serious discussions of artistic theory. Balthasar appears in the paintings wearing "a bristling purple coat"; he has "slanting eyes and a crazy beard of boiling, bubbling orange from which red-hot droplets fall" (27). While he works on his paintings, Nansen is engaged in a continuous argument with Balthasar over the principles to be applied. Nansen maintains that there is "only one action in every painting, and that's the light," and that it is only by means of intense colors, not, for example, by the choice of specific subject matter, that the "imminence of violent acts, and of doom" can best be represented (111). Balthasar expects a less indirect political message to be conveyed in the paintings. His bristling pride and fiery coloring indicate his role as the personification of criticism and protest; his clothing and demeanor suggest certain figures in the works of Ernst Ludwig Kirchner, whose middle name Nansen shares. Unlike Nansen, Balthasar does not believe in nature mysticism and rejects the basis of Nansen's paintings, the "earthy green" from which everything springs (112). Nansen explains Balthasar's credo to Siggi. "Balthasar thinks all that's not enough. He insists that seeing is also exposure. Something gets laid bare in such a way that nobody in the whole world can pretend he doesn't understand" (336). In contrast, Nansen disapproves of this "strip-tease act" (336), and his choice of this term indicates his disparagement of art with a message; for him, the artistic vision is "penetrating and enhancing," "waiting for something to change" (335).[10] But his critical aspect, his potential for protest through art as represented by Balthasar, is only partially expressed in his paintings, which are dominated by a sense of man's unity with nature. In the dualistic self-portrait Balthasar appears in the background, "rather subdued, in fact rendered pretty harmless by means of perspective" (334). It is as if Nansen were trying to obliterate part of his consciousness.

Among Nansen's works, the prototypical picture is *The Great Friend of the Mill*. The Great Friend, depicted as he is about to set the sails of the mill going again, represents a mythic transposition of Nansen's feelings towards the north German landscape: he rises "silent and brown" above the horizon, "a gentle old man, bearded, a creature of aimiable mindlessness and perhaps a worker of miracles, growing to gigantic stature." This dominant figure is an emanation of the landscape, less a person than a natural outgrowth; he may be a "worker of miracles," but he is also "mindless." In many ways he reminds one of Nolde's Great Gardener, who appears to be at once part of nature and its protector. Siggi surmises that by starting the mill again, the Great Friend aims to grind out "a clear day and a better light" (29).

The means by which this is to be achieved is emotional, rather than intellectual: it is the Great Friend's "determined affection" that is to reintegrate and clarify the landscape (29). What is meant by this becomes clear when we are given a description of another painting, a recollection of Nolde's *Sea with Two Sails* entitled *Sails Dissolving into Light*, where all is reduced to "a dreamlike unity" and the light effects become "one single chant of praise." "Here sky and sea were united," Siggi says of the picture (67). This is the sort of work the young narrator most admires, and his idea that the mill sails in the other picture will also ultimately produce clarity of vision indicates the terms in which he evaluates Nansen's art.

Yet there is another aspect to Nansen's work that Siggi only partly acknowledges—the negative, critical view of this landscape which Nansen, through his alter ego Balthasar, presents in a more subordinated way. "True, the pond near the mill expressed its purple doubts, but it would turn out to be wrong; the Big Friend's determined affection would prove the stronger" (29). Here we have the kernel of the artistic dilemma that Lenz wishes us to perceive through the interplay of Nansen and Balthasar. The "purple doubts," a correlative of Balthasar in his purple fox fur, temper the glorification of nature that Nansen portrays, but the latter triumphs over the critical intellect which seeks to undermine it. Of course, even Nansen himself does not view this landscape as entirely positive. He says, for example, that the picture needs "rage" before the mill sails can start turning again, yet the rage he speaks of is not the purple color of Balthasar's doubts, but the dark green color of nature. He wishes nature itself to avenge the outrage perpetrated upon it; he does not even entertain the thought of political action or a clearer political message.

Nansen's position within the political complex of the Third Reich is brought into sharper focus in his painting of the man in a red cloak, *Suddenly on the Shore,* alternatively titled *Fear* (169). The picture shows a confrontation between Siggi's brother Klaas and a goblin-like figure in a red cloak, set against a desolate shore on the North Sea. After being inducted into the army, Klaas has tried to evade military duty by cutting off his hand. This leads to his confinement in a military hospital, from which he escapes to his home territory, where he is grudgingly taken in by the painter Nansen. His function in the novel is partly to provide a jolt to Nansen's conscience: the painter takes him in but makes no secret of the fact that he feels himself compromised by this action and thus even more liable to observation by the police. That he paints Klaas at all indicates the importance of this confrontation with him. Klaas is depicted in the painting as consumed by "greenish-white flaming fear," but his fear is not the fear of one on the run from the authorities; it is a more elemental fear of the strange figure in a red cloak that remains elevated even though its wearer is dancing on his hands. "Just two or three more hesitant steps, one could see even now, and Klaas would be running, driven across the beach by his fear, running towards the indifferent skyline, anywhere—just to get away from the man standing on his head in the red cloak" (169). But how could a man standing on his head, even one whose cloak completely defies the laws of gravity, have evoked such fear in Klaas, who was capable of cutting off his own hand? I suggest that it was the acrobatic nature of the figure's actions which was so threatening. To please Klaas, the man in the red cloak "was trying to do it by—of all things— walking or dancing on his hands, which he did, it must be admitted, with the greatest of ease." The man's body was delicate ("How thin his wrists were! How delicate the curving, poised body!"), but he had "an ancient face," in which "an ancient cunning was very perceptible indeed" (169). This is clearly an indirect reference to Gottfried Benn's famous definition of the artist as acrobat. The earthy wisdom of the Great Friend is combined with a new element, the idea of an artist concerned only with technique. Klaas, involved with actual political events, cannot accept this image of the artist's role; he is not convinced, but is instead disturbed by the artist's display.

Nansen achieves this critique of the function of pure art with the aid of his imaginary friend, the "invisible know-all Balthasar" (170). The painter's arm feels it must overcome a certain resistance as it works; it hurts him to have to depict Klaas' fear of his art. Lenz thus brings an interesting point of view to bear on Expressionism of this type, since he indicates that it is not only dangerous in the sense claimed by the Nazis but also in another sense, in that its aesthetic mode partially conceals the very sense of doom it simultaneously conveys.

Klaas' later development bears out the criticism implicit in the painting. Not only does he become a close friend of the anarchist Hansi, he is an artist in his own right, a prize-winning photographer whose work, so we are to assume, is epitomized by his series *Dead Hamburgers,* which Siggi sees hanging in Klaas' hallway: "photographs of the people who had been drowned, battered to death, stabbed, strangled, shot, run over in the street, and also some who had died peacefully in their beds" (432). This type of social realism is, of course, at the opposite pole from Nansen's landscapes "dissolving into light."

Nansen does, however, attempt a different type of political criticism that goes beyond the inarticulate rage which motivates his landscapes. This he does in his *Invisible Pictures,* which he draws during the Nazi prohibition on his painting. One is immediately reminded of Nolde's *Unpainted Pictures,* but, in fact, only the title is similar. Despite their vitriolic colors and their use of motifs considered by the Nazis to be decadent, Nolde's landscapes and portraits from this series contain virtually nothing that can be interpreted in the political sense as a criticism of the Third Reich. The protest consists less in their content than in the very fact of their creation. In contrast, Nansen's drawings are critical in both form and subject matter. Like their predecessor, the caricature of policeman Jens Jepsen (*Black-headed Gulls on Duty*), they seem to have been created specifically to irk the lawkeeper. The better part of the paper is blank; what remains are "hints and pointers," as Teo Busbeck calls them, to a more complete context. There is, for example, the torn uniform jacket which "revealed itself as a witness" or the garlanded north German chair "secretly suggesting that perhaps even the north German bottom that might sit on the chair was garlanded" (263). In the movement from Nolde to Nansen we see the direction that an artistic protest against nazism might have taken. Merely continuing to paint is not in itself sufficient: the works themselves need to have a more political emphasis, even if it may be impossible to give anything more than hints and pointers to be completed in the imagination of the beholder.[11]

While Siggi's father regards the *Invisible Pictures* as merely a stupid attempt to fool him, Siggi himself is powerfully affected by the implicit criticism contained in the pictures. He trembles noticeably during the inspection of the papers, although he himself has unearthed them for his father to confiscate. Why should Siggi tremble, we ask ourselves, at Nansen's relatively subtle hints and pointers?

Although Siggi is fascinated by Nansen's work, its appeal seems to be based neither on Balthasar's nor on Nansen's notions, but on a far more literalist view of art. Unknown to him, it is precisely this simplistic mentality that he shares with his father, even though it takes a somewhat different direction in each. An incident mentioned only by the psychologist Mackenroth illustrates Siggi's understanding of art, namely, Siggi's interference with the painting *Nina O. of H.* Mackenroth writes that Siggi changed the little girl's dress from purple to green, apparently because he "couldn't stand" the purple color. With his passion for exactitude, Siggi corrects the psychologist's account, pointing out that he painted the dress not green but yellow: "At least colors are something we want to get right. As for the rest of it, you can work it up as wildly as you like, to serve you as a thesis" (271). Several aspects of this interchange are important. First, in insisting that the change was from purple to yellow, Siggi disengages himself from the controversy between violet and green that marks the painter's own dualism. Had he changed the color of the child's dress to green, he would have been making a daring and crucial correction of Nansen. As we later discover, Nina is a retarded child, one of those who Siggi's mother—still following the Nazi line of thought even after the war—claims should be avoided in case their sickness should somehow be contagious. To identify Nina with green would have reclaimed her from the strangeness with which the purple color had endowed her. Second, Siggi's alteration shows that he has failed to take to heart the painter's admonition that "seeing" does not mean "putting on record" (335). Siggi dresses the girl in yellow, not because this color has a symbolic value for him, but simply because the child did, in fact, wear a yellow dress.

Even at the end of the narrated events, Siggi defends Nansen to Hansi by means of arguments based on the idea of literal accuracy: "in the window-dresser's works," he says, "the perspective's always right," and even his fantastic creatures "really exist, they're there in their own right" (437). Siggi's view of Nansen is thus only a partial one, and he excludes from his conscious mind those aspects which constitute the basic strengths of Expressionism—the resistance spirit of Balthasar. The pictures he takes to his hideout seem to bear this out, since they are not those which celebrate the unity of nature but those in which harsh colors deviate from literal reality and place a critical cast on the subject. When we look below the surface, beyond the point of view that Siggi as narrator gives us, we can see the ambivalence in his view of these paintings. When the hideout in the mill finally catches fire, it contains a strange mixture: magazine pictures of princes, emperors and horse-riders, as well as several of Nansen's works: two *Invisible Pictures*, *The Man in the Red Cloak,* and *The Applepickers* (the last being really Klaas' possession). Later, he attempts to steal *The Money Changers,* and he succeeds for a time in concealing the hedonistic picture of his sister dancing by the shore.

Just as the policeman Jepsen, in his attacks of second sight,[12] sees the obverse of the war, the defeat of the Germans, which his conscious mind cannot perceive, so his son Siggi sees, in similar moments, the critical aspects of the paintings he tries to deny. Subliminally, he recognizes the threatening element that emanates from the pictures and casts doubt on his everyday view of things. He justifies his theft of the paintings by claiming that he was trying to keep them from confiscation by his father, but this is not his sole purpose. From Mackenroth (not from Siggi, who at first conceals this piece of information from us) we learn that Siggi has also been in the habit of collecting locks and keys. From Siggi himself we learn, rather indirectly, that these have been stolen with the intention neither of breaking in anywhere nor of preventing anything from being locked. At first it appears that Lenz has introduced this motif in order to invalidate Siggi's moral seriousness, to indicate that, like the rest of his family, he may not be psychologically well-balanced. But this would not be consonant with the whole tenor of the book. The chapter "Biology" reveals the secret of the apparently senseless key collection. As if incidentally, Siggi mentions the biology showcase: "a cupboard with two glass doors, which was kept permanently locked—one of the keys having become a valuable item in my collection a long time ago" (300–301). Although the locked cabinet does not prevent the teacher from carrying on with biology lessons, it does present the narrator's attitude towards this particular subject. The way in which biological science was subsumed into the Nazi ideology is well known, but Lenz spares no pains to make this point clear in the course of the chapter. As the children attempt to identify fish roe under the microscope, their teacher takes advantage of the moment to offer a lesson in the survival of the fittest:

> "Selection, don't you know. And always the fight for survival. The weak perish in the struggle, the strong survive. That is the way it is with fish, and that is the way it is with us. Get this into your heads: all that is strong lives on all that is weak. In the beginning all things have the same chance, each single egg, however small, holds and feeds a life. But then, when the trouble begins, the trash"—he actually said: the trash—"falls by the wayside" (298).

If Siggi cannot put a stop to the lessons, at least he can lock away some of the instructional materials.

Just as Siggi's theft of keys prevents others from gaining access to whatever they might unlock, so his theft of Nansen's paintings not only keeps them from the lawkeeper but also keeps their critical message at bay. His real attitude to the paintings is shown most clearly in his reaction to the work *Garden with Masks,* which he sees at the retrospective. The picture is evidently related to certain paintings of Emil Nolde: against a garden background of extravagant colors can be seen, dangling from a tree, two men's and one woman's mask. "Sunlight struck these masks from the side, lighting up one-half of them. There was a terrible certainty emanating from them, some enigmatic authority. Their eye-slits were earth-brown, the sky behind them was bright and cloudless. Were these masks a menace to the garden?" (428). Siggi half-recognizes them, but quickly represses his insight; it is too terrible for him to accept. Who else could express this "terrible certainty" but his own mother and father and Siggi himself? Filled with fear and anger, the young man wishes to behead the masks as if he were clipping the heads off flowers in an attempt to deny his association with the hated authority figures of his childhood. Yet by the time he has finished writing his essay, he is willing to admit that he is, after all, inextricably tied to his home town and to his policeman father (467). Only as he begins to accept the dualism of the painter does he come to have some insight into his own dualism. He admires the transfigurations of north German landscapes, the color, light, and perspective in the paintings, but, at the same time, he recognizes the terrible undercurrent which gives them their power over the viewer. While in one sense he protects the paintings, in another sense he conceals them so that their hidden hints and pointers cannot be seen by others. Just as Nansen himself is caught between protest and passivity, Siggi is caught between resistance to the Nazis and the inarticulate knowledge that he, too, shares some of their qualities and attitudes. The garden masks reveal this only too clearly: the self-righteous gaze emanates from "earthbrown" eyes as they seem to threaten all that is beautiful around them. In its external form, *The German Lesson* resembles the *Invisible Pictures.* Just as the viewer has to complete the pictures in imagination, so the reader has to fill in the missing part of the novel. Lenz emphasizes both the dualistic message and the dualistic influence of Nansen's painting. The question whether Nansen or Siggi is the true protagonist of the novel is a moot one, since each is equally important, and the one appears as the reverse image of the other.[13] Whereas Nansen allows the nature ideology to dominate and his critical streak to surface only indirectly, Siggi overtly resists the Nazi system, yet shares the psychological constitution of his Nazi father. Even the minor characters in the novel can be shown to embody different degrees of resistance to nazism and thus to form a scale against which Siggi can be measured.

Of all the characters in the book, Klaas is the only one to take positive action, even if this action ultimately has consequences only for himself and his family. His self-mutilation and desertion from the army show how much he is willing to sacrifice for his protest. In contrast, Nansen, when compelled to take him in, resents the sacrifices it involves ("Do you have any idea, any idea at all, what you're asking of me?" [114]). Siggi's sister Hilke carries out her own form of protest, but it is directed solely against her family. She asserts her independence from the family views by choosing for her boyfriend an epileptic accordion player, a person these adherents of nazism condemn on the grounds that he is both sick and racially suspect (in their minds a gypsy). When her mother finally takes drastic steps to prevent her from seeing Addi again, Hilke is crushed, but contrary to Siggi's expectation, she does not take action herself by moving out of the family home. While she claims to have remained to support her younger brother through his childhood in this repressive household, she does not aid him in sorting out the moral dilemma in which he becomes involved. And when she poses for Nansen's picture *The Dance on the Waves,* of which her mother says: "It's terrible what he's made out of you: the foreign thing, the alien thing that peers out of it" (404), her rage against her parents remains essentially inarticulate. She does not make a clear decision about which side she is to take. For example, when Siggi and Hilke are caught in a thunderstorm and take shelter at Nansen's house, Hilke occupies herself by symbolically sweeping the studio clean while at the same time taking manifest delight in Nansen's satiric portrait of her father, *Black-headed Gulls on Duty* (51).

As we have seen, Siggi's resistance to the forces of nazism is similarly ambivalent. He has difficulty making value judgments and has only a nebulous understanding of the political aspects of the situation. When asked at school to write a composition on the topic of a shining example, he chooses a fictitious model. Why does he not pick a real person, he asks himself: why not his father, his brother, Nansen, or Busbeck? "I already sensed the way everything in this essay was going to clamor for evaluation, to culminate in evaluation. And because I couldn't manage, never would manage, to evaluate people I knew in the way Treplin wanted, I had to seek my shining example in some other place, some other time" (388). The fictitious person he takes as his model is a warden of the Kaage Island, whose task is to protect the wild geese who breed there from the bombardments of novice RAF pilots. This man, whom Siggi names Heinz Martens, becomes famous (according to Siggi's story) for his rather futile protection of the geese's nesting place, futile because the red flares with which he has been provided to warn the pilots do not adequately protect the geese, many of whom are still killed. If this is a theme requiring evaluation, how is one to evaluate Siggi's model? Is it enough to be famous primarily among the members of English societies for the protection of animals? Is Siggi's protection of the paintings an action of the same order?

In the very moment that the composition nears its conclusion, Siggi realizes that the red light burning around him is not part of his fiction but signals, in fact, the burning of his secret hiding place, the mill in which he was keeping Nansen's paintings. Yet even now Siggi still fails to realize the significance of this fire. Nansen draws a lesson from it which Siggi is as yet unready to absorb: "You don't have to see a thing again to make it remain. There are some things you have to lose before you can possess them in peace" (397). Here again is the concept of the invisible pictures, now in the sense that images of the mind are more important than those committed to paper. But there is another, more crucial aspect, and that is the idea of starting over again. "You'll have to get used to the fact that in this life things get lost, Witt-Witt. Perhaps it's just as well. After all, one mustn't get stuck with what one has. One must always keep on making a fresh start" (398). The inability to make new beginnings is something Siggi shares with his father, and it is this that prevents him from adjusting to the situation after the war, when his father's continued confiscation of the paintings is illegal and Siggi is free to take action against him.

Significantly, when Siggi is dismissed from the reform school after his twenty-first birthday, he has no plans for the future. During his time on the island, he has achieved much: he now knows the secret psychological connections between himself and his father, and he begins to question even further the values of his fellow countrymen. He realizes, moreover, that his task has no end. But his future still takes no distinct form: "What then was left for me? What was in store for me? What had I still to hope for?" (466). At the end, he is at least able to say ironically that both he and Director Himpel will feel that they have won (416); and to the extent that each has understood in his own way some of the insights to which Siggi's essay has led, this is indeed so. Himpel correctly, if pretentiously, describes how the essay has become a self-laid trap for Siggi: "He had been struck by the way that memory had become a trap into which I had fallen, and he wanted me to extricate myself unaided" (465). For his part, Siggi recognizes that this is not a trap from which the victim can escape; it is, rather, a question of making things finally fall into place. On one of her visits to him at the reform school, Hilke brings Siggi one of those little puzzles in which one has to get several metal balls to rest simultaneously in various holes. In this case, the holes are mousetraps and the balls represent mice. "Perhaps I shall actually succeed," says Siggi at the end, "in getting all three mice at once into the traps" (471). The three mice, it must be assumed, are Siggi, his father, and Nansen, the three "criminals" whom Siggi has still not succeeded in trapping.

It is no accident that the child Siggi identified with the windmill without sails, for his own opposition to the forces around him lacks impetus, and his resistance is essentially a retreat from engagement, a retreat whose correlative is his hideout in the mill. Rarely do we see Siggi in the open; when he ventures into the landscape he invariably does so furtively, to escape detection by his father. The focal points of his existence are all enclosed spaces: his parents' house, Nansen's studio, the mill, the reformatory. Siggi's guilt lies in this pattern of retreat.[14]

Only when the guilt of the novel's two central characters is discovered can Lenz' political intention become apparent. Although it is not uncommon for modern novels to require that they be read against the grain, the reception of *The German Lesson* indicates that in this case few readers have done so. Most significantly, the role Balthasar plays in evaluating Nansen has not been noted in the secondary literature. And while Siggi's imperfections have been recognized, it has been maintained by many critics that the novel remains on the same level of insight as does Siggi. Defenders of the novel have remained very close to Siggi in their viewpoint, identifying with his moral dilemma and sympathizing with him as a victim of Nazi ideology. Detractors claim that the novel, set in the solitary north German landscape, removes the political conflict from its true arena into a provincial idyll.[15] From this latter point of view, the confrontation between art and politics is not really the central problem of the book.[16] In an interview with Lenz, one critic even suggested that the political dimension of *The German Lesson* could have been more effectively developed had Lenz taken as his model the politically less ambiguous case of Ernst Barlach. "That would have been another book," Lenz retorted.[17] After all, what had most interested him was the ambiguity of Expressionists like Nolde, whose very kinship with certain aspects of nazism made their conflict with it all the more problematic. Neither the supporters nor the detractors of the novel have fully understood its basic point: that nothing is clear-cut, either for the Siggis or for the Nansens of this epoch—both of them more typical than our idealistic image of the resister of nazism. Both are driven by a combination of motives, only some of which are clear to themselves and their contemporaries. Only in hindsight, by means of the juxtaposition of these characters, can we complete the invisible picture and follow up the hints and pointers it contains.

Lenz does not condemn Nansen; his sympathetic descriptions of the paintings show a basic sensitivity to the artistic value of such products of Expressionism. Yet sympathy with Nansen need not preclude criticism of him on other grounds, just as the novel's closeness to Siggi does not prevent us from understanding him better than he can himself. As in Nansen's painting, the Great Friend of the Mill dominates the atmosphere of this novel, told from Siggi's imperfect perspective.

The surface effect is harmonious and conciliatory, but the "purple doubts" are there too. We must be wary of identifying Hansi's simple-minded criticism with the more viable criticism of Balthasar, who has, after all, been a presence in the book all along. Insofar as Balthasar represents explicit criticism of the Nazi regime, the novel clearly has a less conservative point of view than has hitherto been supposed. Mackenroth's thesis title, "Art and Criminality," has many levels of reference within the book, applying to Siggi himself in ways not dreamed of by his young psychologist friend. But it also applies metaphorically to the painter Nansen and by implication to the position of the artist under nazism. Again and again, the question is raised: what forms of resistance to the regime were open to the individual and how effective could they have been? And the converse: what sins of omission on the part of one who could well have protested more loudly might be construed as having led him close to the border of criminality?[18] If some critics find this novel pallid and innocuous, perhaps it is because they fail to hear the spirit of opposition, Balthasar's "hissing disappointment," at their backs. Unlike *Cat and Mouse,* where the missing Heracles can only be found by inverting the image of Mahlke presented by the narrator, *The German Lesson* makes no attempt to conceal the counter-image to Siggi and Nansen. Nonetheless, Balthasar's status as an imaginary figure has hampered recognition of him as a central element in the novel's treatment of the resistance to nazism. By restoring him to his rightful place as a critic of ambivalence and as the model the painter fails to follow, we help complete the quest for Heracles that Lenz's novel has made us undertake.

CHAPTER EIGHT

NARRATIVE BYWAYS
Johannes Bobrowski's *Levin's Mill*

We like to have firm opinions, says Johannes Bobrowski at the beginning of his novel *Levin's Mill: 34 Sentences about My Grandfather* (1964), and we are reluctant to have our clear vision dimmed by a more precise knowledge of facts. Were this not so, he goes on, art would scarcely be as serene as traditional German theory (derived from Schiller) would have it, and stories would be a good deal more difficult to tell. Bobrowski determines not to take art so lightly and deliberately sets out to break down firm opinions and fixed schemes of thought. The cost he will pay for this, as he clearly recognizes, is the disruption of the narrative's free and easy flow; what he has to tell can no longer be encompassed by linear thought. This is a story that demands a judgment on our part ("then [I must] get on and tell the story, otherwise you can't form an opinion about it" [6]),[1] but it is also one that is all too likely to be prejudged by its readers. Bobrowski speaks to a public which thinks that it understands its past and knows how to apportion blame and praise. His aim is to upset this balance through a narrative that approaches its goal tentatively, circuitously, and disturbingly.

Since the turn of the century, the modern novel has made much of its inability to narrate in a straightforward manner, or even to narrate at all in the traditional sense of the word. Yet Bobrowski's novel should not be seen as part of this earlier mode. Novels in the first half of this century reflected a more general problem: the limitation of individual consciousness and the inaccessibility of a total world view once held to be within the writer's grasp. Bobrowski's concern is less a philosophical than a moral one. He wants us to see that our accustomed categories of thought may often prevent us from taking account of details that do not seem to fit. Not only will these details interrupt the smooth flow of the story, they will at first appear irrelevant since they lie outside our usual blinkered vision. The story itself will seem to take a roundabout path, approaching the truth only indirectly. Chronological, conventionally ordered narration cannot find the truth that underlies the apparently simple fable of *Levin's Mill*. "I think it's wrong if you know in advance exactly what you want to say and how long it's going to take" (5). Bobrowski hopes to undo the deviousness of thought by a counter-deviousness of narration.

Order thus becomes, in a newly defined sense, a key ingredient in the story itself and in its telling. The narrator's attempts to organize his thoughts parallel the various apothegms of his grandfather to which he constantly refers. "Sort things out a bit," the old man says, referring to sinister plots of his own; and on another occasion, "all this confusion has got to stop" (212, 205). These maxims function on two levels, with an ironic displacement between the grandfather's conception of "confused times" and the narrator-grandson's reversal of these views. Order, we begin to understand, is not absolute. This applies not only to narrative but also to social and political complexes; in fact, the whole point of *Levin's Mill* is to demonstrate the interweaving of fiction and history. The form of the novel is by no means random: it depends on the narrator's underlying conception of the historical period he is treating. And this turns upon his answer to a question posed in the very first paragraph, "but where am I?," a significant query for a writer who has been claimed by both East and West. Where does Bobrowski stand? Despite the critical controversy, the novel is not as ambiguous as might be expected of one narrated in such an indirect fashion. The author realizes from the outset that his narrative bypaths must eventually lead into clarity, and in the end we do know exactly where he stands. From the start, he invites us to take a critical position: "I said before that whether it is right and proper or not depends on where I am, so I must establish that first and then get on and tell the story, otherwise you can't form an opinion about it" (6). As he struggles with the task of narration, we, too, are drawn into the process, impelled to ask again and again: how much do we really know? (202). Questioning, not assertion, is the dominant mode.

The narrator's constant groping for the correct formulation is like the continual refocusing of a precision lens. His first task is the location of what is central and what is peripheral to the story, symbolically indicated by the geographical imagery of his first pages. "The Drewenz is a tributary in Poland" (5), his first stab at an opening sentence, is soon found to be misleading, since it suggests that the nationality of the area is clear; the imagery of tributary and mainstream suggests the relation of the narrative byways to the central truth as well. It turns out that it is a little millstream leading into the Vistula tributary, not the tributary itself, that forms the focus of the story. Although it will be a circumlocutory tale, it will lead in the end to a new sharpness of vision. So the thirty-four sentences and their subsidiary clauses swell to a short novel at first confusing but ultimately revealing.

We have seen a number of novels from the postwar period in which different historical epochs are superimposed, but Bobrowski employs this method in an original, even idiosyncratic, manner. He removes his analysis of relationships between Germans, Jews, and Poles from the immediate past into the year 1874, while at the same time maintaining, through the assertion that the novel is about his grandfather, a clear connection with the present. Grandfather Bobrowski is revealed in a distinctly negative light as the evildoer who has washed away his Jewish competitor's mill by opening a dam and releasing the floodwaters. Grandfather derives no advantage from his wreck of Levin's mill; instead, he is driven out of the village and forced to move to the city. Levin, for his part, seeks help from a group of wandering gypsies. The musician Habedank and his friends Geethe, Weiszmantel, and Willuhn are the ones who conduct the real resistance to the inhumane laws Grandfather hopes to exploit, and it is Habedank and his fellow musician Weiszmantel who compose the satirical ballad in which Grandfather's evil deed is exposed. Gallant Aunt Huse, long a renegade from the Baptist church because the minister has refused to allow unmarried mothers to attend services, becomes Levin's chief witness at his grandfather's trial, although she only knows the story at second hand. The gypsies, the drifters, and the Polish mill workers join in a concerted action by which Grandfather's personal and business ruin is assured and the dismissal of Levin's court case to all practical purposes reversed. And the Bohemian flutist, Johann Vladimir Geethe, provides a social analysis that points to the materialism of the well-to-do as the cause of what at first appeared to be racial and national tensions. "Well the simple answer . . . is that it's all because of money . . . the one lot because they have some and want to hang on to it and the others because they want it and get paid for running errands" (174–75).

By telling a story against his own family, Bobrowski unmasks the East German myth of a resistance heritage and exposes German guilt at its historic root.[2] No simplistic parallel is drawn between the Nazi period and the late nineteenth century; the latter is merely allowed to illumine the former suggestively. In this way, what might have been an assertion of historical recurrence or the universal patterning of events is modified and placed in its proper context, supported by a wealth of specific historical detail. Simple though it sounds, the plot still needs to be pieced together. Unlike *Cat and Mouse,* where the reader must reconstruct the inverse of the story told, *Levin's Mill* demands that the reader imagine the mainstream into which the narrated tributaries flow. Bobrowski's call for reader participation in reconstructing the hidden truth is supported by his use of colloquial language.[3] The casual style is that of an inveterate yarn-spinner whose voice modulates from pleasant chattiness through wit, irony, and anger. We cannot help feeling personally addressed by this infectiously appealing narrator. At the same time, there is also a darker aspect to his yarn-spinning, and it is no accident that Bobrowski refers to Joseph Conrad as his legendary great-great-uncle from whom he can still learn a lot more about narrative perspective.[4] The whimsical tone of the surface bears a dialectical relationship to the "heart of darkness" the yarn-spinner ultimately uncovers.

Thus, its ironic edge is the most important attribute of this narrator's apparently free and easy style, in which the grandfather's dicta stand out in a way that calls forth the reader's criticism. Their real significance is the opposite of what Grandfather imagines it to be. When he vows, "all this confusion has got to stop," referring to his intention of eliminating the non-German element in the village, the reader also understands it as Bobrowski's determination to clarify the relationship between Germans and Poles, not only in 1874 but also in earlier periods, in the Third Reich, and in the present. In a sense, the entire story is pieced together from quotations, for which it provides a spoken and unspoken commentary. "Well, that's that!" marks the conclusion of the pact by which the families decide to stick together against the Poles, Jews, and gypsies (55). But this remark also indicates a determination that can only be effective for those in power; Levin, for example, never speaks in this tone. "There are people and people," says the narrator, imitating the speech of his characters (181); and his very use of the colloquialism provokes the reader's objection to this unquestioned division of society into acceptable and unacceptable elements. The people regarded as undesirables are almost always referred to in the words of Grandfather and his class; "this girl Marie," for example, is the gypsy girl who becomes Levin's girlfriend. The words of a hymn, "Have done, O Lord," with the addition of "Or I shall have to do it myself" (110) are Grandfather's justification for taking the law into his own hands. A chain of linguistic ironies forms the central core of the novel, indicating both the political stance of the narrator and the critical awareness he demands of the reader.

In view of the GDR's contention that it is the direct descendant of the resistance to Hitler, the narrative stance of *Levin's Mill* is significant. The present-day narrator stresses his family's involvement in late nineteenth-century nationalism, evidently an antecedent of nationalism in the Third Reich. The "fifteenth sentence," he comments, belongs not to the plot but to us: "it is approximately: the sins of the fathers shall be visited upon the children to the third and fourth generation" (129). But the biblical quotation cannot adequately indicate the ramifications of this story set in the past, yet equally valid for the present. "There's no end to it, once we start looking around. We find sinners upon sinners that hold us up and meanwhile maybe, we silently withdraw" (129). The story must be told, regardless of its reflection on the family and regardless of its reflection on the narrator's own generation.

This criticism of the East German heritage model, this willingness to accept his own guilt, is one feature of *Levin's Mill* that has endeared Bobrowski to his West German audience. A song and dance scene in the novel anticipates in miniature the response of the East German reader. Here, the gypsies and outsiders express their anger at the grandfather in a satirical ballad dealing with the ruin of Levin's mill. As the song gathers momentum, its refrain becomes almost menacing: "Hei hei hei hei!" "It's getting positively personal," comments Grandfather (92), starting his own ineffectual counter-dance complete with rude words and gestures. For Bobrowski and his generation, the story does indeed get personal, but "there's no stopping any of it now" (92)—the truth must out.

The truth of the feud between Germans and Poles comes out in ways other than direct narration. It is also revealed through the ghostly apparitions that haunt Grandfather in his drunken stupors. These apparitions bring out the complexities of the family's past political and social role. The final vision sums up the contradictions of the family's national origin. "Very old spirits this time, and very confused ones, who don't know each other's names or families: Strzegonia, Jastrazembiec, Awdaniec, Olawa, Zawora, Starykon, and who confuse the good and bad gods and ghosts: Pomian, Swist Powist, Plon and Plonek and Jescha and Chowaniec. Names, just names. Darkness, a bright day, the shadow swan and the horns. Very old ghosts" (164). The references are to the ancient gods of the region, a topic that plays a considerable role in Bobrowski's poetry. The passage does not simply say that good and evil are inextricably intertwined but points out that the interconnections of Poles and Germans are more complex than Grandfather would like to think. The first apparition speaks of the supposedly noble origin of Poles and Germans who were formerly Poles and now (in 1874) feel themselves to be of ancient German lineage. "Well that's one version of the history of the Polish republic, which can be heard, if only you have the patience to listen and can find the right sort of authority on the subject. One like my grandfather for instance" (21). Grandfather's visions emanate not only from the falsifications themselves but also from his subconscious recognition of them. He would like to identify himself with a period of Polish history when everyone felt himself to be of the nobility: the paradoxical "Republic of Poland," in which the entire nobility had a voice in affairs of state, though only as long as they did not oppose prevailing views. The narrative irony becomes heavier as the unrepublican republic is described. "A thorough knowledge of history is a universal characteristic, one is at home with one's ancestors and expects visions. . . . You just expect visions and think nothing of them, everyone has them, including my grandfather, of course" (22). But Grandfather's refined historical awareness is rapidly dissipated. The ghost turns out to be his ancestor Poleske, a highway robber executed for standing up for what he regards as his rights and claiming to defend the Polish republic by means of his attacks on Danzig trading folk during the reign of Sigismund I. This move onto Danzig territory is significant, for the incident picks up a number of loose threads from Grass' Danzig trilogy, the third volume of which had appeared just a year before *Levin's Mill*.[5] Polish patriotism is no longer as straightforward as it had seemed even in Grass' complex novel cycle. The saving of Poland in 1516 is less nobly motivated than the saving of Poland in 1939, if equally unsuccessful. What Poleske stands for is more ambiguous: "Certainly to defend the honour of the Republic, and the Right, Poland's Right, honour and Right which can be helped with excursions, insurrections, stock-taking decisions, protests and finally, great displays of piety in Gnesen or Tschenstochau" (25).

The empty rhetoric, the disparate coupling of pilgrimages and revolutions, and the critical view of piety cast a new light on Polish nationalism. While the reference to Tschenstochau (Czestochowa) harks back to Joachim Mahlke's reverence for the Black Madonna of Poland, the patron saint is viewed with more scepticism by the narrator of *Levin's Mill*. And Poleske's fellow revolutionary Mattern (perhaps an ironic recollection of that more dangerous Matern in Grass' *Dog Years*) expresses the ultimate ambiguity of the insurrectionists' motivations: " 'It'll be warm enough for us in Poland this winter,' Mattern reflects, 'and it's autumn already' " (24).

Along with the reference to his literary predecessor, Bobrowski introduces an element of current relevance in this passage. With an inversion of the theme of lineage and inheritance, the lines on historical awareness in the Republic of Poland can also be applied to the German Democratic Republic. Just as Grandfather's allegedly German nationalistic background is undermined by the apparition of a Polish revolutionary ancestor who was also a criminal, the East German resistance heritage must be unmasked to reveal the past involvement of certain GDR citizens with nazism.

The second apparition to torment Grandfather is the pious outlaw Krysztof, who hanged himself on a willow tree after the failure of an insurrection he led against the king in 1606. Here the reference is to the armed revolt of Polish gentry, supported by discontented Protestants, against Sigismund III; although beaten down the following year, the insurrection left a legacy of political confusion, blocking reform of the parliamentary system and giving rise to the doctrine of the right of subjects to depose their king. With some modification, the latter issue can be applied to the problem of resistance to Hitler.

Finally, the third vision recalls the death of Grandfather's own father

Michael, burned to death by unnamed persecutors and held to be the victim of an attack by "spirits" (65). Grandfather's identification of these spirits with gypsy spirits and the spirit of Levin he sees in his dream prompts his decision to take revenge on Levin for bringing the lawsuit against him. Since Habedank is one of Levin's supporters, he is now to be the object of Grandfather's renewed attack on Levin: "I'll turf out that Habedank" (97). As ever, Grandfather refuses to learn from the past. He attacks Habedank just as his father, Michael, had been attacked by others. As Michael is said to have been killed by lightning on a clear and stormless day, so Pilch's cottage, the illegal domicile of Habedank, is mysteriously destroyed by fire. History repeats itself, yet with strange twists and turns. The distortions of dream, which make these historical interpolations so difficult to follow, reveal the perversions of history that exist even in the waking mind. It is up to the reader to clarify them and correct them.

But the novel does not rest with this intricate probing of ideology. The tale is more than the story of Polish-German relations. Like other novels of its genre, it also explores the question of the political function of art. Bobrowski's association of the gypsies with music is not merely a stereotype; it provides a telling link between these persecuted figures and the writer himself. Songs, such as Weiszmantel's ballad against Grandfather Bobrowski, occur in significant scenes and carry an important message.

On their way to court, the little group of protesters ironically takes up the sentimental romanticism of German folk songs associated with Nazi nature mythology: "How sweet the peal / O'er wood and field / Of the bugle's lilting song" (170). The echoing refrain is exaggeratedly drawn out, only to be interrupted by the response of a cow in the meadows, nature's reproach to its violation by the song. Marie stops singing, Aunt Huse's soprano hovers in the air, and the reader pauses to reflect on the discrepancy between the song and its singers.

Habedank's song of Moses, which has provoked Weiszmantel's satirical ballad, regards the misfortunes of Levin as part of the history of the Jews:

> Very strange happenings once took place
> When Moses tried to live by the water's face.
> Very fast waters came rushing one day,
> And in their swirl they swept him away.
> Goods and chattels, all he had,
> No more laughter to make him glad (67–68).[6]

Moses' rescue and the ruin of Levin are thus ironically juxtaposed. Songs become a satiric weapon against the Germans, yet they can also be a cry of despair, as in Weiszmantel's elegy: "This time had come, this time I cried, / My soul was sore oppressed" (176). Finally, the Polish orientation of the protesters is expressed in their part-singing with instrumental accompaniment of the Polish national hymn, "Poland Is Not Lost Yet" (190).[7] Here again, the novel must be read as an answer to Grass' trilogy, which is based upon this sentiment.

The identification of the musician characters with art in the broader sense is underscored by the name Johann Vladimir Geethe, clearly reminiscent of Germany's classical poet. Moreover, the painter Philippi is connected with the author himself by a significant scene in which, instead of drawing, he writes lyric poetry somewhat in the style of Johannes Bobrowski:

> Herb, yellow, vault
> Of lips at midday,
> Dry waters
> Scents, mist and once
> Snow,
> I speak into the wind (225).

Like the poet, the novelist speaks into the wind, and it is up to us to catch his words. His insertion of an author-surrogate into the novel gives the narrative an unusual perspective. It is the standpoint of the outsider who is also in some sense an insider, as in a painting in which the artist has put a tiny version of himself into some obscure corner. But at the end of the novel the painter Philippi emerges from his somewhat peripheral position to carry the novel's most important appeal to the reader.

Levin, too, stands apart from the unpleasantly ambiguous characters who populate the village, though he is not without ambiguities of his own. As the victim of Grandfather's wrath, Levin protests too weakly and, in the end, ineffectually; still, the author clearly values him for his openness and spontaneity. His love scene with Marie forms the lyrical axis of the book, a counterweight to the anger and sorrow which permeate the rest of the narrative. Rain is falling, and the lovers begin to count the drops. Then Levin notices the raindrops falling onto Marie's pubic hair, weighing down the separate strands which promptly bounce back up again. Levin laughs. "It's nice here in the meadow. It's nice here in the rain. When was it last so nice?" (126). But the idyll is soon over. Later, the lovers sit listening to the tale of red-haired Lea Goldkron, who caused noble houses to burn down wherever she went and who was finally captured by the prince because of her dangerous beauty. Love and beauty are suspect in this world, even in the present day. With Marie, Levin feels he is living for the first time, yet neither society at large nor their own families accept their union.

In identifying primarily with Levin, the narrator distances himself from his family identity and the biological connection with his grandfather. Turning the tables on his own heritage, he sets up a kind of estrangement effect which extends beyond the merely personal. At the end of the novel, we discover that the geographical location described in such painstaking detail throughout is in reality quite unknown to the narrator. "And now I just wonder if it wouldn't have been better to set the whole story more to the north or still better much further to the northeast, in Lithuania, where I know the whole area, rather than here, where I have never been on this Drewenz river, on the Neumühl stream, on the Struga brook, which I only know from hearsay" (230). Bobrowski has undertaken in *Levin's Mill* a task different from that of his lyric poetry, where he combines material from different periods of history in the context of his Lithuanian heritage. The geographical displacement from Lithuania to Poland is essential to the effect he wishes to create and differs vitally from Grass' Danzig trilogy, which is based on a good deal of semi-autobiographical material. In removing his story both geographically and historically from his real concern, the need to come to terms with nazism, Bobrowski enables us to sharpen our focus on it. We are asked to carry over our critical view of Grandfather to others who share his way of thinking, and we are urged to think twice about historical recurrence and historical continuity.

Even the thirty-four sentences require critical reading. Some need to be read against the grain—"There's very little sense in asking," some with it—"We always need comic characters" (219).[8] In its fine detail, as in its larger structures, the novel's movement is a dialectical one in which weight and counterweight answer each other and point beyond themselves. We are left to find our own way through the intricate mosaic of quotations and commentary. In claiming that the story gives no proofs, Bobrowski suggests that the search for truth continues.

While the end of the book is open, this does not mean that it is ambiguous. Its final emphasis is borne by that amusing personage Philippi, who carries his "good couple of hundredweight" as if it were nothing: "on tiny feet he dances down the street" (220). It is Philippi, with his odd combination of practical joking and academic painting, who gives us our final perspective on Grandfather Bobrowski, mocking and jeering at him for what he has done to Levin. His final roaring "no" as he whirls like a top before Grandfather's eyes, clapping his hands together as if he had caught a fly, is the ultimate expression of protest which forms the novel's concluding sentence. So he joins the spirit-protesters of Grandfather's visions, the dialectical incarnation of that other side of the heritage. In leaving us with this call to resistance, the novel avoids the danger of reducing it to a flat formula. Emotionally, we identify with the resistance of Philippi, yet, at the same time, the novel has shown us, through its various visionary flashbacks, that the value of resistance must be judged afresh in the context of each historical situation.

Unlike Mann's *Doctor Faustus*, which remains ambiguous to the end, *Levin's Mill* resolves its original ambiguities in Philippi's symbolic gesture of protest. With this ending, the narrative byways lead at last onto the main road. And where Mann's analogy between nazism and the Faust pact suggests an underlying pattern to German history, Bobrowski is concerned, in his comparison of late nineteenth-century Poland and mid-twentieth-century Germany, with the specificity of this particular historical development. His irony is not ambivalent, like Thomas Mann's; instead, it is directed against the self-serving justifications of all who, though retrospectively claiming to have been innocent, had in truth been involved in racism and bigotry.

Clearly, *Levin's Mill* deviates from the official requirements of socialist realism in that its positive model is a highly symbolic, peripheral figure rather than one of the two protagonists. In addition, it relies on modernist narrative techniques that are usually frowned upon in socialist realism. The question remains how Bobrowski himself was able to regard it nonetheless as an eminently socialist work and why, despite its difficulty, it was so popular in the GDR. While Bobrowski is often claimed by the West as a renegade from the official line, his position is more complex. It is not enough to regard the novel merely as an expression of sympathy for the underdogs and cast-offs of society. In playing off the past and present against each other, the novel makes us aware of distinctions that are ignored by the characters themselves. Grandfather's justification of his claim to his rights by reference to his ancestors' fight for theirs is shown to be based on false logic. Similarly, the revolutionaries are not wholeheartedly applauded, and the question of an insurrection conducted by members of the landed gentry (a reference to the role of officers and gentry in the resistance to Hitler) is subjected to an indirect critique. Bobrowski's satire cuts in a number of different directions at once, thus demanding that readers east and west rethink their positions.

The salient feature of Bobrowski's attempt to go beyond socialist realism is his attention to the transformations of history into ideology. This is a major contribution to the issue of literary form and its relation to the presentation of the past, one that appears to have gone all but unheeded in the GDR. Bobrowski's use of indirect narrative shows us again and again the determining power of perception. History is accessible only in and through our vision of history. The novel shows us how the past is reconstructed in Grandfather's conscious and subconscious minds, and it juxtaposes these two versions in an attempt to cut through their underlying ideologies. Set off against this interplay is another factor which, in turn, interacts with the complexities of the family heritage. This is the view of history presented by the gypsies and Jews. Both groups of outsiders see the past from a satiric, as well as from an elegiac, aspect. Weiszmantel's mocking ballad and his plaint on the history of persecution represent two faces of the outsiders' view of reality. The narrator's questions, spoken and unspoken, modify these various views of history and urge us to think beyond them.

Bobrowski thus seems to be making an appeal for a more subtle, more dialectical conception of socialist fiction,[9] a conception taken up a few years later by Christa Wolf in *The Quest for Christa T.* (1968). Just as the narrator of *Levin's Mill* stands in a dialectical relationship to his grandfather, so the narrator of *Christa T.* is dialectically related to her friend Christa (who is also, in a sense, her former self). Christa Wolf's husband, Gerhard Wolf, has been one of the most active participants in the GDR criticism on Bobrowski; in his two books and various essays, he has made some of the most astute comments to have appeared in that country on Bobrowski's narrative technique.[10] In particular, he repeatedly points out that the narrative byways of *Levin's Mill* are no mere frivolous toying with modernism for its own sake, but a deliberate attempt to give new direction to socialist literature. Christa Wolf's *Model Childhood* should be read as a continuation of this effort, against the backdrop of the strong criticism of *Christa T.* in East Germany, where its dialectical form went largely unobserved. In *A Model Childhood* the dialectic becomes overt in the narrator's reflection on her own younger self, and the confrontation with the Nazi past is simultaneously made more explicit than in *Christa T.* All three of these novels set out to activate the reader, using their own inner dialectic instead of the more orthodox positive models. This technique is particularly suited to the probing of ideology that all three undertake, since it involves what we may think of as a transposition of the Brechtian alienation effect into the realm of prose fiction.

In an interview, Bobrowski once explained that his view of art was not to represent the past for its own sake, but from the perspective of and with reference to the present, "so that these two phases, the historical period and our present-day witness to it, constantly interpenetrate each other."[11] This dialectic of history is more than the model case it has usually been adjudged in East German analyses, since it assumes a continuing dialogue with its readers.[12] Bobrowski justifies this practice by reference to nineteenth-century realism (often held up as the exemplary predecessor of socialist realism), in which he notes a degree of subtlety not customarily acknowledged in the view of realism derived from Georg Lukács. Unlike Wolf in *Christa T.*, however, he does not refer here to the German provincial realists, but to that sophisticated realist Flaubert, whose letters, Bobrowski claims, adumbrate positions similar to his own. His stories need to have "open forms," he explains in this connection, because this allows him to set up the kind of sharp contrasts he is after, as opposed to "well-greased joints," closed structures, and simplistic plot outlines as promulgated by the party line. "I like to bring a little levity into these serious stories and hope that in this way they will be a sort of mild shock therapy."[13]

In terms of literary history, *Levin's Mill* forms a productive connection between West German confrontations with the Nazi past such as Grass' trilogy and the unorthodox modulations of socialist confrontations in Wolf's *Christa T.* and *A Model Childhood*.[14] In this way, Bobrowski's belief that literature has a message is fulfilled in a sense he himself would doubtless have approved. The task of literature, he points out, is not to deal with past guilt once and for all; it is to allow our inability to come to terms with it completely to become a potent motivating force for the future. "I'm in favor of stating over again all that is usually called 'unresolved,' but I don't think that doing that will 'resolve' it. It has to be done, even if only hopefully."[15] If literature works slowly, its advantage, Bobrowski suggests here, is that it avoids the short circuit of the common supposition that merely by expressing our guilt we are able also to exorcise it.

Within this framework, Bobrowski, more overtly than Wolf in *Christa T.*, pleads for the special role that art can play in unmasking ideology. Through the musician figures and the artist Philippi, he indicates his view of art in an oppressive age as a prime articulator of resistance.[16] This is most forcefully brought out in the final sequence of "sentences." An unidentified voice (or voices) utters the penultimate three: "Come, let us sing. In Gollub the gypsies are playing. If we don't sing, others will" (230). Singing, art, is necessary; if we don't employ it in our own cause, Bobrowski says, others will in theirs. And the novel concludes with Philippi's vehement protest against the grandfather's pleas to be left in peace: "No." Thus *Levin's Mill* urges a continuing resistance that resonates beyond the novel's end and connects past, present, and future without resort to simplifying typologies.

Bobrowski's later novel, the posthumous *Lithuanian Pianofortes* (1966), moves the scene of the action back to his home territory and closer to the present, placing it in Lithuania in the year 1936. Once again a connection with the past is established, this time through the eighteenth-century Lithuanian poet Donelaitis, whose biography is to be performed as an opera at the annual festival of the National Women's Club. The two days of the fictional present are thus subsumed into an entire national history. Though pivoted around a fight between Germans and Lithuanian Nationalists, the consciousness of the novel is dominated by the figure of the schoolteacher Potschka, who has so totally identified himself with Donelaitis that he lives in a visionary world of the past. His final illumination serves to break the illusion and to call him back to his rightful place in the present. The disillusionment of musicologist and concertmaster, confused and depressed over the disruption of their opera rehearsals by the nationalist incident, forms a counterpoint to the unspecified optimism of Potschka's return from his dream world. But the suggestion of a productive relationship between past and present remains no more than a hint, and the past is seen at too many removes for a true dialectic to emerge. The whimsically personal dialectic of villain grandfather and narrator grandson in *Levin's Mill* had more successfully turned the socialist myth of the resistance heritage into a genuine weapon in the fight for resistance.

CHAPTER NINE

THE DISCONTINUOUS SELF
Christa Wolf's *A Model Childhood*

"What is past is not dead," writes Christa Wolf in *A Model Childhood;* "it is not even past. We cut ourselves off from it; we pretend to be strangers (3)."[1] We have already seen how this estrangement from the past is deliberately cultivated in the GDR, though at a cost to the psychological need to come to terms with experience under nazism. In her most recent novel, Christa Wolf addresses precisely this issue of the discontinuous self. In her "Workshop Interview," she takes issue with the tendency of the GDR, still prevalent when the novel appeared, to appropriate as its antecedents the anti-fascists and resistance fighters and to ignore the fact that the majority of its members, no less than the citizens of West Germany, were in need of a therapeutic reckoning with the past and an exploration of their own involvement in guilt.[2] This is the gap that *A Model Childhood* sets out to fill.

To the best of my knowledge, it is the first and so far the only GDR novel to deal with the issue on this level. As fictionalized autobiography it shares the difficulty experienced by West German writers in applying that genre to the reckoning with nazism: the fact that many Germans had not been involved in the resistance efforts and had, in fact, been scarcely aware of their existence. In presenting the past through the eyes of an ordinary person, it can be grouped with other autobiographical works that have since appeared in West Germany, such as Kempowski's family saga or Hermann Lenz' novel *New Times* (1975). But it goes beyond these works in its recognition that straightforward (or even mildly ironic) autobiography cannot adequately reproduce the discontinuity experienced by the individual in the transition from nazism to the present. Whereas Hermann Lenz only thinly disguises his former self in Eugen Rapp and Walter Kempowski is only slightly distanced in his treatment of the younger Walter, Christa Wolf dramatizes the discontinuity more starkly. To herself, both in the days before and immediately following the war, she gives the name Nelly; Wolf as she is in the present is referred to in the form of meditation and reflection as "you" until on the very last pages the first person singular pronoun is finally permitted to emerge.

By constructing her novel in this manner, Wolf reverses a traditional pattern of epic narration that had been outlined by James Joyce in Stephen Dedalus' description of the old ballad *Turpin Hero:*

> This progress you will see easily in that old English ballad *Turpin Hero* which begins in the first person and ends in the third person. The dramatic form is reached when the vitality which has flowed and eddied around each person fills every person with such vital force that he or she assumes a proper and intangible esthetic life. The personality of the artist, at first a cry or a cadence or a mood and then a fluid and lambent narrative, finally refines itself out of existence, impersonalizes itself, so to speak.[3]

According to this view, epic objectivity is attained by a progression from individuality to impersonality; the artist's task is to transform tangible experience into something more abstract and general; the subjective becomes objective. Why does Christa Wolf choose to reverse this familar process? The reflective asides interwoven with the narrative portions of *A Model Childhood* (some of which are unfortunately omitted in the English translation) furnish a clue to the conception of character and character development underlying the novel. The narrator comments: "Fixation of personality; the shrinking of its possibilities or its illusion of possibilities it never had." This idea that characters in a novel shrink rather than expand in potential during the process of writing also implies a shrinking of the "sacred ego," "the royal self";[4] Wolf explicitly distances herself from what she calls the fictional sense, a deceptive feeling of invulnerability on the part of the author. This amounts to something not dissimilar to what Joyce meant when he described the author of a work of literature, in the famous passage that follows Stephen's remarks about *Turpin Hero,* as comparable to the "God of creation." For Wolf, the artist no longer has this sense of sovereignty. By casting her experiences into the third person, she allows herself to be subjected to the same processes as her characters. In reversing the *Turpin Hero* scheme, she seems to be asking whether it is appropriate to the present situation to refine characters out of existence or to transform oneself into a God-author.

To bring herself into existence, Christa Wolf begins by discussing general aesthetic issues and then moves rapidly to the unfolding of her childhood experiences. Much of the story concerns events that reviewers have seen as trivial or tedious. If this is true, perhaps there is no other way in which the piecemeal memories of the girl's forcibly repressed childhood can be re-created. Part of the novel's aim is to show what Nelly's life was like from her point of view, and this inevitably includes the child's emphasis on day-to-day events at the expense of wider political issues. Thus, Nelly spends a disproportionate amount of time trying to discover how children are conceived while remaining scarcely aware of certain political events going on around her. That her mother was critical of nazism, an attitude we can gather from various little hints, escapes Nelly completely. Only in the recounting does this begin, though still rather dimly, to take on clearer contours. Indirectly, the novel takes issue with other works that have purported to portray the Nazi past from a child's-eye view. Oskar, the perennial three-year-old, and Siggi, the twenty-one-year-old still not far removed from his ten-year-old self, are not adequate models for the kind of problems Wolf wishes to treat. Showing the past from a distinctly, even grotesquely, inadequate standpoint, as Grass and Lenz do in these novels, deliberately estranges readers from their own experience of the past. Wolf's Nelly is in many ways more typical of her time. Furthermore, in claiming that the narrator is not really Nelly, Wolf tells us unambiguously how to read the story. By this means, she adheres in essence to East German literary theory, according to which ironic or open-ended structures are an invitation to a dangerous plurality of interpretation.[5] And while *A Model Childhood* makes much of the gap in consciousness created by the transition from the prewar to the postwar years, this type of gap is not at all equivalent to the "blank spots," or deliberate omissions, that West German writers like Grass or Lenz use to activate critical reading. Although the discrepancy between the narrator and her Nelly could easily have been used in this way, Wolf stops short of this kind of dialectic.

One major reason why the novel's dialectical potential is unrealized lies in its reliance on the concept of patterns. In her asides, Wolf makes much of various compounds of the word *Muster* ("pattern"). As a depiction of "patterns of childhood" (the literal meaning of the German title), the novel implies that this childhood is less individual than typical. In addition, Nelly's childhood patterns are set against those of the narrator's daughter Lenka. As the book progresses, the concept of patterns of perception creeps in increasingly frequently. One of the novel's most urgent questions concerns the validity of this concept, which in many ways conflicts with East German theory. In addition to exploring the patterns of childhood and the patterns of perception, Wolf is also concerned with the patterns of memory. The many interruptions and asides and the interweaving of various time planes are part of her attempt to discern a pattern in what appears fragmentary, chaotic, and discontinuous.

Among the interspersed theoretical comments on the nature of memory is the following observation on different kinds of memory. "One distinguishes the following types of memory: mechanical, gestalt, and logical, verbal, material, action memory. The absence of one category is acutely felt: moral memory" (36). With this statement, Wolf

makes it clear that she is attempting to do more than merely demonstrate the commonplace that memories, especially childhood memories, tend to be incomplete, inaccurate, and inchoate. Instead, she tries
to examine what happens to memory when it must be evaluated in this
unusual historical period, where one inculcated view of morality has
suddenly been supplanted by another. In this context, individual perception is shown to be determined by learned or externally imposed
patterns; it is not the free action which it appears to be to the subjective mind. The shift in moral perspective during her growing years
accounts for the unevenness that characterizes the narrator's reminiscences. Just as, once the war is over, she must learn to say "Guten
Tag" instead of "Heil Hitler," so she must substitute a new moral code
for her original sense of right and wrong. "For quite a while she thinks
she's done the right thing. For quite a while longer—as you understand
it today—it's not a question of right or wrong" (352). Not surprising,
except to the narrator herself, are the repressions, as when she forgets
the most optimistic line of a poem otherwise intact in her memory
("We bid you to hope," from Goethe's "Symbolum" [290]). What she
does remember—all too well—are details other members of her family
would prefer her to forget: for example, line after line of the Hitler
Youth songs she had collected in a special notebook during her teens.
On their flight before the advancing Russians, Nelly's mother burns
the incriminating book, but the songs cannot be erased from the narrator's memory. The novel's representative of today's younger generation, Lenka, protests vehemently against the unearthing of this material, even though she herself is constantly brimming over with popular
songs. Of course, Lenka's songs, which express solidarity with the
struggle against oppression in Spain, are politically the opposite of the
songs her mother persists in recalling.

A metaphor for these discontinuities is given in a conversation between the narrator and her brother Lutz. The idea of black holes in
space is Lutz' contribution to the discussion. "Now I can see my sister's
brain waves rev up into high gear," Lutz comments (295), as she
digests his information about those superheavy spaces left by collapsed
white dwarf stars. It is Lutz who draws the connection that turns the
astrophysical theory into a metaphor for the state which bridges his
sister's childhood and her adulthood: "collapsed horizon of events"
(295). When the white dwarf disintegrates, it becomes a black hole in
which neither time nor space exist and the laws of physics cease to
operate. The collapse of Germany represents a similar situation for
Nelly. In contrast to the "black box" (281), or memory blank, that
Nelly had experienced during the flight (when she suddenly realized
that the infant she was holding for a fellow refugee had died unnoticed
in her arms), the black hole is not a gap in reality but a different kind

of reality. Whereas the black box is a state where the mind is incapable of forming and absorbing impressions (282), the black hole is a state where thought follows laws unknown to the rational mind.

Nelly's own breakdown coincides with the collapse of her country. The coordinates that have hitherto made her world meaningful are no longer operative, but there is as yet no new set of coordinates to provide her with orientation in the new situation. "She believed that she wouldn't return home ever again, yet at the same time she still considered the final victory possible. Better to escape into absurd thinking than to give in to the unthinkable" (296). At the time, she is unaware of what has happened to her. Only later is she able to recognize it as a kind of mental breakdown, and even then only because she is suddenly made conscious of how others see her. "Months later, in May, she read in the eyes of a U.S. Army officer that he seriously thought she was insane, but she understood only years later that his almost shocked look meant nothing more than that" (297). Because his mental framework has remained intact, the American soldier perceives what she cannot; not until Nelly has constructed a new framework for herself can she understand the meaning of his gaze.

In contrast to her brother, the narrator accepts the place of black holes in the scheme of things. Like those East Germans who insist on cutting off their past experience, Lutz would be happier to believe that black holes do not exist; he would prefer to regard them as the result of scientific miscalculation. He even goes so far as to say that he would deny them, however probable their existence. To him they represent a threatening element in an otherwise consistently organized universe. Other people would also react this way, he claims; in fact, they would rather accept makeshift solutions as long as their world views remain constant: "You considerably underestimate the number of people who are willing and able to live without black holes" (296). This interchange between Lutz and the narrator, embedded in the parallel account of Nelly's experiential and moral turning point, is the crux of the novel. It dramatizes Christa Wolf's opposition to the official line taken at that time in East Germany, where one's actual experience of nazism was to be denied if it was not consonant with the notion of a resistance heritage. The emotional turmoil experienced by Nelly in the transition from one regime to another is something on which Lutz would prefer not to dwell. He fails to understand that the psychological black hole is an essential clue for Nelly in her reevaluation of past and present categories of thought.

This underlying thesis explains why the narrator takes such pains to describe for us the patterns of Nelly's childhood. We come to see that the fabric of memory contains holes of crucial significance. The narrator attempts to fill these gaps by foraging among old newspapers in the library of her home town. The press excerpts she quotes provide a counterpoint to Nelly's recollections by revealing historical events that lay beyond Nelly's awareness. They indicate, too, that the often made claim that certain news was withheld from the people by the Nazis is not entirely correct. For example, while Nelly can quite correctly claim that she knew nothing of the resistance movement because it was not discussed in her family, she discovers that it did not go unreported in the newspapers. In retrospect, Nelly's confirmation in the Christian church appears almost shocking when set against events that were occurring at the same time in the outside world. "But not even the slightest indication that the names of Sophie and Hans Scholl [members of the Catholic resistance movement; executed in 1943] were ever mentioned in Nelly's presence. No mention ever of the uprising of the Jews in the Warsaw ghetto, which must have been at its height at the time Nelly was kneeling at her Christian altar" (257). Contrasting her memories of that time with what the newspapers reported of it, the narrator realizes that in comparison with the Christian faith of the White Rose resistance group, Nelly's own religious piety was unconsciously corrupt. In eliminating any but such brief references to the resistance movement, Wolf shows sovereign disregard for the idea of an East German resistance heritage (and certainly she makes no mention of the Communist resistance, which is what is meant by this term). The narrator becomes painfully aware that she failed to resist the thought patterns thrust upon her by Nazism. For her, the concept of resistance was in another sense a black hole, something that lay beyond and was an inversion of her world. Had her family entertained the idea of resistance—and there are repeated hints that Charlotte Jordan, Nelly's mother, is not entirely bound to the Nazi way of thought—then like astronauts entering a black hole, they would have virtually shriveled up into nothingness for Nelly. Even in the narrative present, Lutz prefers to see the black hole concept as a product of nihilistic thought. But for the narrator, the black holes can be windows that open up new perspectives.

These two contrasting views find a correlative in Dali's well-known painting *The Persistence of Memory* and the narrator's reflections on it after she first sees the original during her trip to the United States. Like matter in a black hole, Dali's objects, the limp watches and the disembodied sleeping eye, are not subject to the ordinary laws of physics. The unreal colors, the uncanny light, the darkness that threatens to engulf the picture, and the blurred boundary line between light and dark—all these constitute for the narrator a depiction of "what one would not think possible," the landscape of memory (258). Memory, in other words, acts like a black hole, converting received impressions into entities of another world. But the world shown here is not the productive opening of windows the narrator seeks; rather, it is the nihilistic and destructive vision feared by her brother. She comments on the coldness that emanates from the painting, identifying it with the political cynicism later revealed by Salvador Dali. There is still a long way to go before she can find a positive counterpart to Dali's uncanny landscape of memory.

Her progress towards the new vision she seeks is part of her general progress from the third to the first person. But here we must be cautious. The coalescence of the two persons is not actually shown in the novel, even though the first-person pronoun ultimately appears at its conclusion. Nelly recedes more and more into an unreachable distance: "The closer she gets to you in time, the less familiar she becomes" (211), she says at one point, and later still: "Unmistakably, this girl, still called Nelly, recedes instead of gradually coming closer."[6] Even in her postwar existence, Nelly is too caught up in predetermined ways of thought to perform the task the narrator has undertaken: to straighten out the limp watches and restore the deformed past to the wholeness of restrospective judgment. Of this task, the narrator says: "you are forced to shuffle the details in order to get close to the facts" (56). Nelly's details must be transformed into the narrator's facts.

Wolf illustrates this phenomenon by observing the progress of her dreams. After her flight from the town L., she often suffered from nightmares in which she could not repeat the names of its streets (even though, oddly enough, she could still do so when awake). A long period ensues during which she no longer dreams of L. at all; however, once she has returned on a visit, she dreams of it once again, this time with the street names intact. Memory is like the deforming dream, narration like the rectifying return. What the narrator seeks is a pattern different from the conscious pattern of her childhood. Nelly, in both her earlier and her later versions, must disappear into the black hole to allow her narrator to emerge into newly aligned categories of thought.

In *A Model Childhood* (in contrast to *Cat and Mouse,* for example), the closeness of narrator and object of narration adds a new dimension to the problem of narration. The child who, along with the patterns of childhood themselves, had been absorbed into the narrator's consciousness cannot be unearthed and worked through in a psychoanalytical manner; rather, she is a discrete personality paradoxically related to the narrator's present self. This self is referred to throughout the book (until the last pages) as "you," and it is this second-person pronoun that is ultimately replaced by the first person. The use of the second person leaves room for another consciousness which is invoked at the novel's conclusion and which exists on a different level from the woman who made the trips to L. and America. In the novel's last paragraph, this new voice gives expression to a dream, a dream that, paradoxically, is set into the realm of future hope, not of actual experience.

> At night I shall see—whether waking, whether dreaming—the outline of a human being who will change, through whom other persons, adults, children, will pass without hindrance. I will hardly be surprised if this outline may also be that of an animal, a tree, even a house, in which anyone who wishes may go in and out at will. Half-conscious, I shall experience the beautiful waking image drifting ever deeper into the dream, into ever new shapes no longer accessible to words, shapes which I believe I recognize. Sure of finding myself once again in the world of solid bodies upon awakening, I shall abandon myself to the experience of dreaming. I shall not revolt against the limits of the expressible (407).

The fluid transitions; the constantly changing, insubstantial being; and the beautiful image represent an ideal of freedom from the constraints of patterns, from the bounds of the self, from the limitations of language. Here is a positive counterpart to Dali's *Persistence of Memory*, a transposed reality that is no longer cold and threatening. The narrator knows that she must accept the firm contours of waking reality; she is even grateful for their existence. But, at the same time, she welcomes the vision of another level of being.

Yet while the hypothetical dreamer speaks of different modalities of existence, there has been nothing in the novel itself that would make such flexibility seem possible. The relation of the dream person to Nelly remains unclear, and the vision itself has not yet taken place. That the series of questions immediately preceding this passage is unanswered suggests that the spell of the past and its division of the self into a second and third person is not completely broken.[7] Conscious and subconscious mind remain unintegrated, related to each other only by the same type of inversion as that which relates the laws of physics to the theory of black holes.

This basically unresolved discontinuity of self is paralleled by two other discontinuities: the gap between the older and the younger generation and the difference between East Germany and the West as represented by America. These discontinuities explain the necessity for the inclusion of the third time level in the novel. We shall look first at the generation problem, as revealed by the contrast between the narrator and her daughter Lenka, then at the question of the cultural and political differences revealed by the narrator's trip to America.

Like some of the other subsidiary characters in the novel, Lenka is curiously two-dimensional, her function appearing to consist primarily in voicing the reader's impatience at the mother's tedious reflections. A closer look reveals, however, that through Lenka another network of coordinates is set up, another pattern of childhood that bears striking resemblances to the narrator's and is at the same time an inversion of it. Both Nelly and Lenka give shape to their lives through the songs that express their beliefs; the songs plot the points that constitute the respective patterns. It is as if the two lives were two languages, mutually unintelligible but sharing some of the same structures. They, too, relate to each other as the black hole relates to ordinary space.

The trip to America uncovers a similar relationship. What most concerns the narrator is the problem of transferring old thought patterns to an unfamiliar situation. "It seems to go without saying that sleep, too, is subject to laws here that are different from those at home" (259). The appropriate categories constantly elude her; the new language overlaps but frustratingly fails to coincide with familiar meanings. How can *flavor* mean both natural taste and an artificial additive (259)? Or worse: how can *fair*, in German a loan-word applicable only to moral contexts, in English also mean *blond* and *beautiful* (254)? These observations give credence to the narrator's theory that we are defined by acquired or inculcated schemata of perception, such as those of which she had written earlier. An interview she had seen on American television with a well-known psychologist casts her previous thoughts on patterns of perception into confusion. She begins to ask some crucial questions. To what extent are patterns of perception permanently laid down in the early years of childhood (through language, as well as by other determinants), and conversely, to what extent can individuals be said to perceive things differently if the structure of nerve cells in the brain differs from one person to another by only 1 percent (156)? An answer to these questions is essential if the narrator is to be able to understand, and relate to each other, the perceptual patterns of the child and the adult. In connection with these issues, another difficulty emerges. This is the problem of reconciling the psychologist's view that all essential patterns are laid down irrevocably in the early years of childhood with the socialist view of the individual's ability to change. "What does it mean: to change?" she asks (141).

It is this novel's explicit concern with the question of change that distinguishes it from both those based on the autobiographical reminiscence schema and those which posit a clean break with the past. It also contrasts with the novels of Böll, Grass, and Lenz, which presuppose the possibility of change in the individual even though they often present it *ex negativo*. One difficulty for the narrator of *A Model Childhood* is that the change in Nelly is not presented as a process. It is simply a reversal, a reversal that takes place as a result of external causes, rather than individual reflection.[8] While this accords with historical fact, there is no place for it in the Marxist theory of change, especially as it pertains to the conception of the literary protagonist.

Perhaps aware of this, Christa Wolf projects her heroine's internal change into two external figures, the two teachers who serve her as role models before and after the war. Julia Strauch, her teacher during the period of the Third Reich, is shown at first as Nelly then saw her, an admirable influence on the girl's developing intellect. When Maria Kranhold becomes Nelly's mentor after the war, the girl experiences a jolt of discontinuity. During her service as a housemaid, Nelly finds an old box of books she had first read in copies borrowed from Julia, and, as she re-reads them, she is struck by a kind of "phantom pain" (368). For the first time she realizes how ingrained in her Julia's literary preferences had become. It is almost impossible for her to accept the suggestions Maria Kranhold makes for her reading. When Maria lends her a copy of Goethe's play *Iphigenia,* expecting it to have a special relevance to the girl, Nelly remains strangely unmoved. "She felt nothing as she read the heretofore unknown words. Her Goethe was the one whom her teacher Julia Strauch had recited to her with vibrant voice" (392). With some perplexity, she comes to understand Maria's view that Julia had created a "false conscience" in her pupils (391), but her internal change is not yet in step with the external change wrought by the collapse of the Nazi regime. While the conversations with the two teachers had helped her to align herself with prevailing views at the two different times, they had not helped her to develop her individual identity. The internal change, the movement from the postwar Nelly to the narrator's present self, is not shown.

This problematic aspect of the book is paralleled by another inadequately resolved problem, the relationship between its various levels. An East German reviewer comments that only when continuity and discontinuity are both effectively present can the demands of dialectic be satisfied.[9] That this is not the case in *A Model Childhood* can be seen from a comparison with the dialectically better developed *Quest for Christa T.* (1968).

In this earlier novel, Christa Wolf uses a technique for indicating discontinuity different from the "Nelly" strategy of *A Model Childhood.* In *Christa T.,* the narrator uses the author's first name to designate a character who supposedly is not herself at all. Despite this fiction, it becomes apparent in the course of the novel that Christa T. is in a sense another self of the narrator, a self that must be allowed to die at the end for what it is not, yet is also to be remembered for the positive qualities it represented. The connection between the two novels lies not only in this formal structuring: a direct reference is actually made to Christa T. in the later work. This reference is never followed up and appears at first to be merely a hermetic joke: "[Nelly] fleetingly thought that Julia was overlooking the real danger: it wasn't Hella and Isa, with their love of impudent pranks, . . . but Christa T., the new girl from the Friedberg area, who didn't show off and had no need for Julia, and from whom Nelly had just extorted the half-hearted promise that she would write to her during the Christmas vacation" (227). The details are sufficiently precise to identify Nelly as the narrator of *The Quest for Christa T.* who had once begged a similar promise from Christa T. Other details also confirm the connection between the two books and suggest that the one is in part dependent upon the other, such as the references to that exemplary Nazi youth Horst Binder in *Christa T.*[10] which are elaborated in a different context in *A Model Childhood.* The passing reference to the danger threatening Nelly from the new girl Christa T. is not fully explained here, however. We must turn to the earlier novel for the answer. There, Christa T. is seen as the prototype of the independent person. She is energetic, high-spirited, and forthright; the leitmotif for her provocative good humor is her echoing cry "Hooohaahoo" in the midst of a busy street. "She doesn't need us," comments the narrator. "We need her."[11] Her real significance is less what she is than the function she performs in respect to others: "At last I understand the role Christa T. played in her [Gertrud Dölling's] life: she put it in question."[12] Christa's provocative questioning is missing in Nelly Jordan, and because the new girl is only briefly alluded to in *A Model Childhood,* our perspective on Nelly cannot be quite complete. But even the half-reference indicates what is not allowed to surface in *A Model Childhood:* the possibility of resistance to accepted patterns, the courage to be different.

The questioners in *A Model Childhood* are of a different sort from Christa T. Nelly's second teacher, Maria Kranhold, claims to have been critical of nazism; actually, through trick and subterfuge, she simply managed not to pay lip service to it while it prevailed. In *A Model Childhood* the questioning takes place after the Nazi period and within another set of clearly defined thought patterns. Even the questions of the narrator are problematic. While she raises many important issues, she tends to frame her questions in such a way as to make them virtually unanswerable, such as whether one's perceptual patterns are set in the first years of life or are capable of further change. In contrast to the mutual interplay between the perspectives and value systems of Christa T. and her narrator, the relationship between Nelly Jordan and her narrator is simply one where the earlier viewpoint is put into its proper context and corrected by the later one. The consonance of the narrator's judgment of Nelly with the judgment of current readers is too thorough to be provocative. By contrast, *Christa T.* had used the same kind of reader-activation technique employed in *Cat and Mouse* and *The German Lesson:* it requires us to extend the lines formed by Christa T.'s and the narrator's development to their implied point of convergence beyond the end of the novel itself.[13] *A Model Childhood,* by contrast, essentially frames the past within the perspective of the present.

This is not to say that the novel's intention is completely spelled out. The reception of *A Model Childhood* both in the East and the West indicates that certain levels of the narration are not fully worked out or not satisfactorily integrated with the others. The problem appears to lie in the novel's relevance to contemporary events. Socialist and non-socialist criticism does not divide neatly in this regard. One typical approach to the novel is to see it as a kind of allegory of the East German situation. Thus, the rigid thought structures of nazism would appear as an unspoken parallel to the rigid policies of the GDR, and what purports to be a reckoning with the past would actually be a code language where the past, in effect, stands for the present. Even some Marxist critics have viewed the novel in this way.[14] On the other hand, Wolf has also been accused of referring only to those events of contemporary politics that happen to suit her purpose, so that while she mentions Vietnam and Chile, she refrains from dealing with "Prague and Budapest and the Polish Uprising and. . . ."[15] According to this view, her comparison of the Jewish uprising in the Warsaw ghetto with what she regards as a lack of effective protest among American blacks against a system that oppresses them is partially invalidated by her failure to discuss the problems of protest within socialist regimes. Both charges can hardly be true at the same time, however. If *A Model Childhood* is intended as an allegory of socialism, a critique of the GDR by comparison with the Third Reich, one wonders why so much time has to be spent on the minutiae of Nelly's personal life. The very complexity of the questions Wolf raises about continuity and discontinuity surely militate against so simplistic a reading. Similarly, the political events that are not mentioned are omitted because they fall outside the horizon of the person whose problematic and incomplete coming into being is the novel's central focus. Thus, what makes the book most original, its attempt to deal with the past on a personal level, is also its major weakness, since this intention by nature prevents a full exploration of political issues in a wider sense.

Yet, significantly, younger people, especially in the GDR, have responded more positively to Wolf's use of the personal mode. In this respect, *A Model Childhood* fulfilled an important need in East Germany for an account of "what it was really like" in Hitler's Reich.[16] Some readers have found the book's most refreshing figure to be the narrator's daughter Lenka, largely because Lenka is more politicized than was the young Nelly (Lenka spends sleepless nights worrying about the war in Vietnam).[17] It seems unlikely that Lenka is meant to carry so much of the book's political burden; Wolf seems to depict this East German teenager of the early seventies as a somewhat equivocal character, since her almost wholesale condemnation of everyone and everything as "pseudo" partially invalidates her other judgments. Actually, Wolf's treatment of the younger generation is comparatively perfunctory, yet to demand that more attention be given to Lenka's problems would be to turn it into another book.[18] If Wolf's exploration of a discontinuous self is to be effective, then others, such as Lenka, must function essentially as foils.

Beyond its concern with the self, *A Model Childhood* is important for the fictional presentation of nazism because of the way in which it incorporates reflections on writing into its narrative structure. Although the non-Marxist tradition has long relied on this technique, it was relatively new to GDR literature, and it is the one aspect of the novel by which Wolf most subtly confronts the official East German conception of art. But it is important to distinguish Wolf's reflections on writing from those that have so long been fashionable in non-socialist literature. Wolf's concern with the function of art goes well beyond such platitudes. She is aware that her own works cannot easily be subsumed into familiar conceptions of literature, and she takes up the question again and again in her essays, in discussions with readers, and, as here, within the works themselves. She knows that literature is one of the things that determine our view of the world, and that it is also one of the ways in which we shape our individual identities. Christa T. resolves the turmoil within herself by making a conscious decision in favor of a particular kind of literature that corresponds to only one part of her being: she writes her dissertation on the late nineteenth-century realists rather than on the more complicated modernists, such as Thomas Mann, in whom she is also interested. In contrast, Nelly and her narrator come to understand the detrimental effect that a particular selection of reading matter can exercise upon the growing mind. "Interview question: do you believe in the influence of literature? Certainly, though probably not as you do. I believe that the mechanism which deals with the absorption and processing of reality is formed by literature; in Nelly's case, this mechanism was severely damaged, although she was not aware of it. How did we become what we are today? One of the answers would be a list of book titles" (368–69). With this in mind, the narrator points out that literature must avoid becoming a moral tract ("the accursed falsification of history into a moralistic tale" [361]) or blinding our moral judgment by its aesthetic persuasion ("art triumphing over morality" [373]). How can all these requirements be met? In her essay "Reading and Writing," Wolf expresses a literary aim that also has bearing on the later work *A Model Childhood*. "Apparently we need for our life the support and acquiescence of fantasy. That is to say: play with unlimited possibilities. But there's something else going on inside us, every day, every hour—a gradual, almost unavoidable process: hardening, petrifaction, habit. It attacks memory in particular."[19] Applied to *A Model Childhood,* this would mean that the petrifaction of memory must be undone, to be replaced by the free play of unlimited possibility. But short of Dali's surrealism or the longed-for but unrealized dream at the end of *A Model Childhood,* it is hard to imagine how memory can be made so infinitely flexible. Even the concluding vision, the imaginary dream, is not adequate to the task. It does not develop as a logical consequence of the (quite different) views on change and determinism presented in the body of the novel; it seems to emanate from another sphere, one more appropriate to the German romantic writer Novalis. In addition, it envisages a state in which the individual is dissolved and removed from place in chronological time, a state that goes beyond the bounds of what can be articulated in language. Thus the dream projection, with its indeterminate fluidity, invalidates the concept of historical change and the necessity for the individual to change in time consciously.

The questions so provocatively asked in *Christa T.* have been reduced in *A Model Childhood* to abstractions so vast and timeless that the reader must either capitulate before them or recede into the black hole of the concluding vision. The conception of *A Model Childhood* is a bold one, but an imperfect dialectic prevents its probings from becoming a genuinely activating "play with unlimited possibilities."

CHAPTER TEN

INNOVATION AND REALISM
Versions of the Documentary

Implicit in this study from the outset has been the question whether the reckoning with the Nazi past has altered the way fiction deals with history. To what extent did the break in historical continuity also give rise to a break in literary tradition? From their allegorizing beginnings to the development of ironic and open-ended structures, postwar writers have asked whether traditional forms are suited to the portrayal of their experience under Hitler. Realism in its nineteenth-century form had been partially invalidated by the modernist period of the earlier twentieth century, with its demonstration of the importance of individual consciousness. There obviously could be no return in the postwar period to the omniscient narrator of earlier historical novels. A new approach had to be found for incorporating reality in fiction. Could it be done more directly than was the case in the ironic novels of Günter Grass or Siegfried Lenz?

One attempt to achieve this might be seen in the documentary method. Although primarily a dramatic mode, it had its influence on the novel as well. Documentary implies that other forms of literature manipulate the elements of reality on which they are based; its basic tenet is that facts should be allowed to speak for themselves. But when applied to the reckoning with nazism, the documentary poses problems of reception that have not always been successfully resolved. At its most effective, it depends no less than other literary forms on contrasts and ironies, however heavily it accentuates its basis in fact. Thus in Rolf Hochhuth's play *The Deputy* (1963), the Church's involvement in political machinations and its refusal to speak out against the mass exterminations of Jews is set off against our knowledge of its later protestations of ignorance and helplessness; in Rolf Schneider's drama *Trial in Nuremberg* (1967), claims of innocence are juxtaposed with evidence of their falsity; and in Peter Weiss' play *The Investigation* (1965), an apparent change of attitude between the prewar and post-war periods is revealed as an ominous continuity. Documentary drama of this sort relies on a particular arrangement of the evidence it presents. In *The Deputy,* this ultimately has the effect of transforming the act of resistance into the scheme of conventional tragedy. But tragedy implies a kind of inevitability that does not pertain to the heroic sacrifice on which this drama centers. Moreover, since Hochhuth's resister is shown to have been helpless in the face of the overwhelming forces of evil represented by his opponents, resistance itself is made to appear a hopeless cause.

Pre-formed structures such as tragedy do not exist in the same degree in the novel, and one would expect it to be more open to the documentary technique. Yet there have been only a few attempts at a documentary novel on the Nazi past. Of these, the best known is perhaps Uwe Johnson's *Anniversaries* (1970–75), in fact only partially a documentary. Here the retrospective material is cast in the shape of conventional fiction, and attached to Gesine Cresspahl, a character from Johnson's earlier novel, *Speculations about Jacob* (1959). Only the contrasting material from the seventies is given in documentary form.

This use of documentary created the impression that Johnson had moved to a more realistic mode than had been the case in his previous works, but *Anniversaries* remains in essence a novel of consciousness, differing only in superficial technical respects from its predecessors. Johnson himself claims that the documentary inserts, extracts from the *New York Times* of 1967–68, are not so much a montage of material collated by the author as an integral part of Gesine Cresspahl's consciousness.[1] If we compare the extracts and their placement in the novel to the montages of newspaper items in the works of Alfred Döblin or John Dos Passos, the difference in intent becomes obvious. No longer are the press clippings part of an ironic commentary mounted by the author as a critique of his character, as in Döblin's *Alexanderplatz, Berlin* (1929), nor are they dispassionate amplifications of the political and social settings, as in Dos Passos' *U.S.A.* (1937); they are passages noted by the protagonist herself. In essence, they are Gesine's mental underlinings of her morning reading matter. This makes *Anniversaries* a peculiarly modern sort of diary-novel whose form is no longer that of conventional notation. Essentially, we are given a logbook of Gesine's thoughts and activities in the course of the year, partly as tape recordings, partly as newspaper extracts, partly as narration from her own point of view. Rarely, if at all, are the newspaper articles quoted in full. Instead, we are given only salient paragraphs or sentences, presumably those which have caught Gesine's attention. And Gesine does not often comment on these extracts; her attitude, her political views, are deduced from recorded conversations and reminiscences. The backbone of the book is formed by the interplay between the political situation of 1967–68, especially the American involvement in Vietnam and political developments in the Czechoslovak Socialist Republic, and the narration of events in Germany from 1933 to the early postwar period. The relation between the two time levels is not, strictly speaking, a dialectic, but neither is it a cheap or simplistic parallel.[2]

As in Johnson's earlier novels, the central dilemma for the characters in both present and past is that of individual freedom, choice and action. "Love it or leave it," the popular slogan of the Vietnam war years, suggests a problem that had already been a concern of Johnson's, although in a different context. His own emigration from the GDR to the FRG and his portrayal of similar emigrations (or decisions against emigration) on the part of his characters had brought the issue to the fore in all of his earlier works, and Johnson had repeatedly made it clear that the choice was by no means as clear-cut, the individual's motivation by no means as unambiguous, as might be supposed.[3] The novels are permeated by a sense of pessimism which suggests that the individual is inextricably caught in an irresolvable dilemma, a choice between alternatives that are either not desirable or not viable. Conclusions only implied by the earlier works become explicit in *Anniversaries*, where Johnson demonstrates on a multiplicity of fronts that life involves "playing with an unavailable alternative."[4] The blind patriotism of "love it or leave it" is transposed in Johnson's more elaborate paraphrase into the view that if the crimes of one country weigh upon one's conscience one can simply move to another. Again and again characters are depicted who do precisely that, and we are impelled to ask whether their action is sufficient. Gesine herself, who has gone from East to West Germany and from there to America, is the prime example. Heinrich Cresspahl provides a counterpart to his daughter, but the motivations of the two are very different, as are their resolutions of the moral dilemma. While Gesine remains essentially passive during her stay in America, Cresspahl becomes involved in espionage activities for the British after his return from England to Nazi Germany. To be sure, his motivation is not entirely selfless. Albert Gosling's revelation of his unintentional retention of illegal sums of money in an English bank account makes it possible for the British to persuade Cresspahl to work for them. His wife Lisbeth's return to Germany and her loyalty to the arch-conservative family from which she comes is contradicted by her profound belief in Protestant Christianity ar.d her suicide following the murder of a Jewish child during the *Kristallnacht*. Abstract principles and personal psychology create in almost all of Johnson's central characters a complex mixture of motivation that gives the lie to any simplistic analysis.

Two interlocking features of Johnson's basic philosophy as expressed in the novels deserve special consideration: first, his insistence on the hegemony of individual consciousness, and second, his underlying pessimistic belief in determinism. We have already seen how typical this ambivalence is in fiction dealing with nazism in the late fifties and early sixties. But whereas his earlier novels, *Speculations about Jacob* and *The Third Book about Achim,* had presented reality as a set of conjectures posited by an individual consciousness, a position expanded only slightly by the dual focus of *Two Views* (1965), *Anniversaries* no longer stresses the conjectural so heavily. Yet the narration only appears to be more reliable; now the central consciousness no longer merely reflects events but also reacts to them. The newspaper is one of the several things in her new life that set Gesine thinking. Her eleven-year-old daughter Marie is an equally, if not more, vital stimulus, as is to a somewhat lesser extent her affluent and highly Americanized friend D. E. Furthermore, Gesine's reflections on the past, intended as explanations for Marie but just as much addressed to herself, are no less conjectural than Johnson's earlier narratives had been, despite their more straightforward form. Even the account "Through Cresspahl's Eyes," which is appended to the second volume of the German version, is given in the subjunctive of indirect speech and represents a fairly liberal account of Cresspahl's contributions to a father-daughter conversation; its gaps are particularly evident in Cresspahl's refusal to explain his motivation. Commentators have noted other gaps in the body of the novel, such as the fact that Cresspahl does not join the Nazi party, although we are told that he did pick up an application form. Along with Gesine, the reader can only attempt to piece together the past. Lisbeth Cresspahl's innermost thoughts and feelings can only be deduced, and imperfectly, from her actions; Heinrich Cresspahl's taciturnity gives rise to numerous lacunae in his own account. Thus, past events that could be guides for action in the present become instead a source of confusion. Her parents' motivation appears even more complex and ambivalent viewed through the filter of Gesine's present consciousness and as a result of her attempt to relate the two time levels to each other. In spite of the parallels that she and Marie try to draw between past and present, and in spite of the very real similarities that actually do exist, the two periods prove incommensurable in the last analysis. No infallible guideline can be drawn from the one to the other.

Complicating this is Gesine's view of her father's attempt to resolve the dilemma between choice and determinism. This has been described as a "rather 'Kantian' interpretation of his situation in which free-will and compulsion co-exist," in which Cresspahl, by accepting and acquiescing in his own fate, manages to feel that his own free will is still operative.[5] His return to Germany upon Gesine's birth is the key example of his Kantian solution: although his wife has manipulated his return by returning to Germany herself for the baby's birth, Cresspahl, in retrospectively conceiving of her trip as having taken place with his permission, constructs a personal control over events that he does not actually possess.

This view of individual action, which becomes increasingly evident to Gesine in the course of her narration, casts a particular light on Cresspahl's resistance to nazism and consequently on the potential within the family to follow suit. If Heinrich Cresspahl's resistance (becoming a spy for the British) was not only inspired by mixed motives but also in a sense determined by a situation beyond individual control, what implications does this have for Gesine's or Marie's opposition to the Vietnam war? Gesine's refusal to participate in anti-Vietnam demonstrations is the direct outcome of the pessimism she feels as the result of her reflection on the past; the dispassionately non-partisan newspaper she now reads may be a protective "auntie" to her (as she describes it), but it does nothing to prod her out of this basic passivity. While Marie is more disposed to join the demonstrations, she, too, is overwhelmed by the powerlessness of the individual and implores her mother not to expect her to stop this war when her mother could not stop the war of her own generation. A continuing theme is the socially conditioned need to disguise beliefs that are in opposition to prevailing ones: young Gesine was taught to believe in nazism so that she wouldn't arouse suspicion amongst her classmates; young Marie is instructed not to speak of the family's political views at her exclusive New York Catholic school. Different modes of resistance or of maintaining moral integrity are explored in the various time levels and characters in the book. But whether it be undercover work, suicide, emigration, demonstration and public protest, rejection of honors offered by corrupt governments, or active support of political alternatives, each avenue is negated by its impure motivation or its basic impracticability. In ending the fourth volume of *Anniversaries* on the day of Soviet intervention in Czechoslovakia, Johnson sustains the work's underlying pessimism about the possibility of effective resistance.[6]

Yet with its single, limited, central consciousness, its interplay between two time levels and between document and response, *Anniversaries* has many elements of a truly activating novel. Indeed, its not inconsiderable virtue is its demonstration that resistance is not a simple issue, that it involves problems of free will, as well as political, moral, and psychological dimensions. None of these is clear-cut. The novel demonstrates, moreover, that learning from history is neither as easy nor as straightfoward as is generally supposed. Accompanying these theoretical ramifications is a degree of historic specificity hitherto unattained in novels dealing with nazism. Most readers and critics have presumed this specificity to be due to the inclusion of documentary materials, in other words, the newspaper extracts. Yet the same specificity is also present in the conversational portions of the novel, which directly take up many of the topics reported in the press clippings, as well as in the fictional reflections on the past. In some ways, these dialogues seem more realistic and detailed than the often very brief newspaper items. In viewing the documentary portions as supplements to Gesine's perspective rather than as aspects of it, critics have been led to charge Johnson with the creation of an unrealistic character.[7] But Gesine is not a character in the ordinary sense; she is also a fictional stand-in for a large segment of Johnson's own political engagement. "Who's telling this story, Gesine. We both are. Surely that's obvious, Johnson" (169). This playful merging of author and character permits Gesine to do exactly what Johnson did during his trip to the United States: assiduously read the *New York Times*. Johnson himself points out that a newcomer to the country would be unlikely to read a more local newspaper.[8] More important is the function of the documentary method here. The selectivity of the extracts and the relationship between them and the non-documentary portions make it clear that the newspapers are being read from a very particular point of view, in which predilections and limitations become increasingly apparent. Gesine's special use of the newspaper information and Johnson's implied critique of the *New York Times'* presentation have been commented on by several critics.[9] Still, the interplay between Gesine's consciousness and the newspaper she reads is only superficially the crux of the novel. More vital is the relationship between past and present as it develops in the course of her day-by-day analysis. Why does Johnson fail to convert this into a genuine dialectic? The answer lies in the essentially pessimistic view of individual action that is implied in virtually every aspect of the two time frames. Genuine alternatives are "unavailable." Thus, what flexibility the novel has gained by its subtle combination of document and fiction is counteracted by the fact that its various strands ultimately point in the same direction. Just as Johnson's first novels treated personal psychology as something inherently inaccessible, so *Anniversaries* makes the mesh of individual and political situation seem impenetrable and the problem of resistance irresolvable. By subordinating document to fiction, Johnson divests it of its objective reality and makes it as impenetrable as subjectivity itself.[10]

There are some novels about nazism, however, that do leave document as document. The most notable is Alexander Kluge's account of the German attack upon Stalingrad, *The Battle* (1964). In completely deadpan manner, Kluge mounts a revealing mixture of evidence on this phase of World War II: official communiqués from the field, instructions to the press on the required tenor and format of reports on the Stalingrad battle, manuals for soldiers on techniques of winter warfare and survival, and interviews with army officers and doctors, together with a large number of other accounts, excerpts, and notations of unidentified origin. What is rapidly revealed through these juxtapositions (aided by the ironic underlayer of our knowledge about the actual outcome of the battle) is the deceitfulness and manipulation at the official level, the coming catastrophe that was well foreseen but not officially admitted, and the attempt to transform senseless carnage into a heroic sacrifice. This method may be compared with the more conventional realism of Theodor Plievier's *Stalingrad* (1948). Based on detailed reports from participants in the battle, it is presented in an objective narrative format that owes a good deal to its forerunner, Arnold Zweig's novel series on World War I. Whereas Plievier's novel, with its shattering account of human devastation, has the greater power to arouse the reader's compassion and sense of outrage, Kluge achieves a different impact through his documentary montage, which requires us to play off the various idioms of reportage against each other before we can arrive at an actual picture of the battle. Kluge's technique unmasks propagandist jargon and reveals delusions in a way that realistic methods cannot; in its dry manner, it allows contrasts and ironies to speak for themselves.[11] The second half of the book, which gives a day-by-day account in what approximates a history student's notebook full of unattributed sources, is less successful than the first. Despite this weakness, *The Battle* is important in the development of the documentary novel. It demonstrates that the documentary method is not, as one might expect, a close neighbor of literary realism, but rather its theoretical opposite. Novels like *The Battle* remain basically open-ended; they point to judgments they do not themselves spell out. Even Uwe Johnson, in abandoning his version of the *nouveau roman* for the documentary, has not opted for a more realistic mode of presentation. To be sure, *Anniversaries* is more readable than its predecessors, but it still requires a considerable amount of piecing together on the part of the reader, whose task it is to relate the newspaper excerpts to the fictional layer. At its best (and Kluge and Johnson do not always rise to this level), documentary demands reader participation of a relatively sophisticated kind. In making us aware of ironies and discrepancies, it tunes our critical faculties more finely and enables us to perceive that documents, like "reality," must not be taken at face value. By leaving the evaluation of the evidence to the reader (or spectator, in the case of drama and film), documentary attempts to encourage independent thinking. Sometimes, as in the section "Reckoning with the Past" in Günter Wallraff's *13 Undesirable Reports* (1969), conflicting presentations of "facts" make the truth apparent to anyone willing to compare the versions. Yet sometimes documentary leaves too much freedom. Joachim Fest's documentary film about Hitler, put together from old newsreels and the like, unintentionally prompted some viewers to develop a positive image of its subject. Such reactions show that documentary alone cannot be expected to carry the whole critique of the Third Reich. If it throws the weight too heavily upon fact, the documentary implicitly rejects the idea of a productive relationship between reality and fiction.

Precisely this relationship is examined by Alfred Andersch in his whimsical use of documentary in *Winterspelt* (1974). Framed by extracts from historical accounts (given, in contrast to many of Kluge's, in accurate bibliographic detail), the novel sets out to perform a "dry run" (*Sandkastenspiel*), a depiction of an unrealized possibility. Kluge's *The Battle* is clearly the reference point against which both the documentary frame and the realistic narrative are to be measured, though Andersch sets his novel on the western, not the eastern, front. The documents extracted from German, English, and American sources clarify the military position and indicate the tactical possibilities open to the Germans in 1944. The novel then enacts what Andersch calls "Phases of a Transition from Documentary to Fiction," the working out of the theoretical model. Referring throughout to the fictional material as a report, Andersch tells the story of an imaginary Major Dincklage of the 416th Infantry Division and his spontaneously conceived plan to set up a formalized truce with the Allies. Andersch emphasizes his choice of an infantry division for this act of military resistance, in opposition to elitist groups such as the conspirators of 20 July 1944. With heavy sarcasm, he comments: "In the 416th Infantry Division and in the entire German armed forces, there never was an officer, in 1944 or before or after, who entertained such plans as are here attributed to Major Dincklage. Consequently, the 416th Infantry and the German Army as a whole need not feel implicated in this narrative."[12] Nonetheless, he dedicates the book to an "extremely reliable" person, who, having spent the years 1941–45 on the western front, takes issue with this assumption and urges Andersch to revise it. The book is the fictional realization of this revision. But: "History relates what happened. Fiction plays out a possibility," Andersch reminds us.[13] In the course of the novel itself, the issue is taken up in discussions between the principal characters. When the former schoolteacher Käthe Lenk protests that it doesn't make much sense to speak in the conditional when referring to historical events, her friend, resistance fighter Hainstock, objects: "That is the most reactionary statement I have ever heard. . . . If we refuse to imagine what might have been, we shut off the chance of imagining any better possibility. Then we are just accepting history as it comes."[14] For Andersch, fiction is the answer to fatalism; yet even the fictional playing out of this possibility ends negatively. The concluding "Phases of a Transition from Fiction to Documentary" draws the parallels that have been implicit all along, notably the comparison with the conspirators of 20 July and their inability to gain satisfactory conditions from the Allies.

Within the documentary frame, the story is told in a straightforward manner, except for occasional interpolations to insure the reader's continued consciousness that it is only a play of possibilities. The story thus reveals the obverse of the coin that can only be hinted at in pure documentary. However, in taking this approach, it also has to deal with the inherent problems of literary realism, and one layer of the novel consists of reflections on this issue. That Andersch is a master of realistic technique had already been amply demonstrated in his earlier works, which had effected a brilliant transformation of autobiographical material into fiction. But the spy-story atmosphere of *Zanzibar* and the romantic element in *The Redhead* (1960) had appeared suspect to serious German critics. *Winterspelt* is doubtless a response to this criticism, an attempt to stay closer to the experience of his readers. The underground resistance is not absent, but it is toned down so that the focus can rest on Dincklage's refusal to obey military orders.

In *Winterspelt*, realism and documentary augment each other to point up their respective inadequacies. At the same time, *Winterspelt* brings out one of the latent issues in postwar literature: the inability of realistic narration to reveal the hidden potential for resistance in the person who did not, in fact, resist nazism. Its most intriguing feature is its use of a reportage style to narrate fiction and comment on document simultaneously. In using this style, Andersch presents his fiction as if it were document, though the reader knows, of course, that it is not on the same level as the genuine documents with which it is framed. In consequence, historical reality, the fictional plot of the novel, and other permutations of the plot conjured up in the mind of the reader all come to have the quality of alternative possibilities, any of which might equally well have taken place. In contrast to Johnson's "playing with an unavailable alternative," Andersch's dry run through an unrealized possibility of history allows us to rethink the past according to multiple variations. The basic similarity of *Winterspelt*'s conclusion to the outcome of the assassination plot against Hitler does not invalidate this; instead, it points all the more clearly to the quite different course history might have taken. Andersch's fictional documentary is remarkably open-ended.

Like *Winterspelt*, Peter Weiss' fantasy autobiography, *The Aesthetics of Resistance*, with which this study began, is a hypothetical account of a sequence of events that never happened: an imaginary and idealized version of Weiss' own life. An ambitious combination of the historical novel, the documentary, and the novel of education, Weiss' book links the story of the Communist resistance with the fictitious account of a young worker's attempt to educate himself through reading. Anchored in meticulous historical research and summarizing in almost overwhelming detail the entire spectrum of art and literature relevant to socialist theory, this provocative novel is, nonetheless, somewhat cumbersome in its structure. More an extended essay than a novel, it tries to contain its amorphous bulk by its initial reference to the missing Heracles figure. Despite this resonant image, the book as a whole remains a recalcitrant mixture of myth, fantasy, and reality. The fictional framework is little more than an excuse for summaries of novels and descriptions of works of art which the young workers are supposed to have studied in the course of their political development. Its reflection on resistance takes place on a plane far removed from the familiar arena of fiction, and its perception of reality is quite remote from that of the readers it addresses, most of whom would have been more passive participants in the Third Reich.

The mixed success of this combination of fact and fiction gives added urgency to the question of literary technique. Why had more traditional methods of narration proved unsuited to an ethically sophisticated reevaluation of the Nazi past? If realism is an effect created by virtual coincidence of the historical and the fictional points of view, a unity of "objective presentation" and "subjective evaluation,"[15] this means that to appear realistic, a work of literature must correspond closely to the expectations of its readers and to their perception of reality. In postwar Germany, this relationship no longer existed, and the integration of history and fiction could no longer follow traditional models of literary realism.

What literature had to do was to point up its basis in ideology. This it could best do by drawing attention to the fact of subjective presentation, by the use of unreliable and non-omniscient narrators. The major novelists of the sixties adopt what I regard as the most fruitful solution to this problem: the novel of consciousness, which demands a particular critical awareness from the reader prompted either by an open-ended or an ironic fictional structure. By breaking down mythic structures, these novelists simultaneously break down our passive acceptance of events; by questioning narration they call forth reconstruction and response. If we can learn to read their novels correctly, we can acquire a more critical stance for our perception of history itself. As long as novels do not close off the possibility of change, we can look to the future more confident of our own power to resist what may at first appear to be inevitable. Just as the historical resistance to Hitler failed, so too do Mahlke, Balthasar, and Levin; and the novels themselves create a new awareness of the need for resistance. The fictional rethinking of nazism becomes a dialectic to be completed in the future.

In the late sixties, when other issues came into the foreground, the experience of nazism became more of a contrastive backdrop for immediate concerns. Now a new technique was used to evoke a critical response in the reader. The Nazi past became a point of reference, an evaluative guide for contemporary events, whether they be the Vietnam war, the student unrest, terrorism and violence, or the punitive measures enacted to control them. Realism of this type requires a new transference of reflections on history into the present day. Against this background, it is not surprising that Grass contrasts the plan of a high-school boy to demonstrate against the use of napalm in Vietnam with his teacher's recollections of his anarchist past as a member of a youth gang in Hitler's Germany (*Local Anaesthetic*, 1969) or that he counterpoints his account of Willy Brandt's election campaign of 1969 with the tale of a Jew who spends the war years hiding in a cellar (*From the Diary of a Snail*, 1972). Similarly, Böll's depiction of the burning of a stolen army jeep as a protest in *End of a Mission* (1966) or of the oppressiveness of modern mass media and their relation to violence in *The Lost Honor of Katharina Blum* (1974) are meant to be read against the implicit background of the Nazi period. In *The Model* (1973) Siegfried Lenz shows the effect of literary and historical models on young people and thus provokes renewed reflection on the recent past. And Uwe Johnson employs an explicit juxtaposition technique in *Anniversaries* (1970–73). These works and many others are symptomatic of a continuing influence exerted by the reevaluation of the past on individual writers' responses to the present.

In contrast to the juxtapositional novels, which still demand critical distance and active reconstruction from their readers, there was also another trend, relying on identification rather than estrangement. Obviously more questionable than the dialectical works, these novels capitalized on an upsurge of interest in the Third Reich characterized by a sentimental or nostalgic streak. Exploited by Walter Kempowski in *Tadellöser & Wolff* and its sequels (1971–75) and by Hermann Lenz in *New Times* (1975), they were only very slightly ironic about the mentality they depict. But their audience saw little of this irony. When Kempowski's novels were shown on German television, the primarily middle-aged, middle-class audience was fascinated chiefly by his skillful evocation of their childhood and remained unaware of the series' critical implications. The German public urgently needs a work that addresses its ambivalence about childhood in the Third Reich more directly. What many remember as a time of great social and family security is not a time of which they can now be proud. Alongside this problem of the middle and older generations, there are also the needs of the younger generation of Germans. For several years there has been a growing concern about the young people's often inadequate knowledge of the Nazi period, and a concerted attempt to give them a more accurate picture of the German past is now under way. There is as yet no literary work that gives the facts and relates them, in a sensitive and non-sensationalist way, to problems of the present.

Novelists still appear to be casting around for an appropriate way to approach this complex problem. But if they are to be successful, they must take a lesson from their forerunners. It will not be enough to draw a simple parallel between past and present: rather, forms must be developed that productively play off the one against the other, contrasting the two while making the reader work toward new solutions. If their readers are to move beyond mere acceptance of historical events, these works must make them, in effect, look for the missing Heracles in the panoramic depiction of struggle. The more actively we must search out this image, the greater the likelihood that we will be required, at the same time, to rethink basic presuppositions about individual freedom and responsibility.

NOTES

NOTES TO THE INTRODUCTION

1. *Die Ästhetik des Widerstands,* vol. 1, rev. ed. (Munich, 1976), p. 11; my translation.
2. *Ibid.,* p. 316.
3. For the genesis of nazism as treated in recent literature, see Franz Futterknecht, *Das Dritte Reich im deutschen Roman der Nachkriegszeit* (Bonn, 1976), and Hans Wagener, ed., *Gegenwartsliteratur und Drittes Reich* (Stuttgart, 1977). On the problem of giving literary expression to the atrocities of nazism, see Lawrence Langer, *The Holocaust and the Literary Imagination* (New Haven, 1975), and Hamida Bosmajian, *Metaphors of Evil: Contemporary German Literature and the Shadow of Nazism* (Iowa City, 1979).
4. See in particular Peter Demetz, *Postwar German Literature: A Critical Introduction* (New York, 1970); R. Hinton Thomas and Wilfried van der Will, *German Literature and the Affluent Society* (Manchester, 1968); R. Hinton Thomas and Keith Bullivant, *Literature in Upheaval* (Manchester, 1974).
5. See Terry Eagleton, *Criticism and Ideology* (London, 1976).
6. On this point, see Theodore Ziolkowski, "The Literature of Atrocity," *Sewanee Review* 75 (1977), pp. 135–43, esp. p. 139.
7. Bosmajian, *Metaphors of Evil,* p. 21.
8. See "Realismus in der Prosa," in *Tendenzen der deutschen Literatur seit 1945,* ed. Thomas Koebner (Stuttgart, 1971), pp. 179–275.
9. For example, Gisbert Ter-Nedden, "Allegorie und Geschichte. Zeit- und Sozialkritik als Formproblem des deutschen Romans der Gegenwart," in *Poesie und Politik: Zur Situation der Literatur in Deutschland,* ed. Wolfgang Kuttenkeuler (Stuttgart, 1963), pp. 155–83.
10. Theodor W. Adorno, *Noten zur Literatur III* (Frankfurt, 1965), p. 125.

NOTES TO CHAPTER ONE

1. Cf. Hans Egon Holthusen's poem of the same name in *Hier in der Zeit* (Munich, 1949); Frank Trommler, "Der 'Nullpunkt 1945' und seine Verbindlichkeit für die Literaturgeschichte," *Basis* 1 (1970), pp. 9–25; Heinrich Vormweg, "Keine Stunde Null," in *Die deutsche Literatur der Gegenwart,* ed. Manfred Durzak (Stuttgart, 1971), pp. 13–30.
2. For a general survey and analysis of this period, see Frank Trommler, "Der zögernde Nachwuchs: Entwicklungsprobleme der Nachkriegsliteratur in Ost und West" and "Realismus in der Prosa," in *Tendenzen der deutschen Literatur seit 1945,* ed. Thomas Koebner (Stuttgart, 1971), pp. 1–116, 179–275. Cf. also Guy Stern, "Prolegomena zu einer Geschichte der deutschen Nachkriegsprosa," *Colloquia Germanica* 1 (1967), pp. 233–52, and *Gegenwartsliteratur und Drittes Reich,* ed. Hans Wagener (Stuttgart, 1977).
3. See Charles W. Hoffmann, *Opposition Poetry in Nazi Germany* (Berkeley, 1962); Theodore Ziolkowski, "Form als Protest: Das Sonett in der Literatur des Exils und der inneren Emigration"; Reinhold Grimm, "Innere Emigration als Lebensform," in *Exil und innere Emigration,* ed. Reinhold Grimm and Jost Hermand (Frankfurt, 1972), pp. 153–72, 31–73.
4. Karl Krolow, *Aspekte zeitgenössischer Lyrik* (Berlin, 1961), p. 37.
5. A version of these views was presented at the Amherst Colloquium of 1973 in a talk entitled "Die 'innere Landschaft' in der Literatur des zwanzigsten Jahrhunderts." Cf. also Judith Ryan, "Nelly Sachs," in *Die deutsche Lyrik von 1945 bis 1975,* ed. Klaus Weissenberger (Düsseldorf, 1981), pp. 110–18.

6. For an excellent critical analysis of *The Indelible Seal,* see Ehrhard Bahr, "Metaphysische Zeitdiagnose," in Hans Wagener, ed., *Gegenwartsliteratur und Drittes Reich,* pp. 140–46.
7. The basic principle of the novel is expressed in the phrase, "life is a chain of repetitions" (*Die Stadt hinter dem Strom* [Frankfurt, 1947], p. 194; my translation). On the allegorical structure of the novel, see Ehrhard Bahr, "Metaphysische Zeitdiagnose," pp. 137–39.
8. *Die Stadt hinter dem Strom,* p. 315.
9. *Das Los unserer Stadt* [The fate of our town] (Freiburg, 1959), p. 93; my translations.
10. *Ibid.,* p. 94.
11. *Ibid.,* p. 279.
12. *Ibid.,* p. 80.
13. *Ibid.,* pp. 80–81.
14. *Ibid.,* p. 81.
15. *Ibid.,* p. 144.
16. *Ibid.,* p. 111.
17. Horst Steinmetz also points out the danger of historical fatalism latent in this play (*Max Frisch: Tagebuch, Drama, Roman* [Göttingen, 1973], p. 68). On parabolic structures in postwar German dramas, see Andreas Huyssen, "Unbewältigte Vergangenheit—Unbewältigte Gegenwart," in *Geschichte im Gegenwartsdrama,* ed. Reinhold Grimm and Jost Hermand (Stuttgart, 1976), pp. 39–53.
18. Hellmut Karasek compares Frisch's technique with that of Brecht, which by its very nature includes the possibility of choice (*"Biedermann und die Brandstifter,"* in *Über Max Frisch,* ed. Thomas Beckermann [Frankfurt, 1971], p. 145).
19. Reinhold Grimm and Carolyn Wellauer have observed that, in spite of Frisch's criticism of his time, his novels tend to illustrate a retreat from time ("Max Frisch. Mosaik eines Statikers," in *Zeitkritische Romane des zwanzigsten Jahrhunderts,* ed. Hans Wagener [Stuttgart, 1975], p. 295).
20. "Einleitung zur *Panne,*" in *Theaterschriften und Reden* (Zurich, 1966), p. 80.
21. *Romulus der Grosse,* in Dürrenmatt, *Komödien I* (Zurich, 1957), p. 19; my translations.
22. *Ibid.,* p. 73.
23. *Ibid.,* p. 75.
24. *Ibid.,* p. 58.
25. *Ibid.,* p. 74.
26. *Theaterprobleme* (Zurich, 1955), p. 14.
27. Unfortunately, Brecht's own plays about the Nazi period, *The Private Life of the Master Race* (1935–38) and *The Resistible Rise of Arturo Ui* (1941), were written during his exile and before the complete development of his dramatic theory. While he was pleased with their popularity in the postwar years, he felt that he had progressed beyond them.
28. *Das Los unserer Stadt,* p. 49.
29. For summaries of East German literary treatments of the Third Reich and World War II, see Karl Heinz Hartmann in "Das Dritte Reich in der DDR-Literatur: Stationen erzählter Vergangenheit," in *Gegenwartsliteratur und Drittes Reich,* ed. Hans Wagener, pp. 307–28; Therese Hörningk, "Thema Krieg und Faschismus in der DDR-Literatur," *Weimarer Beiträge* 5 (1978), pp. 73–105.
30. Cf. Hans-Albert Walter, *Deutsche Exilliteratur,* vol. 2 (Darmstadt, 1972); Hans Dahlke, *Geschichtsroman und Literaturkritik im Exil* (Berlin, 1976); Grimm and Hermand, *Exil und innere Emigration;* Peter Uwe Hohendahl and Egon Schwarz, eds., *Exil und innere Emigration II* (Frankfurt, 1973).
31. See Gertraud Gutzmann, "Schriftsteller und Literatur: Ihre gesellschaftliche Funktion im Werk von Anna Seghers" (Ph.D. diss., University of Massachusetts, 1979).
32. Cf. Kurt Batt, "Zum Seghers-Lukács-Dialog," *Weimarer Beiträge* 5 (1975), pp. 136–37.

NOTES TO CHAPTER TWO

1. *Doctor Faustus*, trans. H. T. Lowe-Porter (New York, 1948), here slightly adapted. Page numbers in parentheses throughout this chapter refer to this edition.
2. Hans Rudolf Vaget, "Kaisersaschern als geistige Lebensform. Zur Konzeption der deutschen Geschichte in Thomas Manns *Doktor Faustus*," in *Der deutsche Roman und seine historischen und politischen Bedingungen*, ed. Wolfgang Paulsen (Bern, 1977), pp. 200–235.
3. Cf. T. J. Reed, *Thomas Mann: The Uses of Tradition* (London, 1974), p. 400.
4. Vaget, "Kaisersaschern," pp. 206–11.
5. *Ibid.*
6. Meinecke, *Die deutsche Katastrophe* (Wiesbaden, 1946); Ritter, *Europa und die deutsche Frage* (Munich, 1948). For a compact account of the significance of these works, see Georg G. Iggers, *Deutsche Geschichtswissenschaft* (Munich, 1971), pp. 340–41.
7. Franz Futterknecht, *Das Dritte Reich im deutschen Roman der Nachkriegszeit: Untersuchungen zur Faschismustheorie und Faschismusbewältigung* (Bonn, 1976).
8. Hans Rothfels, *Die deutsche Opposition gegen Hitler* (Frankfurt, 1949); Gerhard Ritter, *Carl Goerdeler und die deutsche Widerstandsbewegung* (Stuttgart, 1955); Iggers, *Deutsche Geschichtswissenschaft*, pp. 345–46.
9. Thomas Mann, *Die Entstehung des "Doktor Faustus": Roman eines Romans* (Amsterdam, 1949).
10. For a helpful discussion of the Leverkühn-Zeitblom relationship in terms of Mann's studies of Luther, see Herbert Lehnert, *Thomas Mann: Fiktion, Mythos, Religion* (Stuttgart, 1965), p. 195.
11. "*Doktor Faustus* und die deutsche Katastrophe," in *Kunst und Menschheit* (Vienna, 1949), pp. 37–97. The most notable account of this position to appear more recently has been Horst Meixner's article "Thomas Manns *Doktor Faustus*: Zum Selbstverständnis des deutschen Spätbürgertums," *Jahrbuch der Deutschen Schiller-Gesellschaft* 16 (1972), pp. 610–22. Paul Rilla takes an opposing view in *Essays: Kritische Betrachtungen zur Literatur* (Berlin, 1955), p. 255.
12. Heinz Peter Pütz lays to rest the controversy over the hallucination issue by showing that the ambiguity is not meant to be definitively resolved (*Kunst und Künstlerexistenz bei Nietzsche und Thomas Mann* [Bonn, 1963], pp. 112–15).
13. Cf. Erich Heller, "*Doktor Faustus* und die Zurücknahme der Neunten Symphonie," in *Thomas Mann 1875–1975: Vorträge München—Zürich—Lübeck*, ed. Beatrix Bludau, Eckhard Heftrich, and Helmut Koopman (Frankfurt, 1977), pp. 173–88.
14. Käte Hamburger sees a discrepancy between the theme of modern music and the "anachronistic devil symbolism" in the novel ("Anachronistische Symbolik: Fragen an Thomas Manns Faustus-Roman," in *Thomas Mann*, ed. Helmut Koopman [Darmstadt, 1975], pp. 384–413).
15. This manner of thinking doubtless owes much to Theodor W. Adorno.
16. Cf. J. Elema, "Thomas Mann, Dürer und *Doktor Faustus*," *Euphorion* 59 (1965), pp. 91–117.
17. See T. J. Reed, *Thomas Mann*, pp. 372–77. Reed's discussion of the political potential of Leverkühn's music is extremely helpful, but he does not sufficiently stress Zeitblom's role in this connection.
18. For a comparison with Nietzsche's attempt to transcend modern scepticism through a return to myth, see Heinz Peter Pütz, *Kunst und Künstlerexistenz*.
19. Jonathan Leverkühn is drawn after Dürer's portrait of Melanchthon. Cf. Gunilla Bergsten, *Thomas Manns "Doktor Faustus"* (Stockholm, 1963), p. 61.
20. Cf. Donna Baker, "Nazism and the Petit Bourgeois Protagonist: The Novels of Grass, Böll and Mann," *New German Critique* 5 (1975), pp. 77–105.
21. Thomas Mann, *Entstehung des "Doktor Faustus*," p. 82; also Eckhardt Heftrich, "*Doktor Faustus*: Die radikale Autobiographie," in *Thomas Mann 1875–1975*, pp. 135–54.
22. Donna Baker also sees this as a fault of the novel ("Nazism and the Petit Bourgeois

Protagonist," p. 86). Others have taken an opposing view, e.g., Margrit Henning, *Die Ich-Form in Thomas Manns "Doktor Faustus"* (Tübingen, 1966), pp. 133–34. T. J. Reed regards the ultimate coincidence of Zeitblom's theory with Mann's as one of the positive features of the novel (*Thomas Mann*, p. 402).
23. On the ambiguity of Echo, see Pütz, *Kunst and Künstlerexistenz*, pp. 142–44.
24. Ehrhard Bahr sees this more positively. He defines the form of *Doctor Faustus* as an "antinomic allegory" whose advantage for the rethinking of the Nazi past consists in the fact that the Third Reich thus becomes the subject of continuing reflection ("Metaphysische Zeitdiagnose: Hermann Kasack, Elisabeth Langgässer und Thomas Mann," in *Gegenwartsliteratur und Drittes Reich*, ed. Hans Wagener [Stuttgart, 1977], p. 153).
25. Futterknecht points out that the problem of aesthetic mediation remains unresolved in *Doctor Faustus* (*Das Dritte Reich im deutschen Roman*, p. 107).

NOTES TO CHAPTER THREE

1. Peter Pütz maintains that Mann's influence on postwar literature has been primarily indirect; he does not identify *The Tin Drum* as a possible response to *Doctor Faustus* ("Thomas Manns Wirkung auf die deutsche Literatur der Gegenwart," in *Thomas Mann 1875–1975: Vorträge München—Zürich—Lübeck,* ed. Beatrix Bludau, Eckhard Heftrich, and Helmut Koopman [Frankfurt, 1977], pp. 453–65).
2. For a fuller account of *The Tin Drum* see John Reddick, *The "Danzig Trilogy" of Günter Grass* (New York, 1974); Keith Miles, *Günter Grass* (New York, 1975); Jürgen Rothenberg, *Günter Grass: Das Chaos in verbesserter Ausführung* (Heidelberg, 1976); Hanspeter Brode, "Die Zeitgeschichte in der *Blechtrommel* von Günter Grass: Entwurf eines textinternen Kommunikationsmodells," in *Günter Grass Materialienbuch,* ed. Rolf Geissler (Darmstadt, 1976), pp. 86–114.
3. *Doctor Faustus,* trans. H. T. Lowe-Porter (New York, 1948), p. 141.
4. *The Tin Drum,* trans. Ralph Manheim (New York, 1961). Page numbers in parentheses throughout this chapter refer to this edition.
5. *Cat and Mouse,* trans. Ralph Manheim (New York, 1963), p. 86.
6. For a more detailed analysis of Dürer's *Melencolia I,* see Erwin Panofsky, *The Life and Art of Albrecht Dürer,* 4th ed. (Princeton, 1955), pp. 156–71.
7. Donna Baker does not make this distinction ("Nazism and the Petit Bourgeois Protagonist: The Novels of Grass, Böll and Mann," *New German Critique* 2 [1975], pp. 77–105). On social class in Grass see also Helmut Koopmann, "Günter Grass: Der Faschismus als Kleinbürgertum und was daraus wurde," in *Gegenwartsliteratur und Drittes Reich,* ed. Hans Wagener (Stuttgart, 1977), pp. 163–81.
8. Georg G. Iggers, *Deutsche Geschichtswissenschaft* (Munich, 1871), p. 354.
9. One of its most important publications was Reinhart Kosellek's *Preussen zwischen Reform und Revolution* (Stuttgart, 1967).
10. Theodore Ziolkowski does not take up the question of the Jesus myth in *The Tin Drum* in *Fictional Transfigurations of Jesus* (Princeton, 1972).
11. *Tristram Shandy,* Everyman's Library (London, 1912), p. 79.
12. On the concept of a convergence point beyond the end of a novel, see Wolfgang Iser, *Der implizite Leser* (Munich, 1972), p. 74.
13. For a discussion of the literary context in which Oskar's madness must be seen, see Theodore Ziolkowski, "The View from the Madhouse," in *Dimensions of the Modern Novel: German Texts and European Contexts* (Princeton, 1969), pp. 332–61.
14. Cf. Volker Schlöndorff, *"Die Blechtrommel": Tagebuch einer Verfilmung* (Darmstadt, 1979).
15. "Virtual image" is used in the sense introduced by Wolfgang Iser (*Der implizite Leser,* pp. 68, 74–78).
16. Erich Heller, *The Ironic German* (London, 1958), p. 277.
17. *Ibid.*
18. Jürgen Scharfschwerdt, *Thomas Mann und der deutsche Bildungsroman* (Stuttgart, 1967), pp. 236–38.
19. *Doctor Faustus,* p. 148.
20. *From the Diary of a Snail,* trans. Ralph Manheim (New York, 1972), pp. 302, 293.

21. *Doctor Faustus,* p. 241.
22. *From the Diary of a Snail,* p. 293. I have slightly altered Manheim's translation to bring out the meaning of the original more clearly.
23. *Ibid.,* p. 289.
24. *Ibid.,* p. 302.
25. *Ibid.,* p. 306.
26. *Ibid.,* p. 310.
27. *Ibid.*
28. *Ibid.* Only after completion of this chapter did I come across Henry Hatfield's amusing parenthetical comment: "Perhaps some day some bold fellow will note an analogy between *Die Blechtrommel* and *Doktor Faustus,* though this would probably annoy both Herr Grass and the revered shade of Thomas Mann ("Günter Grass: The Artist as Satirist," in *The Contemporary Novel in German,* ed. Robert R. Heitner [Austin, 1967], p. 125).

NOTES TO CHAPTER FOUR

1. *Sansibar oder der letzte Grund* (Zurich, 1970). Page numbers in parentheses throughout this chapter refer to this edition; my translations.
2. Peter Demetz, *Postwar German Literature* (New York, 1970), p. 183.
3. *Ibid.,* p. 184. Demetz points out that Andersch, while polemicizing against the "arty" style of his contemporaries, nonetheless creates an original and complex method of his own.
4. Quoted in Hans Geulen, "Alfred Andersch: Probleme der dargestellten Erfahrung des 'deutschen Irrtums,' " in *Gegenwartsliteratur und Drittes Reich,* ed. Hans Wagener (Stuttgart, 1977), p. 211.
5. Significantly, Gregor's ruminations about Rerik and Tarasovka were published separately by Andersch in the final issue of the journal *Texte und Zeichen* 3 (1957), pp. 568–78. Livia Z. Wittmann points out other changes in the characters' relation to nature that support this basic symbolism (*Alfred Andersch* [Stuttgart, 1971], p. 36–38). Cf. also Alfons Bühlmann (*In der Faszination der Freiheit* [Berlin, 1973], esp. pp. 140–48).
6. "Kann man ein Symbol zerhauen?" *Texte und Zeichen* 1 (1955), p. 384.
7. I disagree with Wittmann's contention that the multiple-point-of-view technique as used in *Zanzibar* creates an illusion of totality (*Alfred Andersch,* p. 136).
8. Demetz compares *Zanzibar* unfavorably with *The Redhead* on this count (*Postwar German Literature,* pp. 182–83). Cf. also Ingeborg Drewitz, "Alfred Andersch oder die Krise des Engagements. Der Erzähler," *Merkur* 20 (1966), p. 671.
9. "And death shall have no dominion," *The Poems of Dylan Thomas,* ed. Daniel Jones (New York, 1971), pp. 49–50.
10. "Die Blindheit des Kunstwerks," *Texte und Zeichen* 2 (1956), p. 75. For an excellent discussion of artistic autonomy as set forth in this essay, see Peter Demetz, "Alfred Andersch oder die Krise des Engagements: Der Essayist," *Merkur* 20 (1966), p. 677.

NOTES TO CHAPTER FIVE

1. *Billiards at Half-Past Nine,* trans. Leila Vennewitz (New York, 1962). Page numbers in parentheses throughout this chapter refer to this edition.
2. I am not convinced by H. Stresau, who sees the setting of this novel, as of others by Böll, as a metaphorical equivalent of "the peculiar homelessness and defencelessness of the characters" (*Heinrich Böll* [Berlin, 1964], p. 83).
3. Cf. Klaus Jeziorkowski, "Heinrich Böll: Die Syntax des Humanen," in *Zeitkritische Romane des zwanzigsten Jahrhunderts,* ed. Hans Wagener (Stuttgart, 1975), pp. 309–10; Manfred Durzak, "Entfaltung oder Reduktion des Erzählers," in *Böll: Untersuchungen zum Werk,* ed. Manfred Jürgensen (Bern, 1975), p. 33. The opposing point of view is held by K. A. Horst, who sees the lamb and beast categories as a necessary parallel to Robert Fähmel's abstract formulae ("Überwindung der Zeit," in *Der Schriftsteller Heinrich Böll,* ed. Wolfdietrich Rasch [Munich, 1968], p. 70).
4. It is not clear to what extent this adoption represents a solution for Hugo, who, after

all, accepts it quite passively. W. J. Schwarz exaggerates the case when he claims that the adoption saves Hugo from becoming a victim of society (*Der Erzähler Heinrich Böll* [Bern, 1967], p. 103).

5. Page 212. I have slightly altered Vennewitz's translation to bring out the meaning of the original. This passage would seem to contradict W. J. Schwarz's claim that these puritanically oriented sectarians are a more consistent alternative to the corruption of Catholicism (*Der Erzähler Heinrich Böll*, p. 61).

6. When Karin Huffzsky reproaches Böll for not presenting self-assured female figures, she appears to be ignoring Johanna Fähmel ("Die Hüter und ihr Schrecken vor der Sache: Das Mann-Frau-Bild in den Romanen von Heinrich Böll," in *Heinrich Böll: Eine Einführung in das Gesamtwerk in Einzelinterpretationen*, ed. Hanno Beth [Kronberg, 1975], pp. 29–54).

7. My translation; Leila Vennewitz renders this passage differently (p. 125).

8. *Love and Intrigue*, act 5, sc. 1 (my translation).

9. My translation (cf. that of Leila Vennewitz, p. 254).

10. Roy Pascal, "Sozialkritik und Erinnerungstechnik," in *In Sachen Böll*, ed. Marcel Reich-Ranicki (Cologne, 1968), p. 84.

11. Klaus Jeziorkowski illustrates this throughout his analysis of the novel's time structure: he sees Johanna as the only one capable of perceiving and making evident the "totality of time" (*Rhythmus und Figur* [Bad Homburg, 1968], pp. 126–27).

12. For a discussion of Johanna's insanity in the context of similar complexes in the modern novel, see Theodore Ziolkowski, "The View from the Madhouse," in *Dimensions of the Modern Novel: German Texts and European Contexts* (Princeton, 1969), esp. pp. 340–41.

13. Cf. Jeziorkowski, "Die Syntax des Humanen," p. 309.

14. On the problematic nature of Böll's technique of characterization, see Rainer Nägele, "Heinrich Böll: Die grosse Ordnung und die kleine Anarchie," in *Gegenwartsliteratur und Drittes Reich*, ed. Hans Wagener (Stuttgart, 1977), pp. 183–204, esp. p. 198.

NOTES TO CHAPTER SIX

1. *The Tin Drum*, trans. Ralph Manheim (New York, 1961), p. 124.

2. Oskar's final development is clearly intended as a criticism of those who take nostalgic refuge in memories of their childhood. Grass' irony is not recognized by Gertrude Cepl-Kaufmann, who identifies the author too much with his characters (*Günter Grass: Eine Analyse des Gesamtwerks unter dem Aspekt von Literatur und Politik* [Kronberg, 1975]).

3. *Local Anaesthetic*, trans. Ralph Manheim (New York, 1970), p. 221.

4. For example Karl H. Ruhleder's farfetched interpretation of the religious imagery ("A Pattern of Messianic Thought in Günter Grass' *Cat and Mouse*," *German Quarterly* 39 [1966], pp. 599–612) and Ilpo Tapani Piirainen's overly mechanical linguistic analysis (*Textbezogene Untersuchungen über "Katz und Maus" und "Hundejahre" von Günter Grass* [Bern, 1968]).

5. The first view is represented by Johanna E. Behrendt ("Die Ausweglosigkeit der menschlichen Natur: Eine Interpretation von Günter Grass' *Katz und Maus*," *Zeitschrift für deutsche Philologie* 87 [1968], pp. 546–62; "Auf der Suche nach dem Adamsapfel: Der Erzähler Pilenz in Günter Grass' Novelle *Katz und Maus*," *Germanisch-Romanische Monatsschrift* 19 [1969], pp. 313–26). The second position is taken by Gerhard Kaiser (*Günter Grass: "Katz und Maus"* [Munich, 1971]).

6. John Reddick, *The "Danzig Trilogy" of Günter Grass* (New York, 1975).

7. The term was introduced by James C. Bruce in his key article "The Equivocating Narrator in Günter Grass' *Katz und Maus*," *Monatshefte* 58 (1966), pp. 139–49. On Pilenz' deceptive narration, see also Theodore Ziolkowski, *Fictional Transfigurations of Jesus* (Princeton, 1972), pp. 238–50.

8. *Cat and Mouse*, trans. Ralph Manheim (New York, 1963). Page numbers in parentheses throughout this chapter refer to this edition.

9. The one partial exception is a reference to the portrait of the Führer in the school auditorium (p. 86).

NOTES TO PAGES 98–116   173

10. Kaiser sees Mahlke as a product of the fatherless generation (*Günter Grass: "Katz und Maus,"* pp. 26–35); Helmut Koopmann regards him as suffering from an inferiority complex ("Günter Grass: Der Faschismus als Kleinbürgertum und was daraus wurde," in *Gegenwartsliteratur und Drittes Reich,* ed. Hans Wagener [Stuttgart, 1977], p. 176).
11. Cf. Ingrid Tiesler, *Günter Grass: "Katz und Maus"* (Munich, 1971), p. 132.
12. Hans Bahlow, *Deutsches Namenlexikon* (Frankfurt, 1972), p. 328.
13. Günter Grass, *Gesammelte Gedichte* (Neuwied, 1971), p. 201; my translation.
14. In both of her articles, Johanna E. Behrendt takes as the ultimate level of meaning a universal one ("Die Ausweglosigkeit der menschlichen Natur"; "Auf der Suche nach dem Adamsapfel").
15. John Reddick, *The "Danzig Trilogy" of Günter Grass,* pp. 118–19.
16. Later on Mahlke does put the phonograph to use, but his way of using it is a mocking one. The two records he plays, the "well-known 'Ave Maria,' as long-lasting as a wad of chewing gum" (81), and the songs of Zarah Leander, which prophesied that "Onedayamiraclewillhappen" (82), show Mahlke's sense of the appropriate use for the German machine. With respect to Zarah Leander, Pilenz comments, "It was all greased with the same oil"; p. 82, my translation.
17. *Über das Selbstverständliche: Reden, Aufsätze, Offene Briefe, Kommentare* (Neuwied, 1968), p. 183; my translation.
18. *Ibid.,* p. 184; my translation.
19. *Null Acht Fünfzehn* [Zero eight fifteen] (Munich, 1955), vol. 3, pp. 395, 396, 398. I am grateful to Willy Schumann for drawing my attention to this work.
20. *Ibid.,* p. 398.
21. *The Tin Drum,* p. 252. Cf. also Grass, "Der Dichter," in *Gesammelte Gedichte,* p. 105.
22. *The Tin Drum,* p. 84.
23. Manheim's translation of this sentence is inaccurate (*Cat and Mouse,* p. 157); the version given is my translation.
24. Tiesler, *Günter Grass: "Katz und Maus,"* p. 54. Cf. also the passage about different types of crosses in *The Tin Drum,* pp. 139–40.
25. Kaiser (*Günter Grass: "Katz und Maus,"* p. 18) shows how Pilenz' intentions ultimately work against themselves (*ibid.*).
26. *Der Spiegel* 36 (1963), p. 72; cf. Tiesler, *Günter Grass: "Katz und Maus,"* p. 53.
27. *Der Spiegel* 23 (1961), pp. 1, 20–24. This issue appeared in May; *Cat and Mouse* was published in September of the same year.
28. *Ibid.,* p. 23; my translation.
29. *The Tin Drum,* p. 251. Grass explains "Pan Kiehot" is the Polish version of Don Quixote.
30. Günter Grass, "Pan Kiehot," in *Gesammelte Gedichte,* p. 117; my translation.

NOTES TO CHAPTER SEVEN

1. *Die Expressionismusdebatte: Materialien zu einer marxistischen Realismuskonzeption,* ed. Hans-Jürgen Schmitt (Frankfurt a. M., 1973), pp. 256, 253.
2. Siegfried Lenz, *The German Lesson,* trans. Ernst Kaiser and Eithne Wilkins (New York, 1962). Page numbers in parentheses throughout this chapter refer to this edition.
3. Excerpts from Jens' speech are reprinted in Emil Nolde, *Ungemalte Bilder 1938–1945* (Seebüll, 1971), p. 18 (my translation).
4. Walter Laqueur, *Weimar: A Cultural History* (New York, 1974), pp. 86–87.
5. Lenz has taken great pains with these descriptions; close examination should dispel Jörg Drews' views that they are extremely vague ("Siegfried Lenz' *Deutschstunde,*" *Neue Rundschau* 80 [1969], pp. 362–66).
6. Lenz has confirmed that he was primarily thinking of Nolde when he created the character of Nansen (see his interview with Manfred Durzak in *Gespräche über den Roman* [Frankfurt, 1976], pp. 177–203). Wilhelm H. Grothman overlooks the critical aspect of Lenz's adaptations of Nolde ("Siegfried Lenz' *Deutschstunde:* Eine Würdigung der Kunst Emil Noldes," *Seminar* 15 [1979], pp. 56–69).

7. Cf. Martin Urban's essay in Nolde, *Ungemalte Bilder*, p. 5.
8. Kurt Batt regards this ambiguity as a result of the author's uncertainty in evaluating his character (*Revolte intern: Betrachtungen zur Literatur in der Bundesrepublik Deutschland* [Munich, 1975], p. 144).
9. I have slightly altered Kaiser and Wilkins' translation of this sentence (334).
10. Some readers have allowed the distinction between Nansen and Balthasar to become blurred. Trudis Reber assimilates Balthasar's credo to Nansen's views, and Nansen's to Lenz' (*Siegfried Lenz* [Berlin, 1973], p. 80); Dietrich Peinert also equates Balthasar and Nansen ("Siegfried Lenz' *Deutschstunde:* Eine Einführung," in *Der Schriftsteller Siegfried Lenz: Urteile und Standpunkte*, ed. Colin Russ [Hamburg, 1973], pp. 173–82).
11. Manfred Bosch is not convincing when he contends that the pictures have given up any attempt at resistance ("Der Sitzplatz des Autors Lenz oder Schwierigkeiten beim Schreiben der Wahrheit," *Text und Kritik* 52 [1976], pp. 16–23, esp. p. 22).
12. Wilhelm Johannes Schwarz takes this phenomenon seriously (*Der Erzähler Siegfried Lenz* [Bern, 1974]); Jörg Drews regards it as a blind spot in the novel ("Siegfried Lenz: *Deutschstunde,*" p. 364).
13. Cf. Manfred Durzak, who puts forward the view that Siggi is the real protagonist of the novel and that it is not primarily about Nansen (*Gespräche über den Roman*, p. 212).
14. On the theme of guilt in Lenz, see Albert R. Schmitt, "Schuld im Werke von Siegfried Lenz: Betrachtungen zu einem zeitgemässen Thema," in *Festschrift für Detlev W. Schumann*, ed. Albert R. Schmitt (Munich, 1970), pp. 369–82.
15. Cf. Jörg Drews, "Siegfried Lenz: *Deutschstunde,*" p. 364. Hans Wagener argues against this view, pointing out that it is not Siggi but the reader who is meant to mature (*Siegfried Lenz* [Munich, 1976], p. 68). On the question of reader activation, see also Theo Elm, *Siegfried Lenz' "Deutschstunde"* (Munich, 1974), pp. 109–16.
16. Batt, *Revolte intern*, p. 144; Durzak, *Gespräche über den Roman*, p. 212; Drews, "Siegfried Lenz: *Deutschstunde,*" p. 366; Theo Elm, "Siegfried Lenz: Zeitgeschichte als moralisches Lehrstück," in *Gegenwartsliteratur und Drittes Reich*, ed. Hans Wagener (Stuttgart, 1977), pp. 233–35.
17. Durzak, *Gespräche über den Roman*, p. 212.
18. Kurt Batt claims that Lenz presents neither the seductive power of nazism nor active resistance to it (*Revolte intern*, p. 144). This criticism fails to take into account the role played by Nansen's imaginary disputant, Balthasar.

NOTES TO CHAPTER EIGHT

1. *Levin's Mill: 34 Sentences about My Grandfather*, trans. Janet Cropper (London, 1970). Page numbers in parentheses throughout this chapter refer to this edition.
2. The narrator's family are not actually relations of Johannes Bobrowski, although he exploits the similarity of names, for reasons of irony (cf. his radio interview in *Johannes Bobrowski: Selbstzeugnisse und neue Beiträge über sein Werk*, ed. Gerhard Rostin [Stuttgart, 1976], p. 33). Eberhard Haufe has established the source Bobrowski used for the novel, a story discovered by Georg Bobrowski (not immediately related to Johannes) during research into his own family tree ("Bobrowskis Weg zum Roman," *Weimarer Beiträge* 16 [1970], pp. 163–77). Of particular significance is Johannes Bobrowski's alteration of the ending, which had in actuality favored the Jew.
3. For a subtle account of speech in *Levin's Mill* see Dagmar Barnouw, "Bobrowski's Socialist Realism," *Germanic Review* 48 (1973), pp. 288–314.
4. Rostin, *Selbstzeugnisse*, p. 64.
5. Bobrowski clearly invites comparison with Grass, even down to such fine details as the mention of Prediger Laschinski's name-change to Lasch (p. 72).
6. Siegfried Streller points out that the model for the ballad is a satire on Panje ("Zählen zählt alles: Zum Gesellschaftsbild Johannes Bobrowskis," *Weimarer Beiträge* 15 [1961], pp. 1079–90).
7. Grass refers to this hymn in *The Tin Drum*, trans. Ralph Manheim (New York, 1961), p. 251.

8. I disagree with Brian Keith-Smith's contention that the thirty-four sentences are elevated to "significant truth" (*Johannes Bobrowski* [London, 1970], p. 54).
9. Dagmar Barnouw gives different reasons for her view of the novel as an example of socialist realism ("Bobrowski's Socialist Realism," p. 314). From a different standpoint again, East German criticism also aligns *Levin's Mill* with socialist realism, though it is rather different from most other works in that category (*Zur Theorie des Sozialistischen Realismus* [Berlin, 1974], p. 360).
10. Cf. Gerhard Wolf, who describes *Levin's Mill* as a dialogue between reader and fictional narrator (*Johannes Bobrowski: Leben und Werk* [Berlin, 1976], p. 74). See also Wolf's *Beschreibung eines Zimmers: 15 Kapitel über Johannes Bobrowski* (Berlin, 1973) and his article on *Lithuanian Pianofortes*, in *Selbstzeugnisse*, ed. Rostin, pp. 340–50.
11. Rostin, *Selbstzeugnisse*, p. 43; my translation.
12. Cf. Haufe, "Bobrowskis Weg zum Roman," p. 174; *Zur Theorie des Sozialistischen Realismus*, p. 360. Bobrowski himself may have spoken misleadingly in his radio interview (Rostin, *Selbstzeugnisse*, p. 34).
13. Rostin, *Selbstzeugnisse*, p. 71.
14. Bernd Leistner suggests some attempts to take up Bobrowski's colloquial narrative style in Jurek Becker and Helga Schütz, but he ignores the issue of dialectical structuring ("Der Erzähler," in Rostin, *Selbstzeugnisse*, pp. 336–39).
15. "Benannte Schuld—gebannte Schuld," in Rostin, *Selbstzeugnisse*, p. 20.
16. For more on the function of music in *Levin's Mill*, see David A. Scrase, "Point Counterpoint: Variations on the 'Fest' Theme in Johannes Bobrowski's *Levins Mühle*," *German Life and Letters* 32 (1979), pp. 177–85.

NOTES TO CHAPTER NINE

1. Christa Wolf, *A Model Childhood*, trans. Ursula Molinaro and Hedwig Rappolt (New York, 1980). Page numbers in parentheses throughout this chapter refer to this edition.
2. "Werkstattgespräch," quoted in the jacket text of the East German edition, *Kindheitsmuster* (Berlin, 1976).
3. James Joyce, *A Portrait of the Artist as a Young Man* (New York, 1916), p. 252.
4. These two passages are omitted from p. 84 of the Molinaro and Rappolt translation; my translation.
5. Cf. Manfred Naumann et al., *Gesellschaft—Literatur—Lesen* (Berlin, 1975); Hans Robert Jauss, "Zur Fortsetzung des Dialogs zwischen 'bürgerlicher' und 'materialistischer' Rezeptionsästhetik," in *Rezeptionsästhetik*, ed. Rainer Warning (Munich, 1975), esp. p. 344.
6. Omitted from p. 404 of the Molinaro and Rappolt translation; my translation.
7. The narrator's earlier hope that a "union of the various persons might take place" is thus disappointed (*A Model Childhood*, p. 158).
8. Hans Mayer, "Der Mut zur Unaufrichtigkeit," *Der Spiegel* 16 (1977), pp. 188–89. In an interview, Wolf explained that it was not her intention to write a "novel of transformation"; she differentiates between her experience and that presented in most East German fiction, in which the young hero is encouraged by a wise mentor to develop critical views toward fascism: "not a single book reflected my own experience" (*Sinn und Form* 28 [1976], pp. 866, 874).
9. Heinz Plavius, "Gewissensforschung," *Neue Deutsche Literatur* (1977), pp. 139–51.
10. *The Quest for Christa T.*, trans. Christopher Middleton (New York, 1972), p. 28.
11. *Ibid.*, p. 5.
12. My translation.
13. A convincing analysis of *Christa T.*'s dialectic, especially of the relationship between narrator and protagonist, is given by Heinrich Mohr in "Produktive Sehnsucht: Struktur, Thematik und politische Relevanz von Christa Wolfs *Nachdenken über Christa T.*," *Basis* 2 (1971), pp. 191–233. See also Lothar Köhn, "Erinnerung und Erfahrung: Christa Wolfs Begründung der Literatur," *Text und Kritik* 46 (1975), esp. pp. 14–24.
14. Hans Mayer, "Der Mut zur Unaufrichtigkeit," p. 188.

15. *Ibid.*
16. Cf. Monika Helmeke's review of *A Model Childhood* (*Sinn und Form* 29 [1977], pp. 678–81).
17. Plavius, "Gewissensforschung," p. 152.
18. Cf. Hans Richter, "Moralität als poetische Energie," *Sinn und Form* 29 (1977), pp. 667–78, esp. p. 674.
19. *Lesen und Schreiben: Aufsätze und Betrachtungen,* 2d ed. (Berlin, 1973), p. 211; my translation.

NOTES TO CHAPTER TEN

1. See Johnson's interview with Manfred Durzak in Durzak's *Gespräche über den Roman* (Frankfurt, 1976), esp. p. 442.
2. Heinz Osterle sees the novel's structure as dialectical ("Uwe Johnson, *Jahrestage: Das Bild der U.S.A.*," *German Quarterly* 48 [1975], p. 508). Hamida Bosmajian's view of *Anniversaries* as structured through the "principle of repetition-compulsion" is also unconvincing (*Metaphors of Evil: Contemporary German Literature and the Shadow of Nazism* [Iowa City, 1979], p. 141).
3. This point is convincingly made by Leslie L. Miller in "Uwe Johnson's *Jahrestage:* The Choice of Alternatives," *Seminar* 10 (1974), pp. 50–70.
4. *Anniversaries: From the Life of Gesine Cresspahl,* trans. Leila Vennewitz (New York, 1974), p. 228.
5. Miller, "The Choice of Alternatives," p. 65.
6. The English translation is an abridged version of volumes one and two of the German edition.
7. Durzak especially mentions the improbability of Gesine's newspaper addiction (*Gespräche über den Roman,* p. 444).
8. In his interview with Durzak (*Gespräche über den Roman,* pp. 440–46).
9. Heinz Osterle, "Das Bild der U.S.A."; Sara Lennox, "Die *New York Times* in Johnsons *Jahrestagen,*" in *Die U.S.A. und Deutschland: Wechselseitige Spiegelungen in der Literatur der Gegenwart,* ed. Wolfgang Paulsen (Bern, 1976), pp. 103–9; Bernd Neumann, *Utopie und Mimesis* (Kronberg, 1978), pp. 290–95.
10. I do not share Kurt Batt's view that fiction and document are indecisively balanced against each other (*Revolte intern: Betrachtungen zur Literatur in der Bundesrepublik Deutschland* [Munich, 1975], pp. 150–51).
11. Peter Demetz differs in his evaluation of the two novels (*Postwar German Literature* [New York, 1970], pp. 166–67). R. Hinton Thomas and Keith Bullivant criticize the authorial stand of *The Battle,* but in fact this only applies to the second half of the novel (*Literature in Upheaval* [Manchester, 1974], pp. 93–94).
12. Alfred Andersch, *Winterspelt,* trans. Richard and Clara Winston (New York, 1978), p. 400. I have slightly altered this passage to restore the full sense of the original.
13. *Ibid.,* p. 24.
14. *Ibid.,* p. 87.
15. Robert Weimann, "Kommunikation und Erzählstruktur im Point of View," *Weimarer Beiträge* 11 (1971), pp. 145–55.

INDEX

Judith Ryan is Doris Silbert Professor in the Humanities, Department of German Language and Literature, Smith College. She has published a critical analysis of the poetry of Rainer Maria Rilke and many articles dealing with the works of writers such as Hugo von Hofmannsthal, Franz Kafka, Paul Celan, Nelly Sachs, Günter Grass, and Alfred Döblin.

The manuscript was edited for publication by Carol Altman Bromberg. The book was designed by E. J. Frank. The text typeface and the display face are Mergenthaler VIP Times Roman, based on a design by Stanley Morison about 1932. The book is printed on 55 lb. Glatfelter's Offset Natural paper and is bound in Holliston Mills' Kingston Natural finish cloth over binder's boards.

Manufactured in the United States of America.